OCTOBER EARTHQUAKE

CODE MAP OF THE SUEZ CANAL CROSSING AREA

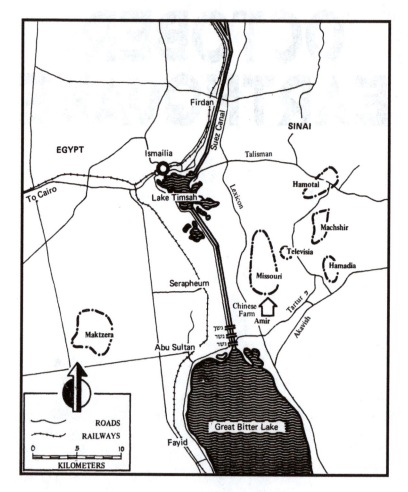

OCTOBER EARTHQUAKE

YOM KIPPUR 1973

ZEEV SCHIFF

TRANSLATED BY LOUIS WILLIAMS

Transaction Publishers
New Brunswick (U.S.A.) and London (U.K.)

Library of Congress Catalog Number: 2012022290
ISBN: 978-0-87855-244-3 (cloth); 978-1-4128-4984-5 (paper)
Printed in the United States of America

Library of Congress Cataloging-in-Publication Data

Schiff, Zeev, 1933-2007.
    [Re'idat adamah be-Oktober. English]
    October earthquake : Yom Kippur 1973 / Zeev Schiff.
        p. cm.
    "Originally published in 1974 by University Publishing Projects, Ltd."
    ISBN 978-0-87855-244-3
    1. Israel-Arab War, 1973. I. Title.
DS128.1.S3413 2012
956.04'8--dc23
                                                    2012022290

CONTENTS

INTRODUCTION

Years will pass before all the facts about the Day of Atonement will be known. And even then the truth will be only one side of coin. The other side can be exposed only when the Arabs choose to open their files. No account of the war can, therefore, be complete.

The problem is made more complex since leaders and generals are cadi presenting their own "truths". Some now claim that they saw shape of things to come. Others have armed themselves with the wisdom of hindsight, which must be at the expense of fellow actors in the drama. The shock of war often prevented the keeping of accurate command diaries. Therefore, when I began to collect the facts and the details, I was faced with irreconcilable contradictions —an Israeli "Rashomon" played out by senior officers.

Nevertheless, I do not believe that journalists have the right to the men appointed to conduct Israel's wars. The Press, with few exceptions, spoke the same language as the Israel Defense Forces and the Defense Ministry. Up to the summer of 1972, I felt that another war between Israel and her neighbors was inevitable. But, in 1973, following Sadat's postponement of war and the Russian exodus from Egypt, I was infected by the optimism prevalent in the IDF. The bug stayed with me until the Defense Minister's declaration, in summer 1973, that no major war was to be expected m the coming decade, and Israel's borders would stay unchanged Airing that period. I then wrote: "Anyone who believes that the present stalemate will long continue is both mistaken and Misleading. In the present situation of military and diplomatic stalemate, it seems that a new war is inevitable."

I have, as much as possible, avoided judging and awarding "grades" That duty must be left to the historians. They will be able evaluate the facts in a wider context, free of personal emotions. I tried in so far as it was possible to base myself on authentic material; recordings of command discussions during the battles, and documents. Some of these details are published here for the first time. Many others served as background, but could not be published far obvious security reasons.

"Earthquake in October' does not have any "star heroes". Through the men mentioned by name in this book, I have attempted to present the items that seem important to me. What happened to them, on the battlefield, in the quartermasters' stores, in the command posts—happened to many others. In collecting the facts, I was assisted by cabinet ministers, senior officers and soldiers. I am grateful to all of them.

The daily diary does not pretend to tell all that happened. On each day, I have chosen the events that I saw as most important. Wars and battles do not stop at midnight, to begin again one minute later—and so, I have allowed actions to cross the "calendar barrier" rather than interrupt continuity for the reader.

One last word for the English-language reader: The war of October 1973 has been variously called The Day of Judgment, The Day of Atonement, Yom Kippur, Ramadan and simply The October War. I have elected not to inflict my choice on history, and so the titles that appear in these pages are governed solely by the needs of the text.

Zeev Schiff
Tel Aviv, September 1974.

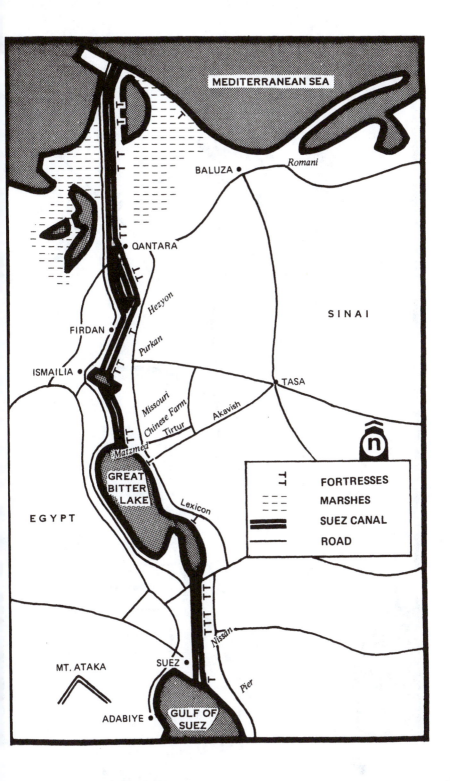

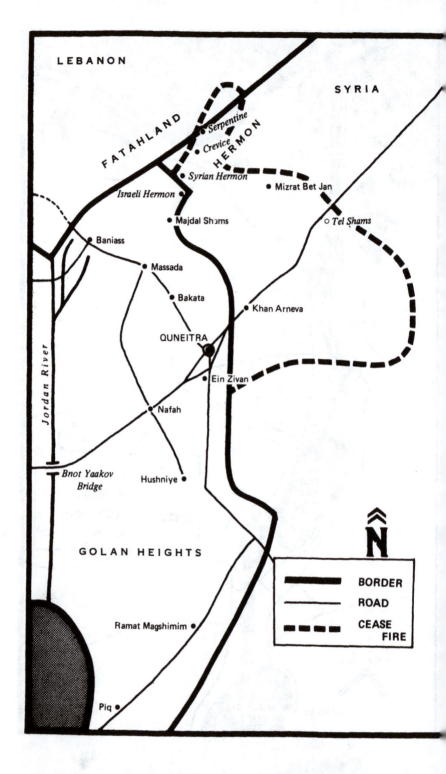

SEPTEMBER 21, 1973

President's Weekend

After a tiring week's work, Egyptian President Anwar Sadat, following morning prayers in his favorite mosque, left with his wife for a weekend at his summer house in Alexandria. Sadat has good reason to rest. His war plans are already complete. Now, he worries only about their implementation – and there is room for anxiety. Sadat is well aware that many plans have failed in the past, and many trusted friends were a source of disappointment. He knows his fate is now in the balance. He promised the "year of decision" in 1971. In 1972, he vowed that – by the next birthday of the Prophet Mohammed – he would push Israel back from the "conquered territories". Broken promises imply military revolution, but military failures invite the same fate.

Towards evening, as the sun sets, Sadat receives the editor of **el Aharam**, Hassanein Heikal, in audience. The meeting takes place on a large balcony overlooking the sea. Sadat's relationship with Hassanein Heikal has always been accompanied by mixed feelings, and his present unease plays its own part. He reveals in deepest confidence that the expected war will take place very soon, and tells Heikal that the Egyptian General Staff have code-named the operation "The Spark" – **el Shrara**.

Israel is used to Sadat's "revenge weeks". So nobody pays any atention to a report in today's Lebanese paper **el-Nahar**, known for its connections with the **fedayin** leaders: Cairo has informed a Palestinian personality that Egypt will shortly embark on an extensive military operation, with the purpose of generating American pressure on Israel.

1

SEPTEMBER 26, 1973

Holiday I

The eve of the Jewish New Year — a short work day, when office and industrial employees finish before noon, and rush home for the beginning of the festival. The roads are packed with traffic. The festival falls before a Saturday, and this means three straight days of holiday. Crowds go off on picnics and rambles. Defense Minister Moshe Dayan decides to spend this — of all days — on an inspection of the Golan Heights. He asks the Air Force for a helicopter, and sets off northwards to the Syrian border. Something bothers the Defense Minister of Israel.

Two days ago, on September 24, another defense minister — the Egyptian — visited his front line. Moshe Dayan and Ahmad Ismail visit for totally different reasons. The latter is playing a role in the great plan to deceive Israel, while Dayan is going out of anxiety and desire to warn the Syrian enemy. His eyes turn northwards.

A small item in the Egyptian press reports that the Egyptian War Minister visited units exercising on the front line. Israel is not the only one to swallow this morsel. American Intelligence has known for some days about Arab concentrations on Israel's border, but also believes it to be part of routine fall exercises by the Egyptian and Syrian armies.

Why is Moshe Dayan worried particularly about the north?

Aerial Overture

On September 13, something exceptional ruffled the fabric of hostile relationships between Israel and Syria. A flight of Israeli fighter planes winged its way north over the Mediterranean, along the Syrian coastline. Between the ports of Latakia and Tartus — 125 miles from Israel — Syrian MiGs tried to shoot down the Israeli aircraft. The Syrians would later contend that the Israeli planes had made a deep photo-reconnaissance in their territory. The battle lasted five minutes. Sixteen Syrian MiG 21s and 12 Israel aircraft – Phantoms, and Mirages that were giving air cover – took part. Nine MiGs fell. An Israeli Mirage was also hit, and the pilot who had downed a MiG parachuted into the sea. Israeli aircraft swept the area for a few hours to protect their comrade. Meanwhile, an Israeli helicopter arrived to rescue the Mirage pilot and a Syrian who was in the sea nearby. Another four MiG 21s attempted to interfere in the rescue operation, but were also shot down.

This was a bitter blow to Syrian pride. Moshe Dayan was convinced that they must exact their revenge. On September 14, the Lebanese press reported Syrian transfer of army units from their Jordanian border to the Israeli front, as a gesture to Hussein following renewal of diplomatic relations between the two countries. The outcome of the aerial battle, and this news, was sufficient reason to increase Israeli alertness on the Golan Heights.

Yet Israeli experts and orientalists read, with satisfaction, news of rows between Damascus and Syria's Soviet advisers following the aerial battle; the Syrian Air Force was not satisfied with the Russian planes, and was demanding MiG 25s – otherwise they could never face the Israelis. Moreover, in a fit of pique, Damascus restricted movements of Russian advisers. It would later be known that these items were deliberate leaks to augment the Arab deception program.

Yet, this "encouraging" news could not deflect Israeli attention from the growing Syrian concentrations on the border.

Anxious Inspection

Moshe Dayan meets representatives of the Golan Heights' settlements. He tells them that the newly-erected Syrian anti-aircraft missile system has grown to dimensions not far short of the Egyptian missile system – reputed to be the densest and most modern in the world. In the

3

presence of journalists, he warns Damascus that the IDF will vigorously react to any Syrian action. This warning comes too late. The Syrian-Egyptian war machine is already moving.

Moshe Dayan doesn't want to upset the Israeli public's peace of mind or spoil the festival. Before meeting representatives of the settlements, he agreed with the O.C. Northern Command, Yitzhak "Haka" Hofi not to prevent festival tourist traffic on Golan – a magnet both to Israelis and foreign visitors. Steps are to be taken for suitable alertness, without scaring the public.

Haka, the amiable O.C. Northern Command, does not for one moment think that in another ten days he will be fighting for Israel's existence in a bitter battle with the Syrians. But, he has been uneasy for months, and has often tried to convince his colleagues that Israel's greatest danger lies to the north, and not in Egypt. He has often quoted the Bible: ". . .out of the north an evil shall break forth." In today's meeting, he again tries to convince Defense Minister Dayan that the Syrian border is more dangerous, and must be reinforced. Haka presents a long list of reasons. The Israel-Syria cease-fire line lacks a natural obstacle to compare with the Suez Canal. The Syrian Army, based primarily on armor and mechanized units, is located close to the line, and only has to start its tank engines. Transition from defensive to offensive disposition, according to the Soviet doctrine of warfare, is simple to implement but difficult to spot. The Syrian Army has, in recent years, gained in strength no less than the Egyptian, which is separated from Israeli population centers by the Sinai Desert, while the Syrians are close to Galilee settlements. If they push the IDF off Golan, they can carry war into the heart of Israel. Moreover, the Soviet Union has supplied Syria with ground-to-ground Frog missiles which, with their 50-55 mile range, are far more dangerous in Syrian hands.

Hofi can see an additional factor that makes the Syrian front more evil than the Egyptian. The distance Syrian aircraft must traverse to reach the Israeli heartland has not

4

changed as a result of the Six Day War. Israel took Egyptian airfields in Sinai, and neutralized others on the west bank of Suez, but the conquest of Golan didn't move Syrian airfields one step back. Another aspect of the air situation worries Hofi; the IDF has always relied on massive and decisive air force support in blocking enemy attacks. But, the Syrians are erecting a dense ground-to-air missile system. In time of war — the Air Force must first eliminate front line missile batteries before it can take care of enemy armor.

Dayan already knows Hofi's opinions. Funds had been allocated to completion of an anti-tank ditch and mine-field, which were destined to claim scores of Syrian tanks.

But all this is a drop in the ocean. In Israel, there is no presentiment of impending storm. Major-General Hofi will later say: "My greatest surprise of this war was that it broke out at all. I feared it could happen, yet did not believe that it would!"

Writing on the Wall

With the force of absolute faith, Israel convinces the United States to disregard information about Arab inten-tions and preparations. Data indicating that Egypt and Syria are about to open an offensive is accumulating in CIA files.

"Are your people aware that an attack on Israel is in preparation?" a senior American representative asks his Israeli counterpart.

"We don't believe it will happen!" — the Israeli replies, thereby calming the anxious American.

INTERLUDE: THE ARAB PLAN

Clearing the Decks

According to all the signs, the Presidents of Egypt and Syria agreed, late in March 1973 to start a war towards

5

the end of the year. Sadat's war plans began to take shape after he demanded, in summer 1972, the removal of Russian military personnel from Egypt. Once they were gone, Sadat no longer feared interference. He told a visiting newsman that, with the Russians out of the way, his critics could no longer argue that anything Egypt will do in the military field could only be a Soviet achievement. One week after the Russian departure, Sadat ordered War Minister Ahmad Tzadek to start planning the war.

In the fall of 1972, Tzadek presented "Operation Plan Granite 1", for limited war based on two moves; a paratroop drop, at brigade strength, in Sinai — and a fifty-plane air attack on Sharm e-Sheikh. The paratroops would dig-in, and Egypt would try to get a UN Security Council decision on cease-fire, with the brigade still in Sinai. The political situation would be changed and the US would pressure Israel for a settlement and withdrawal from Sinai.

The President wasn't satisfied with the details — and especially not with the paratroop drop. His War Minister appeared to lack confidence in Egyptian arms, and feared Israeli Air Force strikes against the Egyptian rear, which he didn't consider prepared for war.

One week later, Sadat announced the appointment of Ahmad Ismail Ali to replace Tzadek. Ismail Ali persuaded Sadat that the Egyptians shouldn't stick to limited moves, which would in any case provoke vigorous Israeli reaction. There was no reason to avoid more extensive action, with its chances of better results. They decided to plan a large-scale crossing of the Suez Canal and, on January 14, 1973, Ahmad Ismail Ali submitted "Operation Plan Granite 2".

Egypt planned to attack in May. The problem now was to prepare the army and convince the Syrians to join in. In March, Sadat received **Newsweek** editor Arnaud de Borchgrave for a long conversation. De Borchgrave mentioned that military experts believed Israel would defeat the Egyptians, and Israeli aircraft would operate against targets

6

in the Egyptian rear. Sadat replied that the last moves of the Vietnam War served as his model. The Vietcong lost 45,000 men in the great Tet offensive, which was a military defeat — but the political turning-point. When the dispute again reached stalemate, the North Vietnamese opened a general offensive in which they lost more than 70,000 men without gaining any ground — but they won; the Americans decided to quit and retire from the battleground.

News of the Egyptian war preparations reached the Americans in late March. A Western dignitary, who was received in audience by Sadat, told US Under-Secretary of State Sisco that Sadat had sworn to keep his promise of war in the next few weeks. Sisco didn't accept the man's evaluation. But the dignitary also talked to Kissinger who did believe, though he wouldn't accept that it was a matter of weeks. Following this conversation, the dignitary tried three times in five days — by his own account — to get an appointment with Ambassador Simcha Dinitz. The Israeli Embassy in Washington replied that the Ambassador had no free time — and, after the third attempt, the man gave up trying.

Busy Summer

Egypt didn't go to war in May because the President of Syria claimed that his army wasn't ready. Egyptian Army personnel also told Sadat that they needed a few more months to complete preparations. A look at Sadat's diary for this period would have revealed frenzied activity. But the comings and goings between Egypt and Syria didn't elicit any interest from the intelligence agencies.

On April 2, Egyptian War Minister Ahmad Ismail Ali arrived in Syria to deal with operative plans. After three days at the Syrian General Staff in Damascus, he returned to Egypt. On May 6, Ahmad Ismail's plane landed in Baghdad. Two days later, he again visited the Syrian General Staff. These meetings were viewed in Israel as ordinary coordination sessions. But Jordan was apparently more alert to the new activity. On May 13, King Hussein circulated a confidential letter among senior Jordanian Army officers; he informed his officers that some Arab states were planning to go to war shortly, but assessed the plan as still incomplete. Details of Hussein's letter were leaked, a few days later, to the Lebanese press.

The Conductor

Ahmad Ismail Ali, the balding Egyptian War Minister, was the hero behind the scenes. Once the principle decision to go to war was taken, the conductor's baton was passed to him. The 55-year old officer was a favorite of the Russians — and a graduate of the Frunze Military Academy in Moscow — while his predecessor as War Minister, Ahmad Tzadek, had often quarrelled with Soviet advisers.

Ahmad Ismail came to the War Ministry from the post of Head of Intelligence and was considered forceful in his opinions. Upon the outbreak of the War of Attrition, he had been Head of Operations in the General Staff, but was appointed Chief of Staff to replace Abdul Munaim Riad who was killed in that war. However he was unlucky. In September 1969, following repeated Egyptian Army failures and an Israeli armored raid across the Gulf of Suez, Nasser dismissed him. Sadat returned him to duty and, in May 1971, appointed him Head of Intelligence Services. Ahmad Ismail's past disgrace acted like an all-consuming fire in his bones. This man's personal motivation, like that of Chief of Staff Saad Shazli, was to play an important role in the preparations for war.

Some ten days after Ismail's visit to Syria, on May 19, a Sadat seven-hour lightning trip to Damascus was suddenly announced. On June 12, Sadat again returned to Damascus to meet Assad. What was Sadat seeking in these visits to Damascus? In Israel — nobody knew. Meanwhile, a Syrian military mission returned the courtesy with a prolonged visit to Cairo.

In August, the activity spread to Jordan. On the sixth, Sadat's special envoy — Hassan Huli — went to Amman.

8

On the face of it this was strange — Amman was considered out of bounds. Four days later, Huli moved on to Damascus, accompanied by Jordanian Prime Minister Rifai. Barely three years ago, Syria attacked Jordan — and now Rifai was rushing to meet Syria's Assad under Egyptian auspices. In Israel, this was explained as willingness of the extremist Arab states to place more reliance on the pro-Western oil producers — like Saudi-Arabia. Sadat and Assad were actually preparing the last item in their military program; securing the Jordanian flank.

On August 29, King Hussein had a visitor — Syrian Defense Minister Mustafa Tlas. He arrived in Amman with the O.C. Moroccan Expeditionary Force to Syria — Major General Abdul Salem Safrawai. The Moroccan force reached Syria in late March. Damascus now wanted to know whether Hussein would agree to transfer of 2000 Moroccan soldiers to Jordan. Hussein rejected the proposal, but they continued to flirt with him. On September 12, a summit meeting attended by Sadat, Assad and King Hussein, ended in Cairo. Egypt and Syria announced renewal of diplomatic relations with Jordan. The end justified the means, and Assad was even willing to suppress those Palestinians who saw this act as treachery.

First Plan Your Move

The Day of Judgement War was the first one that the Arabs planned thoroughly leaving nothing to chance. This time, Arab strategists had the advantages of initiative and surprise on their side.

They initiated the invasion of Palestine in 1948, but their plan was extremely faulty and of low military standard, and coordination between Arab armies was poor. In 1956, Israel opened fire. The initiative was Israeli and Egypt could only react. The same was true of the 1967 Six Day War. Though the Arabs created a **causus belli**, by blockade of the Sharm e-Sheikh Straits and concentration of a considerable army in Sinai, Israel held the offensive initiative. Nasser had hoped to win by political moves

9

without a real fight. The Egyptians initiated the 1968-70 War of Attrition but it was a static semi-war with very limited objectives. The 1973 Day of Judgement War was different. The Arabs set the date and enjoyed surprise, in addition to superiority in weaponry and fire power.

Following repeated defeats, and somewhat slowly, the Arabs did learn a few lessons and draw a number of conclusions. The first was that, in the Middle East, the initiator has an immense preliminary superiority, even if the other side has considerable capacity to absorb blows. Fundamentally, this was a justified conclusion. From understanding that the IDF could react rapidly and was highly capable of manoeuvre, the Arabs progressed to the conclusion that preliminary initiative was not enough; they had to make their main achievements in the first stage of the campaign. Against the event of a military upset in stage two, they had to plan for an international diplomatic operation to prevent Israel tipping the scales. This could be done with Soviet help, and through the Security Council where Arab supporters were in the majority.

Second Front

Another conclusion rested on the assumption that the Israeli Army was built only for blitzkrieg; for economic reasons, Israel couldn't maintain total mobilization for more than 20 days, and her ammunition stocks wouldn't last more than 14 days of intensive fighting. "Israel's fear and nightmare is the possibility of war on two fronts," wrote Hassanein Heikal at the outbreak of war.

In analyzing Israelis' sensitivities, the Egyptians long ago concluded that the best way to undermine Israeli morale is to inflict considerable losses. Before embarking on the War of Attrition, the Egyptian Chief of Staff said that Egypt only needed to kill seven Israelis a day to defeat Israel within a few months.

With all this in mind, the Egyptians decided that taking the initiative was not enough; they had to strike simultaneously on two fronts, and be prepared — after the first

10

surprise blow — for a prolonged war based on large quantities of armaments and manpower from additional Arab countries. Arab quantity would overcome Israeli quality in a long multi-phase war.

When it became clear that war against Israel on three fronts was impossible, the Egyptians and Syrians sought to secure the Jordanian flank while the other two would be active. Hussein promised to concentrate his forces along the Israel border, and guaranteed that the IDF wouldn't penetrate Syria from the south via Jordan. A similar arrangement was made with the Lebanese, from fear of penetration through the Maraj Ayun Valley. Jordan and Lebanon knew nothing of the scheduled date, but were told of the general possibility of a new war. Baghdad was also not a party to the secret of the date, but did promise that, in the event of a flare-up, Iraqi forces would be dispatched to the Syrian front, while the main army would serve as a strategic reserve for both Egypt and Syria.

Strategies

The Arab operational plan was based on the following points:
• The opening would be a general assault, by many hundreds of tanks and tens of thousands of infantry, on both fronts. Even with heavy losses, there would be a reasonable chance of flooding the Israeli lines and gaining immediate achievements.
• The preliminary artillery softening-up and air bombardment would be short in duration and primarily aimed at the front lines to guarantee surprise for the mass assault. Involvement deep in Israel would only spill Egyptian and Syrian Air Force blood in the first stage, so pilots and planes would be, as far as possible, preserved for stage two. Only those planes assigned to stage one would be brought up to forward airfields.
• The IDF holds its forward lines with minimal forces. The first blow must be struck before Israel's reserve army could be mobilized.

11

• The assaulting forces would not pause to deal with Israeli frontline strongpoints on Golan or Suez. The Suez Canal crossing and breakthrough would be between Israeli strongpoints. Infantry would assault by boats. Bridges would then be erected for the armor and additional infantry.

• As darkness would fall, airborne commandos would seize the Mitle and Gidi passes and crossroads. Their role would be to prevent IDF reinforcements and reserves reaching the front quickly, and to upset Israeli activity on the rear lines.

• To increase the shock and surprise, a strike at a large population center will be considered. This would be by means of Kelt missiles — with an operative range of about 65 miles.

• The first stage objective would be seizure of the Suez Canal, and the whole Golan Heights up to the River Jordan. The objective of the second stage — penetration of the Mitle and Gidi passes in Sinai, and breakthrough beyond the Jordan on two axes — the Bnot Ya'acov Bridge and north of the Sea of Galilee.

• In case of mishap, the attacking forces would stop and group in phalanxes of armor. A wall of thousands of anti-tank missiles would be erected in front, while a screen of anti-aircraft batteries would deploy to the rear. Meanwhile, the strategic reserve from other Arab countries would move up to the front.

They selected the Day of Atonement — the most sacred day of the Jewish religion, as **Ayin (D Day)**. The assumption was that complete surprise could be achieved as this is the only day when even Israeli radio and television are silent. There is no traffic on the roads and, psychologically, it would be difficult for Israel's leaders to desecrate this holy day, while most Israelis are in synagogue. (In fact, on this day all citizens of Israel are to be found in one of two places; in synagogue or at home. Once a decision is made, it is easy to mobilize. On any other festival, hundreds of thousands would be out in their cars, blocking main roads, as war and major mobilization begin).

What was the Russian role in planning and in the decision to go to war? Intelligence services are of two minds, and considerable time will probably pass before the full truth is known. The less reasonable opinion claims that the Soviet Union pushed Egypt and Syria into war. Despite Moscow's desire for inter-bloc detente, the Russians were well aware of the U.S. President's weakened status. It was the time for new achievements in the Middle East, before the opportunity passed.

The other opinion contends that the Soviet Union knew of the Arab decision and warned Egypt and Syria that they were not yet militarily ready. But when the Kremlin understood that Sadat and Assad had made up their minds, they decided to play a role behind the scenes. The Russians assisted in operative planning and prepared all the military equipment for stage two. In the event of failure, they could argue that they had warned the Arabs. But the failure had to be prevented, for otherwise Soviet prestige would suffer an additional blow, and Soviet weapons would again be dishonored. In victory, they could pluck the fruits for assisting the Arabs in planning and in aid supplied during the battles.

There is no doubt that the Soviet Union knew the date of attack. To safeguard her advisers and their families, she ordered them to evacuate Egypt and Syria immediately before the war. In parallel, the Russians began a few days earlier to load ships in Black Sea ports — with military equipment for the Arabs.

SEPTEMBER 30, 1973

Troubled Eye

Deputy Chief of Staff Maj.-General Yisrael Tal's fears are growing. He intended this evening to dine with Nehemia Keen, the Quartermaster-General. Tal has just returned from a conference with the Chief of Staff, in which he recommended sending a standing army tank unit to Golan – or mobilizing a reserve armored unit for the purpose. He orders Yigal, his Head of Bureau, to cancel the date with Keen, and asks Eli Zeira, the Head of Intelligence Branch, to join him for a coffee and to set up a meeting with one of his senior assistants – Brigadier Aryeh Shalev.

Tal goes to them. He is worried and wants to question the Intelligence Branch situation reports. He builds for Zeira and Shalev a totally different picture, leading to the opposite conclusion; everything is ready for war. As Tal sees it, President Sadat did intend to attack in May but cancelled the offensive because Assad, President of Syria, didn't consider himself ready. Assad later began a rapid and immense procurement operation. The Russians supplied bridging tanks, Frog missiles, T62s and a staggering quantity of anti-aircraft missiles. Then, the Syrians began to reinforce their forward missile batteries. These are Tal's thoughts and doubts, but he doesn't succeed in convincing his colleagues from Intelligence Branch.

OCTOBER 1, 1973

A Candle in the Dark

The first Israel press report of tension on the borders appears this morning. **Ha'aretz** notes – in an item on an inside page – an alert on the Golan Heights, following Syrian transfer of army units from its Jordan border. The Israeli press is fed such tidbits only by Israeli military sources. The report says that suitable measures of alertness have been taken in the north, but tourist traffic on Golan is not restricted. The explanation is given as the great aerial battle on September 13. In public, the feeling is that it all stems from Syrian anxieties, and there is no reason for Israelis to worry.

On the Suez Canal, observer Corporal Zvi Beitan reports heavy Egyptian Army traffic and the transfer of boats and fording equipment. His reports have been the same for days. His commanding officer retorts: "You're seeing double!"

The reports collect in the Southern Command Intelligence Officer's department. Binyamin Siman-Tov, a young lieutenant who only completed an intelligence officer's course less than a year ago, notes the changes in Egyptian deployment. Siman-Tov's job is to collate details from observer posts and elsewhere, but they don't conform to the situation assessment made by his commanders, and by General Staff Intelligence Branch; the Egyptian Army is deployed for a large-scale exercise − "Tahrir 41". In a report that he submits to his superiors, he raises his suspicions: "It's possible that Tahrir 41 is camouflage for a real operation." His C.O. rejects the evaluation, and informs Siman-Tov that it refutes the Intelligence Branch situation report, and it would therefore be advisable for the young officer to delete his horrible conclusion. The lines are struck off the report − and Siman-Tov remains silent. His relationship with the C.O. is a tense one, and this isn't the first disagreement between them. His silence is accepted as concurrence, but Siman-Tov will tomorrow night prepare another, more extensive, report with the same serious conclusion.

Intelligence Branch also has its seer of evil portents, who isn't prepared to adapt himself to his colleagues and superiors. This officer is the Syrian Desk man in the Research Department. He is more pessimistic than his colleague on the Egyptian Desk. He isn't very conversant with events beyond the Suez Canal, but is convinced that the Syrian Army intends serious action. Nobody agrees with him in Intelligence Branch, but he does draw some consolation from the fact that O.C. Northern Command "Haka" Hofi called him directly − and accepted his opinion about the seriousness of the situation on Golan.

Maj.-General Eli Zeira, Head of Intelligence Branch, reports to a General Staff Session on a large-scale exercise underway on the Egyptian bank of the Suez Canal. Meanwhile, Syria is complaining to the Chief UN Truce

Observer about two Israeli tank battalions that have been brought up to Golan, with a danger of increased tension on the sector. The complaint is routinely forwarded to Israel.

OCTOBER 3, 1973

Cozy Conference

What will prove to be the most important Israeli meeting before the war is taking place this morning. It is a conference of cabinet ministers, with the participation of some generals and intelligence officers, which is now about to give governmental sanction to the intelligence mistake. From the moment the meeting ends, the error will no longer be solely that of the IDF. This is not a formal "cabinet session". Golda Meir, who has just returned from Europe, convenes the forum known in Israel as "Golda's kitchen". The cabinet ministers present are Yigal Allon, Moshe Dayan and Yisrael Galili. The officers are Chief of Staff Lt.-General David Elazar, O.C. Air Force Maj.-General Benny Peled and Deputy-Head of Intelligence Branch Brigadier Arye Shalev; Eli Zeira is ill today and cannot attend. Golda also brings her Head of Bureau Mordechai Gazit and her Military Secretary, Brigadier Yisrael Lior. Dayan asks Golda to call the meeting because he wants to report events on the border, and share his anxieties with her. This is the first time that any forum of cabinet ministers has been made party to recent developments on the Egyptian and Syrian frontiers. Dayan leaves Golda to decide which ministers should attend the conference. In the course of the meeting, he emphasizes that the purpose is to deliver a report; he hasn't summoned ministers to get decisions.

It now becomes clear that IDF Intelligence has a lot of information; full details, from various sources, on events in the Egyptian and Syrian armies. Only a hairsbreadth separates the mass of data from a decision that they do indeed intend to attack. In the light of this fact, as it is

16

presented to the "kitchen cabinet", the assessment of low probability of war represents an exceptional and bold decision on the part of those responsible for it. It seems as though the intelligence officers are recording long columns of data with deadly accuracy, but totalling the final column wrongly.

Stand-in

Arye Shalev is the main spokesman among the military participants. Golda asks a lot of questions of Dayan, Elazar and even of Peled — she wants details. She is obviously troubled. Allon also asks tough questions, mostly about the intelligence data. Galili only makes one comment; he suggests a meeting with Agriculture Minister Haim Gvati, before Yom Kippur, to discuss preparation of the Golan Heights settlements for possible war.

Shalev, equipped with maps and aerial photographs, first reviews the available information, and says that there are worrisome reports of Syrian intent to conquer Golan with five infantry and two armored divisions. From Egypt, there are reports that the army intends to attack in parallel to the Syrian offensive.

In analyzing the Syrian dispositions, Shalev says they are obviously "defensive" and reinforcement gained impetus after the September 13 aerial clash. Nevertheless there are some exceptional aspects, like the bringing forward of artillery and a bridging battalion. Fighter squadrons have also been moved up to forward airfields. The most obvious movement is of anti-aircraft missile batteries. There are now more batteries around Damascus than there were at the beginning of the year. Many more tanks and artillery are also noticeable on the line.

Now Shalev presents the Egyptian picture. He reports on the coordinated Egyptian Army exercises presently taking place in all command echelons. Forces are being moved forward, and ammunition is being issued to units. They are behaving as though it isn't a routine exercise but the real thing, Shalev says. There are a few exceptional

17

aspects, but reliable information confirms that it is only an exercise. The Egyptians are on top-level alert, as in all previous exercises, for fear that the IDF might choose this moment to attack.

Shalev concludes with an evaluation of the data. Happenings in Syria and Egypt are unrelated; in one place a manoeuvre, and in the other an emergency deployment that has been there before. As for Egypt, she assumes herself as yet incapable of total war. So it's unlikely that a coordinated Egypto-Syrian war will begin in the near future.

Golda Meir isn't through with her questions yet; would it be impossible for Syria to begin, and drag Egypt behind her? Shalev explains that Assad is a realistic, cool and balanced leader. Syria does have a few dozen missile batteries, and is more confident of herself, but she won't go to war by herself. Assad is scared that the IDF will reach Damascus. War just wouldn't make sense, and the Syrian deployment is apparently only because of fear of Israeli attack. The Syrians might be thinking of a limited retaliation for the downing of their aircraft, but even this is a low probability. The Syrians remember January 8, when the IDF reacted forcefully to their breach of the cease-fire.

United Front

Shalev isn't alone in his assessment. Elazar is prepared to accept the Intelligence Branch view. He doesn't reject the possibility of an eventual Syrian-Egyptian offensive, but not at this stage. Syria won't attack by herself. If there will be an offensive, at any time, the intelligence warning will be extremely short — especially if it's a limited operation. The Syrians might penetrate Golan, but can't take settlements or the entire Heights. Elazar explains that the Syrians may be interested in creating tension and burdening Israel. They must be angered by the sight of a mere few dozen tanks and 12 IDF artillery pieces facing their hundreds.

18

Moshe Dayan almost reverses the situation evaluation. His analysis of the stationing of missile batteries on the front line, instead of in defence of the capital, is brilliant — but he draws no conclusions. It's not normal or usual for the Syrians to bring-up missiles, nor is it "defensive". They know that Israel doesn't intend to start a war, and they remember that the IDF attacked deep inside Syria. It follows that strengthening of aerial defense over the front line must demonstrate their desire for greater operative ability, under a missile umbrella — on Golan. Dayan goes on to point out that the Syrians have both provocation and temptation. They can already cover Golan with missiles, and it's possible that they can see the Jordan and Roked rivers as better defense lines — after an offensive.

Dayan sees the Egyptian picture differently. If they cross the Suez Canal, they will sustain heavy losses and, in the second stage, the IDF will hit from all sides. They won't solve anything, and will be in a more difficult situation after the crossing, while at present — the Suez Canal protects them. There are even some Israelis who say: "Let them come..."

Golda accepts Dayan's conclusion that there is a difference between Syria and Egypt. While the Egyptians can't risk a Canal crossing, the Syrians might think it worth a try.

Since Dayan isn't asking for any decision, a question now arises about how to treat the information, and how to transfer it to the other cabinet members. Allon suggests that the activity in the Arab armies should be reported to the full Government session on Sunday, after the Day of Atonement. He says that the Government has a right to be informed. They decide not to mention the subject at the next cabinet session, which is to take place immediately after "Golda's kitchen" to discuss her recent trip to Strasbourg and her meeting with Austrian Chancellor Bruno Kreisky. They also decide, upon Dayan's recommendation, not to tell the other ministers in detail about Israel's difficulties in getting modern weapons from the US.

Golda Meir closes the meeting: "On Sunday, we'll lay these problems before the Cabinet, and please God we won't have to. Meanwhile it would be good were we able to send Assad to synagogue on **Yom Kippur**, with Bruno Kreisky. . ." The three ministers and Golda proceed to the Government session, and Elazar leaves for Haifa.

Defensive Briefing

Israel's newspaper editors are today the guests of the Navy at the Haifa shipyards. After a cruise in the new Israeli-built Reshef missile boat, the guests are seated for lunch with Chief of Staff David Elazar. One journalist wants to know what is going on along the northern border. Elazar answers: "There is a state of alert. The Syrians are concentrating forces, but it is a defensive deployment!"

While the Chief of Staff is at lunch with the editors, a strange movement begins in Syria and Egypt. Soviet Aeroflot aircraft are diverting from their regular routes in the Middle East — and even Europe — to land in Damascus and Cairo. They are loading Soviet advisers and experts with their families, and taking off northwards to the Soviet Union.

After the summer 1972 evacuation, there are a few hundred Soviet experts left in Egypt, and many more in Syria — some 2000 men with their families.

This is a strange exodus. Nothing is known of an Arab decision to expel the Russians, so something unusual must be happening in Egypt and Syria.

Premature Party

This evening, Armored Forces Sinai HQ is throwing a farewell party for their departing commander, Maj.-General Avraham "Albert" Mendler, who is to be replaced by Kalman Magen on October 7. Kalman has just returned from a study trip to England. Everyone wishes Albert well in his new post, but he replies in his calm soft tones: "This is a farewell party, yet I know that I won't be leaving. A war is coming fast." Some of his officers are surprised but others, like Albert himself, have sensed something evil happening across the Suez Canal for a few days now.

Albert Mendler is one of the IDF's elite armored corps officers. In the Six Day War, he commanded a brigade that smashed through Syrian lines to take Quneitra on the Golan Heights. Now, he has been appointed O.C. IDF Armor Branch. When he came to Sinai, in 1972, Albert said: "Now it's quiet here, and it doesn't look as though the Egyptians will risk a war, but I'm certain that one bright day while I'm in Sinai — the silence will be broken, and the shooting will start again."

Attention is being paid to Golan, but a decision is made to re-examine the situation across the Suez. Events are now reminiscent of a Greek tragedy in which there is no escape from the inevitable ending. The IDF is making an attempt to acquire data about the other side, but by an unfortunate technical hitch today's crop of information is lost.

And this is the day that the Chief of Staff tells the newspaper editors: "The deployment (on the other side) is defensive!"

OCTOBER 4, 1973

Second Thoughts

Aerial photographs of the west bank of Suez make the Chief of Staff change his mind. He is no longer satisfied with the Intelligence Branch conclusion: "The probability of war is low." He tells the intelligence officers: "You say there is no proof that war is imminent. Do you have positive evidence that there won't be a war?"

An intelligence officer thumbs through his papers and replies: "There is such evidence!"

After the war, Lt.-General Elazar will contend that, had all the information on exceptional activity on the Egyptian front been put on his desk, he would at today's stage have accepted a different assessment, and would have demanded immediate mobilization of the reserve army. According to his later claims, Intelligence Branch does have such information − but it isn't on his desk, nor is he told about it.

Despite Elazar's suspicion that Egyptian deployment has become "offensive", the General Staff session doesn't discuss this subject . Today's meeting is a long one, but the only point on the agenda is "discipline in the IDF". There is no intelligence presentation, and General Zeira is only represented by his deputy in Intelligence Branch.

A number of IDF units which were on stand-by are given permission to issue **Yom Kippur** leave passes to officers. The Armor School is ordered to cancel the alert. Albert Mendler's corps is also given permission to release commanders and deputy-commanders for home leave, but Albert doesn't like it. He has just reviewed the photographs of the deployment on the west bank of Suez, and decides not to allow leaves. Moreover, he orders recall of officers who are already on leave.

After the General Staff session, O.C. Southern Command Shmuel Gonen goes on to visit friends in Haifa. From time to time he receives phone calls from his HQ. Close to midnight, his Intelligence Officer, Lt.-Colonel David Gedalia, phones to tell him: "Everything is quiet, apart from one exceptional matter − but I don't know whether any importance should be attached to it. The Egyptians are also working by night on a number of the embankments in the northern sector." The Egyptians have for a few days been working feverishly at adding height to the canalside embankments, but this is the first time work has continued after dark. Gonen decides to shorten his stay in Haifa and, at 02:00 hours, starts out back to his HQ.

Russian Dunkirk

The Russian evacuation continues. A Russian freighter is anchored in Latakia port, having just offloaded weapons for the Syrian Army. Its departure is delayed by a few hours as Soviet advisers embark. More Aeroflot planes land in Damascus and Haleb. These are bad omens, but ruling circles in Israel feel that the Russian evacuation is evidence of Soviet dissatisfaction and has nothing to do with any impending war. IDF Intelligence is still convinced that this is not war.

In the Central Security Institution, the mood is more pessimistic, but Military Intelligence enjoys pride of place in the Israeli intelligence community. The Central Security Institution only deals with collection, while Military Intelligence controls strategic research and is responsible for the national situation evaluation.

INTERLUDE: DECEPTION

Eye Wool

The basic condition for Arab success in the war was absolute secrecy. To blunt Israel's alertness, the Egyptians deliberately created the impression that they despaired of military achievement, and had turned to the diplomatic battlefield. Emphasis was placed on the use of oil as a weapon and efforts were made to isolate Israel diplomatically. Libya expended vast sums of money on persuading African states to sever diplomatic relations with Israel. In Jerusalem, officials explained that Cairo's resort to oil as a weapon must compel Egypt to compromise with pro-Western Arab countries — Saudia Arabia and the Persian Gulf emirates. As long as Sadat pinned his hopes on oil politics, he would reject any use of hotter weapons. Israel began to swallow the first baited hook.

In late August 1973, UN Secretary General Kurt Waldheim visited the Middle East. To the surprise of many, Syria was prepared to receive Mr. Waldheim, and to discuss Security Council Resolution 242 — a resolution that Damascus violently opposed, because it indirectly recognized Israel's right to existence. Waldheim went from Syria to Cairo. The Egyptians chatted with him, and leaked to the press that they believed in a Middle East settlement.

In parallel, the Arabs began to create the impression that Egyptian and Syrian forces were totally unprepared for war. Rumors spread that Egypt's aerial defense system and anti-aircraft missile batteries were in an especially poor state technically, and their level of usability was low, as a result of the departure of Soviet advisers in summer 1972. From Syria, there was information that Syrian pilots were dissatisfied with MiG aircraft. There were repeated hints of disputes between Syrians and Russian advisers, and indications that Damascus was interested in purchasing new weapons from the West.

The "deception planners" understood that the complicated and difficult stage would be when the attacking forces concentrated along the borders. To sedate Israeli Intelligence, they resorted to "concentration and inactivity". They frequently moved forces up to the border, and took them away again. In June, there was a large "alertness exercise". Israel noticed it. At the end of September, forces were again concentrated in preparation for the Day of Judgement War, but Israel remembered something similar from June.

Winter Sports

Closer to D Day the Egyptians and Syrians spoke openly of winter manouevres, and Israel was convinced that the activity was no more than a large divisional exercise. When military sources were asked to confirm a connection between the Syrian concentrations and the Egypt preparedness, they whispered in the ears of Israeli military correspondents that Egypt was only holding an exercise. Israel had swallowed another baited hook.

The Egyptians played it as a manoeuvre up to the very last moment. The Syrians tried to copy them, but were less successful. The aerial dogfight of September 13 gave the Syrians an unexpected opportunity. They began to com-

plain that Israel intended to attack Syria. As they had
done before the 1967 Six Day War, they methodically
planted news of Israeli concentrations on the border.
Radio Moscow and the Russian papers soon joined in the
campaign to justify concentration of Syrian forces, and the
"cautious stance" adopted by Egypt. Damascus explained
and Israel listened; they did not doubt that Israel intended
to attack before the coming Israeli general election. "The
Golda Meir Government feels weak because of political
and economic failures, so it is looking for achievements in
other fields." The only way to gain more public credit was
via an Israeli military victory, which of course necessitated
alertness and build-up of forces along the borders. In Israel
– there was "understanding" for the Syrian fears, especially after the aerial battle of September 13.

Yet the Arab deception plan would not have succeeded
but for strict secrecy about the date of war. In Syria, only
three men knew – the President, his Defense Minister and
Chief of Staff. The President of Iraq wasn't told. Arab
forces in the field received no information up to one hour
before the attack. They thought they were holding a big
exercise. Arab aircraft were fueled and armed long before
the pilots knew their objectives. Traffic towards the
frontline only moved at night. In Egypt, soldiers from
units that moved into the line were not allowed to enter
the town of Suez or the agricultural belt villages. All leaves
were cancelled on September 28.

Thirty minutes before the crossing, Egyptian soldiers
were strolling along the canal banks, without weapons or
steel helmets. Some had their shirts hanging out over their
trousers to demonstrate that this was an ordinary, quiet
and pleasant day. In some places on the Egyptian side,
children could still be seen working on the embankment.
The critical Wednesday and Thursday, October 3 and 4,
passed in semi-pastoral tranquillity. It was only on Friday
that Israel became really suspicious – but not to the point
of general mobilization. The Arab deception had been
complete and well executed. At a certain stage, some
Israelis had grasped what was going on, but even they

didn't really believe it. When the war began, it was obvious that Arab cunning had, for once, overcome Jewish shrewdness and suspicion.

OCTOBER 5, 1973

A Stitch in Time

The eve of the Day of Atonement. The General Staff today decides that intelligence evaluations are one thing, and precautionary measures are something completely different. Though the assessment is still that there will be no war, the Chief of Staff declares an alert in the standing army; a C Alert — among the highest states of preparedness. Certain steps have already been taken on the Golan Heights, but the alert now covers the entire Israel Defence Forces.

The Government of Israel convenes in extraordinary session in Tel Aviv. Less than half the ministers are present. Most have already left for their out-of-town houses. Deputy Prime Minister Yigal Allon is in **Kibbutz** Ginossar on the approaches to Golan, and other ministers have gone to Jerusalem. Golda invites the Chief of Staff and Major-General Zeira to this session. The Head of Intelligence reports on the information in Israel hands, but suggests that war is not imminent. The Defense Minister and the Chief of Staff do not dispute his evaluation. David Elazar adds that he decided to declare a C Alert in the standing army, and reports reinforcement of forces in Sinai and on Golan.

"What's your opinion?" — a minister asks past-Chief of Staff and present Minister of Commerce and Industry Haim Bar Lev in the corridor after the session. "With the number of tanks now in Sinai, we can even stop 1500 Egyptian tanks," Bar Lev says. He knows that the hundreds of alerted tanks can smash a force five times greater.

26

After the meeting, the Prime Minister asks her secretary to check the whereabouts of the ministers today and tomorrow − the Day of Atonement − in case a Cabinet meeting will be necessary.

Change of Tempo

The evacuation of the Soviet advisers proceeds at a faster rate. It is now clear that reservists are being mobilized, both in Syria and Egypt; not a large-scale mobilization, but these armies are obviously preparing a strategic reserve. Israeli intelligence personnel recollect that Egypt mobilized reservists in June, but the dust then settled and peace and tranquillity returned to the front line.

A number of changes take place over night on the Syrian front. In the Soviet doctrine, these are typical signs of a change to offensive deployment. Medium artillery is brought forward. Sizable quantities of armor attached to infantry divisions are moved up to the front line. In parallel, the tanks of the armor reserve also close in. Fighter bombers move to forward fields. Everything indicates readiness for an offensive.

From the Egyptian front − similar reports arrive. Artillery is flowing up to the front. Forces usually kept around Cairo are moved in to the line. Close to the canal, the Egyptian Army is clearly shifting fording equipment up to the waterline; the small boats and bridges are usually positioned to the rear and well camouflaged. A great many tanks are now stationed alongside the fording areas prepared over recent years. There is no doubt that, technically and operationally the two armies are ready for attack, but will the order be given?

Israel still believes that nothing will happen!

The American CIA is awake to the situation and asks Israelis in Tel Aviv and Washington: "What do you think? Will there be war?"

The reply: Apparently not! Israeli Intelligence is known to be highly conversant with Middle East affairs, and its evaluations have usually been proven correct. The Israeli assessment is again accepted. In fact, American espionage services have no assessment of their own that could contradict the Israeli reports.

The standing army remains in camp. Fighter pilots are told not to leave their bases. Even the personnel of the IDF's Broadcasting Service do not go home. During **Kol Nidrei** evening prayers, military are noticeably absent from the synagogues. Before the start of the **Yom Kippur** fast, at sunset, the Chief Military Rabbi dispatches scores of young Army rabbis to IDF camps to organize religious services.

Albert Mendler, who has already recalled his officers, now cancels the special leaves for **Yom Kippur** long promised to Sinai tank crews.

Around noon, after the decision to impose an alert, Kalman Magen suddenly appears in Mendler's Sinai command post. He has decided to take a look at what is going on, and his impressions are dismal. Everything indicates war. Albert Mendler contacts General Gonen at Southern Command and says: "Shmulik, this is war!" Towards evening, Magen flies north promising to return the following day. In the plane, he reflects that he is to replace Albert within 48 hours.

Aran I

Meanwhile, another soldier, 19-year old Aran Zmora, is on his way north. He is travelling in a military bus, but not home: to the Golan Heights. He has spent the last few days training, with his Brigade Reconnaissance Company, south of Beersheba in the Negev. Two battalions of the brigade have already been ordered to Golan. Now, his company receives the same order. They load their armored-personnel-carriers on transporters, and crowd into two buses. Aran and his comrades know of the alert, but no one thinks that this time tomorrow they will be in desperate battle. The buses have hardly started out on their journey, and Aran's friends are already asleep.

28

Last Leave

Officers from the Golan Heights also come on home leave. Despite the alert, some have received passes. Eyal Shaham arrives at his parents' house in Zahala, surprising them and his sister with the new rank badges on his shoulder. This morning he received early promotion to captain. Eyal is a talented company commander in an armored brigade that has been on Golan for some time. He is following in his father's footsteps; Ze'ev recently retired from the IDF with the rank of colonel. In the Six Day War, Ze'ev Shaham commanded a brigade that broke through into Samaria in Qalkilya district.

Eyal tells his father about the situation in the north: "It's war, father! I see it with my own eyes. Anyone who thinks otherwise is very mistaken! For each of us, they have ten or fifteen!" Ze'ev Shaham is, as usual, cool as a light breeze: "Son, you may be a captain, but leave that to the generals!"

Ze'ev and Gila, his wife, part from Eyal. This is the last time they will see their eldest son. In less than a day, he will go to war to block the Syrian onslaught.

INTERLUDE: AN INTELLIGENCE FAILURE

Shortcomings of Success

Liddell Hart, British military commentator and historian, visited Israel in March 1960. In a meeting with Israeli officers, he stressed that the IDF's greatest danger lies in its success; victorious armies become over-confident. The Israeli Army was then after two victories over the Arabs. Meanwhile another two have been added; the impressive victory of 1967, and the disruption of Arab plans in the War of Attrition and for the **fedayin** organizations. It was only natural to be self-confident, and

29

so Liddell Hart's warning came partially true. The mood could be summed up in one sentence: "The Arabs wouldn't dare!"

Israel's greatest disappointment in the Day of Judgement War was the fact that her intelligence, reputedly the best in the world, failed miserably. What happened?

The Arabs themselves often complained that Israeli Intelligence penetrated every corner of the Arab world. The ironic tragedy of this war was that they had indeed penetrated deeply; there was no lack of information indicating war. Intelligence knew the movements of almost every unit, and the take-off of almost every enemy plane. But a fatal mistake was made in evaluation – the final stage of the intelligence function. Everything indicated war, but in Henry Kissinger's words: "Israeli Intelligence knew the facts, yet dealt in concepts."

Keen Foresight

Israel was awake to the possibility of surprise attack. There seems no better evidence of this than the following remarks of Chief of Staff David Elazar. On June 14, 1973, I asked him about the possibility of a new war. Elazar replied: "The Egyptians wouldn't be idiots to open fire. They have strategic and operative justification – and the motivation. The Arabs have reached diplomatic stalemate, and Egypt's situation in the Arab world is uneasy. Of all her options, the most dangerous [for us] is total war, in cooperation with Syria and with reinforcements – especially aircraft – from other Arab states. This option is dangerous because of its massivity and the likelihood of it being short. The Egyptians may well foresee preliminary, if restricted, gains. They could think that their opening strike will cause us heavy losses, followed by a freezing of the situation on the ground."

Asked whether the Arabs could surprise Israel by such a move, the Chief of Staff said: "It's impossible to start a surprise overall offensive from an apparently tranquil situation. The probability is that they will move to almost-public alert. They will open their offensive in stage two. In such a case, an offensive would be difficult to predict. Yet, I guess that their first blow will not be fatal. In our present situation, we don't need a pre-emptive strike."

If, four months before the war, the Israeli Chief of Staff could virtually forecast an almost complete scenario, how could there be an error in evaluation?

Ominous Precedent

A student of Israel's wars will find that this is not the first time her intelligence services have made a mistake. In 1948, there were intelligence officers who claimed, up to the very last minute, that King Abdullah of Jordan would neither throw his army into the war, nor invade Palestine. In early 1967, Intelligence Branch assumed that war was not to be expected that year; the Egyptians were busy in the Yemen and couldn't be ready before 1970. When Nasser massed forces in Sinai, blatantly inviting Israel to war, her surprise was total.

In 1973, intelligence history had turned its full cycle. According to all evaluations — Egypt wasn't prepared for total war at this time; she was only just making the preparations. Soviet experts were also known to be convinced of this. On the eve of **Rosh Hashana** — the Jewish New year — the Head of Intelligence Branch, Maj.-General Eli Zeira, lectured on the balance of forces. He saw 1975 as the critical year operatively. Based on the increasing size and strength of the Arab armies, and the change in balance of power, he believed that Israel would find it difficult to repel an Arab-initiated offensive in 1975.

Yet these mistakes alone cannot explain the failure of the Day of Judgement War. To do that we must return to 1967. The Six Day War was a turning-point in Israeli attitudes to the regional balance of power. Up to June 1967 the Israeli tendency had always been to over-estimate Arab capability. There was contempt for the individual

31

Arab soldier, but a growing fear of Arab quantity. Intelligence Branch and Israeli commanders always allowed a wide safety margin to guarantee security. As a result, there were often sharp arguments between Western countries and Israel, over the latter's attempts at arms procurement. Washington contended that the balance of power was stable, and Israel need not seek better than a ratio of 3:1 in the Arab favor.

Double Misconception

The Sinai War of 1956 was followed by social and organizational changes in Egypt. Universities were opened, and the number of students grew by hundreds of thousands. Industry expanded, and the Egyptian Army acquired considerable armaments. It also adopted a new doctrine of warfare suited to a mass army of low educational level. The Israeli assessment was that Arab quantity was slowly becoming quality. On the Arab side, an opposite process was taking place. Incorrect "translation" of internal social and economic events led Egyptian Intelligence to an under-estimate of Israel. So there were two diametrically opposed mistakes. Luckily for Israel, her mistake dictated greater caution.

The Six Day War confounded all the preconceptions. The Israeli victory was easy, perhaps too easy. It was felt that Israel had exaggerated Arab strength; the quality gap was a matter of generations. Immediately after the war, Israeli generals spoke of reducing the Army to a minimum, for no war could be expected in the future. Instead of talk about quantities, the subject was now — the qualitative gap. Immense numbers on the Arab side — whether men, divisions, tanks or aircraft — were no longer so impressive. The war, so went the evaluation, was not between 3,000,000 Israelis and 33,000,000 Egyptians, but between 3,000,000 Israelis and no more than the 5,000,000 educated Egyptians who could provide good soldiers.

So began a thought process that was to result in the mistake on the eve of **Yom Kippur**, more a national mistake than an intelligence error. A mental process of Israeli leadership, the IDF Command and the public at large, led to lowered esteem for the Arabs, and rejection of the possibility of Arab-initiated war. Retired army generals, who had been Six Day War heroes, provoked a sharp public debate over Arab capabilities. "Israel was in no danger of extermination in the Six Day War," so said Generals Ezer Weizman and Matti Peled. Others contended that: "Not only are the Arabs incapable of destroying Israel — they don't event want to." If this had been so on the pre-Six Day War borders, then it was certainly so on the new borders. Even those who knew the Arabs could concentrate considerable power,.tended to believe that the 25-year-old Arab fear of vigorous Israel reaction would restrain them. Israel, led by her politicians and Army officers, misconstrued Arab frustration as a stimulant in risk taking.

Defense Minister Moshe ·Dayan, usually known for a pessimistic attitude, was also infected by the bug. In March 1971, in a Weizmann Institute speech, he spoke at length and in a mood of high optimism: "Our situation has never been better, neither militarily nor politically. We were never 'offered such prices for our shares', and this because our situation is based on our power and United States' desires to see us unbeaten. If war will be renewed — it will find us stronger than ever before."

Wishful Thinking

Israeli intelligence data fell on deaf ears. There was no willingness to accept facts at face value. Perhaps Israeli commanders understood what was going on, but they built an impenetrable psychological wall around themselves. Intelligence Branch now became part of an almost inevitable process; instead of influencing they were influenced.

33

They served as good eyes and ears, but the brain and heart assumed that the Egyptians would not dare start a war — as long as Sadat frequently promises it and doesn't deliver. Sadat's first pledge of an attack was made one month after the cease-fire of August 1970 — the end of the War of Attrition. He repeated it three months later, setting a new date for the end of 1971. Then he announced that the "year of decision" would be before the end of 1972. Sadat swore by the Prophet Mohammed, but was in no hurry to keep his vow. Repetition only reduced his credibility both in Israel and in the rest of the world.

Israeli orientalists and intelligence officers slowly came round to the view that there would be no war for many years. There were a few exceptions. One was a past Head of Intelligence Branch, Maj.-General (Res.) Yehoshafat Harkabi, who repeatedly contended that the Arabs have a better understanding of the nature of the dispute; while Israel wallows in her visions of peace, the Arabs are busy with preparation of the technical means for war. Another exception was a General Staff officer, then-Brigadier Abraham Tamir, who was responsible for long-range planning. In April 1973, he contended that, with no possibility of reconciling the territorial demands of both sides, he foresaw war by late 1973. These were voices crying in the wilderness. The others, led by Defense Minister Dayan, felt that the situation of "no-peace, no-war" could and would continue for a very long time. This feeling could not but affect intelligence evaluations.

In May 1973, Moshe Dayan was pessimistic about the possibilities for war. Neither he nor the Chief of Staff accepted the situation evaluation that total war was an unreasonable conclusion. In a General Staff session that discussed the changing deployment of forces on the Egyptian front, Dayan said that the army must prepare against the possibility of war during that year. However, he was voicing different opinions two months later. In an interview granted **Time Magazine**, the Defense Minister said; the borders of Israel will remain as they are for the coming ten years. No serious war is to be expected within

34

that period. That statement was repeated on Israel Radio, and copied by the Israeli press.

No Devil's Advocate

No possibility for a contradictory opinion existed within the structure of the Israeli "establishment". Israel sorely lacked strategic research institutes. Positions contrary to that of Intelligence Branch met with irritable criticism, and the complaint that the proponents would be better off dealing with academic matters instead of pushing their noses into current affairs. Within government, there was no additional body that could double check intelligence appraisals.

Despite Israel's security situation, she had no national defense council. The Ministerial Committee for defense Affairs lacked staff work, and had to base itself solely on data presented by Intelligence Branch, with no recourse to expert re-examination. Intelligence research was the exclusive province of the military.

Over the years, Foreign Ministry research stagnated leaving an uncontested field. The national level situation report was compiled exclusively by the Head of IDF Intelligence Branch.

Nobody appealed against the faulty structure of the intelligence community. Quite the contrary. After the Munich Olympics massacre, at the height of the war against terror, there was a proposal to transfer other intelligence agencies to the defence establishment, thereby increasing the concentration under one roof – and strengthening the one voice.

Dress Rehearsals

October 1973 wasn't the first time that Intelligence Branch was called on to supply evaluation of Arab intent, in the light of concentrations on Israel's frontiers. In December 1972, war-like preparations were evident across the borders. The Chief of Staff was compelled to postpone

35

his promise of shortened conscript service. Armored forces were moved onto Golan, but nothing happened.

May-June 1973 was a full-dress rehearsal for the Day of Atonement. The Egyptians concentrated forces on the front line, apparently as a stage of their deception plan. Reserves were mobilized, missiles were moved from Cairo District, and fording equipment was prepared for action. Units flowed into the front lines. Israeli intelligence knew it all, but assessed the probability of war as low. "The Egyptians realize they are incapable of restricted war, because Israel will immediately escalate. Since the Arabs aren't yet ready for total war, there will be **none** in the near future," so the experts said. The Chief of Staff and his men didn't accept this appraisal. They took extensive precautionary steps, but nothing happened. In hindsight, Intelligence Branch was proven right — for the time being.

By October 1973, Israel and her Supreme Command were ripe to fall into the Arab-Russian deception bag. Intelligence again knew almost everything, but again assumed the chances of war to be very slight. Senior intelligence officers attached no importance to simple indications, like frontline observation reports on movements of fording equipment, and frequent visits by "orders groups" of Egyptian officers. Instead, they relied on information from other sources; they saw not the wood but the trees. Bare minutes before zero hour, they obstinately held to their evaluation of "low probability". Their supreme confidence even convinced US intelligence agencies that there was no danger of war.

This time, Intelligence Branch had partners among their superiors. The Chief of Staff and the Defence Minister relayed their situation reports to the Prime Minister without dissent. Intelligence must judge the enemy's intentions, but it is incumbent on the Chief of Staff and his Defence Minister to weigh his abilities and options. Their responsibility for the final assessment is therefore greater than that of Intelligence Branch. On Friday October 5, Lt.-General Elazar's suspicions were growing, but it was not until Saturday morning, dawn of the Day of

Atonement, that he completely rejected the intelligence appraisal. Israel had never taken into account the possibility of such a crude mistake occurring, and recurring to the very last moment. All plans were based on an IDF model of a minimal 48 hours warning. this time – the warning was limited to ten hours, and the delayed timetable was in force before the first shot was fired.

Mirror Image

Israel was experiencing Egypt's trauma of 1967. There is no need to seek distant and irrelevant examples like the German "Operation Barbarossa" or the sudden attack on Pearl Harbor. Israel had no dictator like Stalin, who could contemptuously dismiss warnings, nor did she suddenly find herself at war with a country which maintained an ambassador in her capital. The similarity between 1973 Israel and 1967 Egypt goes beyond the same elements of error and surprise; it involves the same armies, the same arena and a similar state of mind.

In both cases, 1967 and 1973, the military intelligence agencies of the attacked party misled leadership. When it was clear that the other side was massing force on the frontier, they reported low probability of war. In 1967, Egyptian Military Intelligence assumed that Eshkol's Israel wouldn't dare attack. In 1973, Israel Intelligence Branch made the same assumption for Sadat's Egypt. In both cases, this was not a last minute error but the result of a prolonged process. Both sides were engaged immediately before the war in a security problem of secondary importance, and therefore lost sight of the major threat. The Egyptians in 1967 had invested considerable efforts in a distant war in the Yemen, while the IDF and its Intelligence Branch in 1973 were greatly concerned with the war against terrorism.

Moreover, neither Egypt in 1967 nor Israel in 1973 were satisfied with their defense plans in Sinai. The Egyptians had been arguing over the application ot their "el-Kehira" defense scheme, while within the IDF the dispute was over the Bar-Lev Line. In both cases, despite the concentration of forces, the alert procedures were marked by complacency. In 1967, the Egyptians didn't move their aircraft from the landing strips, and war caught senior officers in the air as the Israeli Air Force pounded landing fields. The IDF's complacent alert will be discussed elsewhere — but again, in both cases, the opening hours were to determine the success of major operations; in 1967, the air strike destroyed the Arab air fleets; in 1973, the Egyptians succeeded in crossing the Suez Canal.

Leadership on both sides fell into the same trap of exaggerated confidence. Nasser in 1967 invited Rabin to go to war if he wanted. In 1973, Dayan promised to "smite them hip and thigh" while Elazar threatened "broken bones". The Egyptian public expected an easy victory in 1967, while the Israelis in 1973 had visions of the "Seventh Day" of the Six Day War. In both cases, many days were to elapse before leaders told their publics the full truth about the battlefields.

The opening scenario was the same, but the actors had exchanged roles. Luckily for Israel, the last act of 1973 was different, thanks to the courage of IDF soldiers who broke the thread of repetition.

OCTOBER 6, 1973 — THE DAY OF ATONEMENT, MORNING

Holiday II

Close to 04:00 hours, the phone rings in three Tel Aviv homes. The three are: the Head of General Staff Intelligence Branch, Maj.-General Eli Zeira; the Prime Minister's Military Secretary, Brigadier Yisrael Lior; and the Defense Minister's Military Secretary, Brigadier Yeshayahu Raviv.

The conversations are very short. "Information has been received confirming that Egypt and Syria intend to start a war today. Zero hour is 18:00!"

38

This is the beginning of a chain reaction. Lior contacts the Prime Minister at her Ramat Aviv home, outside Tel Aviv, and is instructed to summon a number of ministers for urgent consultation at 08:00 hours. Raviv wakes the Defense Minister at his Zahala home, and then phones the Chief of Staff's Head of Bureau, Lt.-Colonel Avner Shalev. David Elazar is awoken at 04:00 hours. A few minutes later, the Head of Intelligence Branch also calls him.

While putting on his uniform, Elazar calls O.C. Air Force, Benny Peled:

"When can the Air Force be ready to attack?"

"As we agreed yesterday. At 13:00 hours."

"O.K., you have a stand-by order to attack at that hour."

The General Staff is already in session by 05:00 hours. All its members are present, but for the regional command generals who have been invited for a later hour; they have a long way to come. Elazar opens the meeting, relays the new information, and mentions the order he has given the Air Force. He orders mobilization of Air Force reservists and a group attached to the General Staff. The first speaker among the staff generals is, according to custom, the Head of Intelligence Branch. Zeira reviews the state of alert and intentions of the Arab armies. Yesterday, he estimated the probability of war as very low. Now, he says that the new information increases the chances of war, but Intelligence Branch still believes the probability to be low. Elazar concludes the meeting: "Nevertheless, I must work on the assumption that the Arabs will open fire this evening. I will demand total mobilization, and hope it will be approved."

A Trip for the Children

Close to 06:00 hours, the Defense Minister arrives at his office and calls for the Chief of Staff and his deputy, Maj.-General Tal. A long corridor connects the Chief of Staff and the Defense Minister's offices. Within minutes, eight men convene in Dayan's room. The tension is great.

"Let's first talk of small things," says the Defense Minister. "What has been done to evacuate women and children from the Golan Heights settlements?" The Defense Minister feels at this stage that this will not be total war, but a large-scale incident on Golan. "We'll organize a trip for the children of the settlers. If there'll be anything serious — we won't take them back," Dayan suggests. As the Defense Minister speaks of women and children in the Golan settlements, Russian advisers' families can be seen at Damascus Airport, carrying overnight bags and small suitcases; a hasty departure.

Now the talk is of big things. Elazar proposes a pre-emptive strike. Dayan vigorously objects. Elazar's dissatisfaction is plain to see. Elazar wants to mobilize the entire IDF reserve system; total mobilization. Dayan again objects. His first suggestion is a reserve armored brigade for the Golan Heights, and another for Sinai. The bargaining begins. At the end of the debate, the Defense Minister softens his approach; he is now prepared to recommend — to Golda — the mobilization of an armored corps for each command. He doesn't approve on the spot, but postpones for the Prime Minister's decision. The IDF's delay now becomes more critical.

Outbidding Opponents

At 08:00 hours, Dayan and Elazar arrive at the Prime Minister's office in the Tel Aviv Government Compound. Ministers Yigal Allon and Yisrael Galili join the discussion. Elazar again proposes a pre-emptive strike. Golda also objects. The Chief of Staff knows that a pre-emptive strike can no longer prevent war, but it might disrupt the Arab offensive, destroy command and communications centers, and damage arsenals and airfields. From a military standpoint, the answer is clear. Any nation desiring to live would react the same way when it finds that, within a few hours, it is to be attacked.

Israel has also done it in the past — in 1956 and in 1967. Golda Meir and Moshe Dayan were among the architects of the 1956 pre-emptive strike. In 1967, Dayan was instrumental in the decision to go to war after blockade of the Straits of Tiran. With them sits Yigal Allon who, in his book, developed the theory of pre-emptive attack, and justified it politically and morally.

Israel's political isolation and dependence on the United States are factors that influence the ministers' decision. The feeling that the occupied territories form a sufficient defensive belt to absorb the first blow, and that the balance of forces is in any case in the IDF's favor, play a part.

Now, the talk is of reserve mobilization; a discussion that is at least 24 hours late. Even with total mobilization, the reservists cannot reach the battlefield before the Arabs open fire. The debate begins:

Dayan: "They'll accuse us of aggression. Because of mobilization, the world will say that we started the war."

Golda: "The world doesn't bother me right now." She turns to the Chief of Staff: "Dado, how many armored corps have we?"

The Chief of Staff answers her, adding that the absolute minimum is 100,000 men. The Prime Minister agrees; a compromise solution. One of Elazar's assistants rushes from the room to phone Deputy Chief of Staff General Tal. The reserve machine at long last begins to move — at approximately 08:30 hours.

The Defense Minister still believes the scope of mobilization is too big. "I won't resign if you decide to mobilize more," Dayan says with a smile, "but I think that some 30,000 men is enough."

Last Resort to Diplomacy

U.S. Ambassador Kenneth Keating is already in the Prime Minister's waiting room. He and his senior staff have known of the Arab concentrations for two days, and were more anxious than the Israelis with whom they spoke. Golda, in a weary voice, explains to Keating: "They're going to war. Now we have no doubt. They must be

41

warned in time. The spilling of blood must be prevented." Keating has only one question: "Will you fire first?" "No!" Golda replies, "I will do everything to convince my colleagues that we should not be the first to open fire."

Golda and her ministers have just made a decision exceptional in the history of warfare; Israel is to announce to her enemies that she knows of their intention to attack, and even the hour when the offensive is to begin. The assumption is that the Arabs may be deterred at the last moment when they realize that their plans are known.

Meanwhile the General Staff reconvenes, now with the addition of the O.C. Southern Command, Shmuel Gonen, who has just arrived. Elazar presents his plans. Today and tomorrow, the IDF will block and parry. Gonen will absorb the first blows while he accumulates strength. Then the IDF will cross the Suez Canal according to the pre-prepared operational blueprints. Tal presents the plans for mobilization. The Defense Minister arrives towards the end of the session. Dayan's greatest interest is in events on Golan. He again asks whether evacuation of the civilian settlements has begun.

The U.S. Ambassador to Israel sets off another chain reaction. In an urgent message, he reports his conversation with the Prime Minister of Israel. The State Department duty officer wakens Secretary of State Kissinger, who immediately contacts U.S. President Richard Nixon at his holiday home in Florida. The sudden tension along Israel's frontiers comes as a total surprise to the President of the United States. He had known nothing of possible and imminent war in the Middle East. Nixon instructs his Secretary of State to activate the "red line," inform the Kremlin of the anticipated danger, and report to U.N. Secretary General Kurt Waldheim. They also agree to send an urgent message to the President of Egypt.

Egyptian Foreign Minister Hassan Zayyat is in New York. "What's the point in your action?" Kissinger asks Zayyat. "Israel knows everything. Within two days, she will mobilize her reserve forces, and deliver a crushing counter-attack. Think about it!"

Zayyat promises to relay Dr. Kissinger's remarks, and immediately calls, from the Egyptian representative offices in New York, to the President's Office in Cairo. Sadat is already in his War Room. Some will later contend that Zayyat's message speeds up the Arab war machine; when Sadat and Assad became aware that Israel knew of the Arab offensive, they decided to advance zero hour from 18:00 hours to 13:50. Another version says that zero hour was changed two or three days earlier and that information given Israel on war at 18:00 hours was a deliberate plant.

Fateful Phone Call

At about the time that Kissinger talks with the President of the United States, Gonen is phoning from the General Staff to the O.C. Sinai Armored Forces, Maj.-General Albert Mendler. Gonen tells Albert that reserve mobilization has been ordered, and an Egyptian-Syrian attack will apparently commence at 18:00 hours.

"Give a stand-by order to the strongholds, but no tank movement before 16:00 hours," the O.C. Southern Command orders. "I don't want the Egyptians to see any movement before time, so they don't start earlier. I don't want them to have any warning that we are prepared," Gonen explains.

An argument is going on in Albert's HQ. An officer says that it's possible to keep the spirit of the order and yet move before the preset time. Albert's hesitation is evident. He wants to follow the dictates of military logic, and yet he remembers the order not to provoke the enemy. Albert is a disciplined soldier, who always expects his men to obey orders. Earlier in the morning, he even rejected a suggestion that the troops on the line should be ordered to wear flak jackets and steel helmets – because the Egyptians might think we are preparing something. An undisciplined soldier could perhaps open fire, or the Egyptians might exploit the tension. There had already been a precedent when, in October 1968, the Egyptians exploited a minor incident to open an artillery barrage along the whole front.

43

After Gonen's phone call, the frontline strongholds are finally ordered to stand-by. The order will save many lives. Some strongholds are instructed to send non-combatants to the rear. The observers at their posts between strongholds are ordered to withdraw to the nearest fortresses. Reports are important, but the men are too exposed. At about 13:00 hours, most strongholds receive the alert and stand-by order; not an order to take position, but to prepare. It implies flack jackets and steel helmets, removing various pieces of equipment from the compounds and preparing for artillery barrage — similar to that of the 1968-70 War of Attrition. The Suez Canal fortresses are manned by Jerusalem Brigade reservists and **Nahal** — Fighting Pioneer Youth Battalions — mostly without canalside experience from the War of Attrition. The tank crews close to the line lack battle experience. The company commanders served in the War of Attrition, and some of the more senior commanders were also in the Six Day War.

Not all the strongholds behave according to the spirit of the alert order. Some will later contend they didn't receive the order. Others, including the garrison of the Pier Position, will say they do remember receiving a stand-by order.

The O.C. Northern Sinai Sector calls Mendler to check whether he correctly understood that he may now move the armor. Albert replies: "No! Don't move the tanks!" Those present in the room will later attest that he says it in a hesitant voice; he is obviously not completely at ease with the order.

The O.C. Central and Southern Sinai Sector collects his unit commanders to tell them that the Egyptians are likely to open fire at 18:00 hours. They must be deployed at 17:00 according to the standing defense plans. Movement will only begin at 14:00 hours, and everything will be ready an hour later.

Quiet Saturday

Three army engineers are standing on the earthen canalside embankment, north of the Great Bitter Lake. One holds a camera aimed at his comrades. They're looking for a convenient pose, where the west bank will be clearly visible on the picture; it's a souvenir. They arrived at the Suez Canal last night to check fuel ignition installations close to one of the strongholds. This morning, they found the fuel sprinkler pipes damaged. This is one of two installations on the line. Tomorrow in Tel Aviv, they will report that the installations are inoperable. Meanwhile, they are using their time to tour the Suez Canal and take photos. They're still standing on the embankment when an armored personnel carrier passes, and the driver calls to them to jump in quickly. A stand-by alert has been announced and they must return to the stronghold.

In the IDF forward position on Mount Hermon, everything is complacency. Close to noon, a member of the garrison contacts HQ. He consults a senior officer on a technical problem, and then says there are signs that the Syrians intend to attack the position. One of the men will later relate that the officer answered: "Everything's known. It's a Syrian exercise, and there's no room for anxiety." And so, the garrison isn't worried; they don't even man their anti-aircraft gun. After talking to the Chief of Staff this morning, the O.C. Northern Command ordered reinforcement of the Hermon position with combat troops. The order hasn't been obeyed — but General Hofi doesn't know that.

Machine in Motion

The IDF war machine has been on the road for hours, but it's climbing a steep slope. Runners are out summoning reservists to assemble at pre-set points. They will go to unit stores to be equipped, and then rush to the front. Many reservists are at home. Others must be called from synagogues. A reservist is walking down the Savyon-Tel

Aviv road dressed in khaki and carrying an army pack. A prayer shawl is draped over his shoulders. In his hand, he holds a prayer book, and his lips mumble the ancient verses. As long as there is no absolute need, he has no intention of desecrating the sanctity of the Day of Atonement by riding to his unit assembly point.

A runner reaches a Tel Aviv synagogue to tell Welfare Minister Hazani, of the National Religious Party, of a government session at 12:00 hours. In another synagogue, Opposition Leader Menahem Begin is asked to come outside to receive a report from the Government Secretary.

In a Rehovot housing estate, a runner knocks on the door of the Levy family, looking for 24-year-old Doron who returned from a short honeymoon yesterday afternoon. On Tuesday he married his girl-friend, and they went to Eilat for three days. Doron is a combat corpsman. According to the ordinances of the Jewish religion, a newly married man is not called to war. His wife and parents accompany him into the street for their last parting before he goes to Sinai.

Waks I

On the Carmel in Haifa, the phone rings in the home of Technion architecture student Moshe Waks. The caller is his friend, Amos Ben David from Nahalal. Moshe and Amos are company commanders in a reserve armored unit. Amos wants to know whether Moshik has already been called. A few minutes later, the call arrives. His parting from his wife Ora is lighthearted and hasty. On the eve of the Jewish New Year, their son Matan was born. He laughingly waves goodbye to the one-week-old baby and his seventeen-month-old daughter. Not even a kiss. Moshik will be the first reserve company commander to go into battle on Golan. Less than 24 hours later, he will no longer be among the living. His comrade Amos will fall in battle later.

46

Agam I

Elsewhere in Haifa, another student is called. Reserve Lieutenant Yitzhak Agam, member of **Kibbutz** Ogen, is in his fourth year of mechanical engineering in the Technion. Twenty-seven year old Yitzhak commands a platoon in the reconnaissance unit of Arik Sharon's reserve corps. He did his conscript service in the Airborne **Nahal.** Now he must get to his assembly point somewhere near Beersheba.

Eleventh Hour

At 12:00 hours, the Government convenes in Tel Aviv. Two religious ministers, Burg and Warhaftig who live in Jerusalem, are missing. So far, only Golda, Allon, Bar Lev and Galili have been involved with the problem of war. A number of ministers now hear of border developments and the possibility of war for the first time. They are told of the decision not to stage a pre-emptive strike, and of the mobilization of reserves. All believe that six hours still remain to the war — if it will come. Not one minister contests the decisions already made, or questions the fact that the entire reserve army hasn't been mobilized.

Close to 14:00 hours, Albert Mendler accompanied by his deputy and signals and operations officers, inspects the command transport. He made a first inspection an hour earlier, and complained about things that weren't ready for battle. In anger, he ordered a second inspection.

A great many tanks are still standing under shed roofs. A suggestion was made an hour ago to disperse the vehicles and reduce the danger of damage in any sudden air raid. Albert vetoed the proposal, contending that the orders require no changes in disposition or external appearances. As he and his officers pass between the vehicles, they suddenly hear supersonic booms. They look up to see Egyptian MiGs attacking Refidim airfield. The war has begun.

While Albert races to the Sinai Armored Forces War Room, Gonen is arriving in Southern Command HQ. He doesn't yet know that war has just begun. His first act is an immediate phone call to Albert:

"I think it might be best to move the brigades forward and not to wait until 16:00 hours."

"Yes, it might be worthwhile!" Albert Mendler replies. "They're bombing Refidim!"

The new order to move the tanks and set the defense plans in motion, arrives too late. Albert calls the brigade commander responsible for the central and southern sector, catching him in the middle of a briefing to his unit commanders. While the brigade commander receives the order to move the tanks forward, four Egyptian MiGs pass overhead, and bomb a nearby camp.

In the multi-storeyed General Staff building – the Head of Intelligence Branch – Maj.-General Zeira is briefing Israeli military correspondents: "If the Arabs open fire, they will later contend that we began." A few moments before 14:00 hours, his secretary enters the room and hands a note to the General. Zeira glances at it briefly, leaves the room and then returns to take his hat and briefcase. "It will be alright!" he says to the tense newspapermen after one asks whether something is happening. "Nothing!" Zeira adds. He doesn't tell the correspondents that the note in his hand reads: "The Egyptians and Syrians have opened fire!"

On another floor of the same building, the Chief of Staff is to begin a discussion with O.C. Northern Command Yitzhak Hofi. Haka Hofi was summoned to Tel Aviv to recapitulate his defense plan, in case the Syrians do attack. Deputy Chief of Staff Tal, and Six Day War O.C. Air Force Maj.-General (Res.) Mordechai Hod, also attend the session. Hod this morning agreed with the present O.C. Air Force, Benny Peled, to go north and serve as Haka's adviser on aerial affairs. The men are sitting around the table when the Chief of Staff's intercom announces: "Sir, they've opened fire. The Syrians – and the Canal!"

In the Cabinet Room, Finance Minister Pinchas Sapir is speaking. A minister raised the question of what Israel should do if Egypt alone opens fire. Should the IDF also act against the Syrians? Sapir heatedly argues against. At that moment, Golda Meir's Military Secretary almost crashes in – and the room is suddenly silent. Brigadier Lior crosses over and whispers in Golda's ear. She raises her eyes to her ministers, and says: "It's begun! The Syrians and Egyptians have begun!"

Afterthought

At about 15:00 hours Israel time, the phone rings in the Rio de Janeiro hotel room of Brigadier Yitzhak Ben Dov, Senior IDF Engineer Officer. Ben Dov is in Brazil for a convention of engineer officers, and knows nothing of tension on Israel's frontiers. He has been discussing various water fording methods and equipment with his colleagues. His caller is a leader of the local Jewish community, who wants to know when to collect Ben Dov for morning prayers of the Day of Atonement. At the end of the conversation, he says: "Incidentally, they've just announced on the radio that war has broken out between Israel and the Arabs." Ben Dov doesn't go to synagogue, but to the airport.

INTERLUDE: COMPLACENT ALERT

Why all the Bother

The IDF's operational alert was a mirror of the over-confidence of Israel in general – and the IDF in particular. The Prime Minister and her ministers took responsibility for a decision not to strike first. The military proposed mobilization of IDF reserves too late. There was fear that total mobilization would result in escalation, and an underlying faith that the Arabs were only holding a large-scale exercise.

The already-late alert in the standing army was declared at 11:00 hours on Friday. But what happened from then till the opening of fire? Was the order properly transmitted to the strongpoints, emplacements and tank platoons? Was it carried out properly? the IDF has appropriate plans for specific situations; were they implemented, or was there a hitch in any vital link? A glance at photos of Israeli prisoners of war is enough to indicate that something strange did happen on the frontline. Some captured soldiers were wearing slippers and sneakers. Can there be better proof that they weren't prepared for battle? Was it because they didn't receive the alert order, or because they disobeyed it?

Condition Red

The IDF maintains three distinct levels of alert, the highest of which is a C Alert, that can only be followed by an order to take position and wait with weapons to hand. A C Alert is not a common thing in IDF command posts and the General Staff, but frontline soldiers need not be surprised by an order to increase awareness, wear steel helmets and flak jackets. The alert is only an order to command posts and units to be prepared and, in the standing army – a cancellation of leave. Commanders activate forward HQs, and the General Staff mans the Supreme Command Post. It is not a specific order to deploy or take up positions.

On the morning of the Day of Atonement, when commanders announced that war was to be expected in the late afternoon, little changed in the field by comparison with the Friday alert; not enough to affect Israel's ability to repel the first assault wave. Most commanders didn't consciously grasp that it meant full-scale mass assault on two fronts. The Golan Heights clearly anticipated a day of battle, or something similar – a frequent occurrence in the past. On the Suez Canal, many thought in terms of an offensive with minor crossings, or perhaps something like the War of Attrition.

In some places it was easier to implement the alert order. Air Force power is concentrated on a limited number of bases where pilots live. Their mechanism is well-oiled, and a small spark is enough to tense it for action. The Navy is also concentrated in a small number of bases. The alert order caught naval units just as part of the warship crews were about to depart for Day of Atonement leave. The base gates were ordered to stop men who hadn't yet left. A small number were stopped; most had already gone to the railway station, buses or the Israeli Army institution of hitch-hiking stations. They had to be caught at home on Friday afternoon or Saturday morning. The Navy's main weapons of war, the missile boats, were in good battle order, as would soon become evident.

Early Birds

On Golan, the alarm had sounded much earlier, though at a lower level, and there was no reason for the surprise to be so great. Many Northern Command officers believed that the Syrians must react to their loss of 13 planes on September 13. Officers in the field saw the Syrian concentrations growing day by day. The Golan Armored Brigade, of two regular and one reserve tank battalions, was reinforced in stages by another brigade. which was known for its high combat performance. In all, there were 177 tanks on Golan on the eve of **Yom Kippur**; not many compared with the waves of Syrian tanks that would assault the Heights, but double what the IDF kept on the northern front in normal times.

When war broke out, the 188th Golan Brigade's tanks were not at their firing points. A C Alert didn't require such deployment. They stood ready for war in their tank parks. Many officers believe that, had the tanks been in position, they would have been unable to stop the onslaught, but all agree that the Syrians would have sustained very heavy initial losses and events may have run a different course.

51

Major Omission

Despite weeks of tension on Golan, the necessary precautionary steps were not taken in the isolated Hermon Position. Northern Command was awake to events, but paid no attention to the mountain. An anti-tank ditch was completed, and minefields laid, but building works on Hermon were not speeded-up. Here, the IDF was caught with its pants down. For some time, it had been known that the position was not prepared to stave off assault. Its bunkers offered shelter against shelling and bombing, but there were no suitable firing points or communication trenches. Some of the positions were on exposed metal watch-towers, like those of the border settlements. Despite the C Alert, additional experienced fighters were not posted to the Hermon Position. The composition of the garrison could easily have been changed. Of more than 60 soldiers, less than a third were combatant. The remainder were administrative or technical personnel.

The biggest riddle of all was in Sinai and on the Bar Lev Line. Unlike Golan, there was no earlier tension but, in Sinai Armored Force HQ, a number of officers' professional noses told them something ominous was happening west of Suez. How else can it be explained that, on Wednesday, October 3, Maj.-General Albert Mendler said war could be expected soon?

Greek Tragedy

Some say that mishaps follow each other in a series. There was such a mishap on the Wednesday before the war. Most attention was being paid to the Golan Heights. Nevertheless, in accordance with good military practice, the IDF sent up a plane to photograph the Egyptian lines. It went and returned with over-exposed film. This was the day the Chief of Staff told newsmen that the Egyptian deployment is defensive in nature. The following day, there was another photo reconnaissance. This time, the film was in perfect condition and contained ample cause for the Chief of Staff to change his mind. When the photos reached Albert, he recalled all his officers who were on leave. This was the day before the General Staff declared the C Alert, automatically cancelling all leaves.

On Friday, Albert decided to send a talented young intelligence officer forward, to report directly from the observation posts. The young officer's first report was: "I don't see anything special on the line itself, but there's a lot of movement further back. I don't like the look of it!" He didn't spot the fording equipment, well-hidden close by the canal. This officer would continue to report directly to Albert's staff until wounded − in the first salvo − and taken captive.

Albert Mendler was a disciplined soldier. When, on Friday, he vetoed forward movement of the armor and an order to the men on the front line to wear flak jackets and helmets, he was obeying the spirit of the order he had received.

On the morning of **Yom Kippur**, O.C. Southern Command Shmuel Gonen phoned Albert to report that there now seemed no doubt about war; the Egyptians and Syrians would apparently start a coordinated offensive in the early hours of evening. But the previous order still held; there was to be no provocative movement. The armor must not advance from central Sinai before mid-afternoon, two hours before the expected offensive. Not before that! There will be enough time.

Spirit Without Letter

Pressure began to build up in Mendler's command post. Somebody said the spirit of the order could be observed, yet movements should begin before the predetermined time. Close to 13:00 hours, it seemed that military logic was gaining in force. Albert ordered increased preparedness, and it seemed that he intended to move the armor. A field commander phoned Albert to clarify whether it was now permissible to move the tanks. Albert thought for a moment and said: "I gave an order, but not the tanks!"

This was a compromise with himself. He apparently decided to advance the special alarm for men on the line, but not for the armored vehicles.

A partial advancement of preparedness, despite fear of escalation, was nevertheless significant. It certainly saved many lives. Men were transferred from small outposts to nearby larger strongholds. Some posts were ordered to transfer non-combatants to the rear. A great many forward observers were ordered to withdraw. Their reports were important, but they were too exposed. After 13:00 hours, the strongholds were ordered to prepare for action. The order wasn't observed everywhere. Some say they didn't receive it and carried on as usual. A number of prisoners who returned from Egypt, including the Pier garrison who surrendered only after a week of war, say they do remember an order. The order was quite possibly not carried out in a number of places because the men were too used to cries of "wolf! wolf!"

Sufficient Force

On the morning of October 6, Albert had 264 tanks in his Sinai command. Lt.-General (Res.) Haim Bar Lev, who later took responsibility for the southern front, had estimated this force capable of repelling up to 1500 tanks, provided it was in suitable defensive positions, and ready for immediate action according to predetermined plans.

The tanks were too far behind. For them, war broke out "too soon". Those in forward positions began to move according to the defensive plan but the greater "armored fist" in Central Sinai was only ordered to move at 14:15, and it reached the battlefield late. The first tanks raced towards the canal, reaching the battle zone within two hours, but their first encounter was 12 miles east of Suez, inside Sinai, where Israeli tanks met Egyptian armored personnel carriers.

Had the tanks been ordered to move earlier, some would have entered the strongholds. Others would have taken up position on the canalside embankment. The remainder would have grouped within ten minutes travelling time. The observers would have been replaced by armor. The bigger steel fist would have been 30 minutes from the canal. It is difficult to know how events would have developed. Some say these forces wouldn't have prevented the crossing. Maybe...

Academic Exercise

Nevertheless, the contention that the IDF would have sustained greater losses if the force had been moved forward − is inadmissible. In any event, the losses in armor were substantial when the tanks were hit on the way to their positions. If the forward force alone had been in the line, it could have considerably hampered the Egyptian crossing, despite the paucity of IDF artillery in Sinai, and would have earned more valuable time. This would certainly have been so had all the armor moved forward. The Egyptians would have sustained very heavy losses, and their gains − if any − would have taken much longer. Lt.-General Bar Lev, during the war, met a wounded armor officer, the young son of an IDF major-general, in a field hospital. The boy, with tears in his eyes, asked: "Why didn't I wait for the Egyptians in position? Why did I have to meet them and their anti-tank missiles while still travelling to my post?!"

The armored fist wasn't moved from fear of an escalation that rebounded in Israel's face. There was an alert in Sinai, but it was complacent. Officers in the field had their doubts and worries, but obeyed orders. For this reason, Israel was defeated in battle for the Suez Canal, the first important battle of the Day of Judgment War. Because the armor wasn't moved in time, the IDF's schedule was even further delayed; a delay that began with acceptance of the Intelligence Branch evaluation of no war and continued through the decision not to mobilize all the reserves.

OCTOBER 6, 1973 — THE DAY OF ATONEMENT, THE WAR

Air Power

Forty-five minutes before Albert and his entourage hear the Egyptian MiGs over Refidim, Sukhoi 7 pilot Captain Sharif Abdul Wahab Mustapha is summoned to his squadron briefing room. Alexandrian born Sharif will be one of the first Arab pilots shot down. On another airfield, Captain Halil Yussuf Halim reviews the maps. Halil, resident of Cairo and a Copt, is the pilot of a Nil 8 helicopter. He, with 25 others, is to transport the first assault wave of commandos into Sinai to block roads and strike at IDF command posts. The Iraqi squadron stationed in Egypt will also come in later. In this squadron is Lieutenant Abd el-Kader Hader, a 27-year-old from Mosul.

Sharif Mustapha's plane is pointing westwards when he is hit and compelled to abandon. Sharif is convinced he is parachuting into Egyptian territory. He sets off a smoke flare to mark his position for his comrades but, in his excitement, holds the flare upside down, badly burning his hand. Within minutes, a vehicle approaches. To Sharif's surprise, Israeli soldiers are sitting on it.

The Iraqi, Abd el Kader, wings in his Hunter to attack an Israeli missile battery. He goes with considerable apprehension. He returned a few days ago from leave in Mosul, to visit a brother injured in a road accident. When he was transferred to Egypt some months ago, he never thought to find himself at war. He was told that the purpose was combined exercises and exchange of know-how with Egyptian pilots. He will be assigned two sorties, but won't complete the second; his plane will crash in Central Sinai.

The Copt, Halil Yussuf, will be brought down by an Israeli Phantom. Halil and his machine gunner will be the only lucky ones of the 25 crew members and commandos. The rest will be killed as the helicopter crashes.

56

Aran II

For 19-year-old armored brigade scout Aran Zmora, war begins as two Syrian MiGs pass low overhead flying westward. Aran and his comrades reached the Golan Heights at 05:00 hours this morning, and were ordered to load their personnel carriers with ammunition. The company commander arrives at 10:00 hours and collects his men under a tree in the camp. He explains: "The Syrians intend to start a war this evening. The plan is for the IDF to hit them first. The company's mission is to penetrate Syrian territory and mark routes for Israeli aircraft."

The men of the company rejoice openly. At last they can prove their abilities. They've been on intensive exercises for 18 months, and haven't yet encountered the enemy. As the MiGs pass overhead in the direction of Kiryat Shmoneh and Kfar Giladi, Aran and his comrades study maps of the area in which they are to operate.

Break the Fast

Further south on Golan, 23-year-old Captain Eyal Shaham calls his tank crews together. Many are members of **kibbutzim.** Eyal intends to broach a delicate subject: "I suggest you stop fasting. "There's every chance that war will break out today, and I don't want you going into battle tired, hungry and thirsty. War takes precedence even over the **Yom Kippur** fast. Less than twelve hours earlier, he told his father that it would be difficult to stop the Syrians because of the ratio of forces. When he left his parents' house, with his wife of four months, Miki, he told her: "Whatever happens − if something does happen − on the first anniversary you come to my grave with a husband." His wife reacted angrily.

Now Eyal instills confidence in his men. Suddenly they hear the commander of a forward position over the radio: "The Syrians are stripping camouflage nets off their tanks! I repeat... the Syrians... "

Further north — complacency on Mount Hermon after their morning conversation with the senior officer who said "there's no room for worry." The position's anti-aircraft gun is unmanned as two Sukhois sweep in to bomb.

No Monkeys Over Suez

A few minutes before 14:00 hours, Yoav Canaan spots the "monkey" on the other side of the canal racing down his observation tower. "Monkey" was the nickname given, during the War of Attrition, to the Egyptian soldiers who sat for hours on trees and observation towers looking out over the Israeli area. Yoav knows this isn't the regular time for change of shift, and notices that the monkey's place is not taken by another Egyptian. His surprise is cut short by the whine of shells and thunder of aircraft.

Further south, observer Zevulun Or-Lev spots two MiGs crossing the canal and flying eastwards. The bombardment begins. A shell injures his commander and damages the radio. Zevulun, a Jerusalem teacher, rushes to a vantage point only to see four boats, laden with Egyptian soldiers, crossing the canal. He opens fire and is quickly joined by other emplacements. Within minutes, the boats sink. Zevulun was told this morning that war was imminent. Then he didn't believe it. Now Zevulun believes he and his comrades have repelled the attack. He isn't yet thinking in terms of a major crossing of the canal.

Yitzhak Sharon's surprise is even greater. A 48-year-old from Beersheba, Yitzhak is a liaison officer with the U.N. on the southern sector of the canal. He is in a swimming costume, with two U.N. men — a Frenchman and a Swede — lolling in the pleasant Sinai sun. He hears the first explosions and sees hordes of Egyptians crossing the canal. With the two observers, he descends into a bunker. On his way down, Sharon remembers reporting, a few days before, that the Egyptians were removing anti-personnel mines from the west bank. The Egyptians will come to the observation post 24 hours later and take

Sharon prisoner. The two U.N. observers will be transferred to Cairo and released.

In the northernmost forward position on the sea coast,
the first shells kill the three-man garrison mortar team.
Yonathan Chizik, a 27-year-old reservist from Herzliya,
rushes to the radio in time to hear the BBC announce :
"Fighting has broken out on the Egyptian and Syrian
borders with Israel."

Holiday III

For the residents of Tel Aviv, war begins with the rising
and falling wail of a siren. It was already clear that
something is happening. Army cars and empty buses race
through the streets; an unusual thing on **Yom Kippur**.
Rumors spread through the city. Many people stand on
balconies and by windows. Not one realizes that, at this
very moment, a young pilot is saving Tel Aviv from severe
damage. The pilot and a comrade are on routine patrol
when ordered to intercept a target approaching from the
sea. "We saw a bright point, high and far away, approaching Tel Aviv, and thought it was a MiG 23 coming to take
photographs. I turned towards it. At this stage, I could see
the silhouette of an aircraft trailing flame behind it. I flew
over it, saw it was a pilotless plane and understood what it
meant. I closed in and hit it with my guns. Chunks of its
right wing flew in all directions. The missile spun into the
water with a loud boom. I was thinking that it could have
smashed the tile roof I was building on the second storey
of my house."

It was a Kelt missile, launched 75 miles away by a TU16
bomber. A missile of this kind carries a warhead weighing
a ton.

Regroup for Defense

The Air Force is the least surprised of all. The
preparation for a pre-emptive strike galvanized its squadrons well before other units of the IDF. Confirmation that

the Egyptians and Syrians advanced the time of attack finds most of the planes armed and ready to take off. The only need is to change the armament of some planes; time is pressing, and some offensive ammunition is dropped in the sea. The first order is "regroup for defense," for fear of mass assault by enemy aircraft. The Egyptians' first attack wave is of 150 planes. At Sharm e-Sheikh, 12 Egyptian planes penetrate and about seven are shot down. The moment the Egyptians move out from under their missile umbrella, they're easy to hit.

The helicopters are simple prey. The Egyptian Army has 20 commando battalions that now try to go into action behind Israeli lines. Dozens of helicopters loaded with Egyptian soldiers, cross the canal and the Gulf of Suez, moving in the direction of the Mediterranean. Their purpose is to seize crossroads and passes, and attack Israeli reinforcements on their way to the front. Many fall in the waters of the Mediterranean. A brace of Phantoms have a ball downing — one after the other — eight Egyptian helicopters. The commando operation is a bold one, but costly with little to show for it; the most expensive act of Egypt's offensive.

At 14:30 hours, Air Force O.C. Benny Peled orders many planes from defense to attack on the Egyptians operating in the canal area. The pilots have only two hours to dark, when the scope of operations will be restricted. The order is to strike any and all targets, but it's no easy assignment, because the Egyptians are already crossing in force and intermingling with IDF units. In these two hours, some 200 sorties are flown along Suez and in the area of Adabieh and Zarfana on the Gulf of Suez. At this stage, few planes go to the Golan Heights. All eyes are on the Egyptian crossing. The planes ignore the missile batteries to strike at enemy troop masses east of the canal. By evening, the Air Force has lost five Skyhawks and a Phantom.

Interrupted Vacation

At his holiday retreat in Florida, U.S. President Richard Nixon receives a phone message that fighting broke out between Egypt, Syria and Israel at 09:00 hours Eastern Time. The caller is Dr. Henry Kissinger, who reports that his efforts to prevent war were in vain. Kissinger has been working at it for three hours. Earlier, he decided with the President that, apart from an approach to Egypt, the "red line" must be activated and the Kremlin informed of impending danger. A report was also to be given to U.N. Secretary General Kurt Waldheim. Nothing helped.

In Miami, Florida, another American hears of the Middle East war. Thirty-eight year old Dr. Harold Bargal is in synagogue when somebody says: "The radio just announced that the Arabs are attacking Israel." Dr. Bargal, an eye specialist, arrived in Miami a few days ago for his brother's funeral. He decided a year ago to immigrate to Israel for a trial period. His family is now in Israel, and he knows that Safad Hospital will expect him. He quickly leaves the synagogue and, within five hours, is on a plane with suitcase and operating instruments. Another doctor rushing to find room on a plane to Israel is Stanley Hirsch, a 41-year-old Pittsburgh surgeon and specialist in blood vessel operations. Four hours after reaching Israel, he is already performing his first operation. His wife arrives a day later. She is a non-Jewish anaesthetist. Lorin Hirsch says that she felt it an obligation. She immediately fits into an operating theater team.

Across the Atlantic in Cape Town, another doctor is shocked by the news of war. Moshe Shine was born in South Africa, but also has a firm bond with the Jewish State. He arrived in Israel after the Six Day War, shortly after finishing his medical studies. He volunteered for the paratroops, rising to the rank of captain. When he finished his service, he returned to Cape Town for advanced studies. He now rushes to the Israeli Consulate in Johannesburg. The consulate tries to calm him down, but Moshe goes straight to the airport to catch a plane for

Rome. There, by brute force, he pushes himself on a flight to Israel. One hour after arriving at Lydda International Airport, he is sent to the Egyptian front.

Media Move In

Thirty minutes after the first shots, Damascus and Cairo radios announce that Israel has started a war. The Syrians say Israeli forces attacked their positions, and their army is returning the fire. The Egyptian radio invents another story: "At 13:30 hours, the enemy attacked our forces in the Bay of Suez, at Zafrana and Sohana. Our army is reacting to this attack." Egyptian Foreign Minister Hassan el Zayyat will cling to this version tomorrow, though with a minor change. He will say, in an American TV interview, that Israel was about to attack in the Suez Gulf, so Egypt took the initiative.

The IDF Spokesman's announcement is more laconic: "At 14:00 hours this afternoon, the Egyptians and Syrians launched attacks in Sinai and on the Golan Heights, in the air and on land. After a series of air attacks on Israeli positions and camps, the infantry launched a land offensive. Egyptian forces crossed the Suez Canal at several places and Syrian forces opened armored and infantry attacks along the lines on the Golan Heights. Israeli forces are active against the attackers, and in both sectors air and land battles are being waged." The dry statement doesn't promise victories, but many Israelis are unimpressed by a later statement that general blackout has been imposed; everybody expects an easy victory.

At 14:00 hours, the Defense Minister tells journalists that the real war will begin tomorrow evening, when the reserves reach the line: "We will turn the area into a gigantic cemetery..." At a later press conference in the Journalists' Association Club in Tel Aviv, in the same hall where he met newsmen on the eve and end of the Six Day War, Dayan declares: "The IDF will smite the Egyptians in Sinai hip and thigh. The war will end within a few days with our victory."

For some reason the Defense Minister doesn't even mention the Golan Heights. Moshe Dayan obviously hasn't yet grasped the significance of an overall Arab offensive, and the dangers it poses for Israel.

Flight North

Close to 15:00 hours, an IDF helicopter tries to land at Mahanayim airfield in northern Israel. Major-Generals Haka Hofi, the O.C. Northern Command, and Motti Hod, past O.C. Air Force, are aboard. Fire rains down on Mahanayim. The Syrians appear to be aiming ground-to-ground Frog missiles at the airfield. During a lull, the helicopter lands and Hofi and Hod set off in a half-track to meet Brigadier Raphael Eitan. After a short discussion, the three decide to fly to Nafah Command Post on Golan. Haka, Motti and Raful arrive at Nafah at 15:30 hours, and enter the command bunker.

Waks II

Meanwhile, Moshik Waks is phoning his wife Ora. He tells her resentfully: "We are just sitting here!" Moshik phones again after five: "It's O.K. We're about to move. The company's ready." This is the last time Ora will hear her husband's voice.

As Moshik moves with his company towards the Golan Heights, the battle for Mount Hermon is already all but over. In parallel with the aerial attack, the Syrian artillery opens heavy fire. Most of the garrison of the Hermon Position congregate in its central bunker. Those remaining outside see three helicopters approaching. For a moment, they aren't certain whether these are Israeli or Syrian. One lands by the upper terminal of the skiers' cable car, and soldiers burst from it. The other two land not far from the position. A Druze farmer will later report that one helicopter was hit and went up in flames.

At the same time, a battalion-size commando force sweeps forward out of the nearby Syrian position. The helicopter-borne force and the commandos open a co-ordinated assault. Their fierce fire drives the Israelis into the bunkers; the firing points are not well enough sheltered. The Syrians quickly gain control over the extremities of the Israeli position, and succeed in opening an emergency exit of the bunker. They burst in and smash radar equipment with gunshots and hand grenades. "The objective was to blind Israel's eyes that look out over Damascus," a Syrian military commentator will later explain. The Israeli soldiers are fighting for their lives. Some retreat into corridors and other rooms in the labyrinth of bunkers, closing iron bulkheads behind them. The Syrians make no attempt to follow, but throw smoke grenades through every crack and hole. Thick suffocating smoke drives some Israeli soldiers out with their arms up high.

Tidal Wave

Ten minutes after the beginning of the barrage, Syrian armor begins to pour through the Israeli line on Golan. It's a flood. While artillery fire rocks the ground, the IDF forward positions try to fire at the armored columns. But the tanks are not attacking them. Their tactic is to bypass in depth and not tangle with the positions on the cease-fire line; there'll be time for them later. They adopt the same attitude to the Golan settlements. The Syrian columns avoid all but one — Ramat Magshimim.

The settlers on the Heights are saved by a miracle. At 09:00 hours this morning, they received an order to evacuate all women and children. Mavo Hamma and **Kibbutz** Merom Golan suspected political objectives; only after an effort were they convinced of the danger. The buses to evacuate women and children are late in arriving. The first arrive at the height of the artillery barrage and the evacuation only ends after dark. The men withdraw at dawn.

Unlike the 1948 War of Independence pattern, the border settlements of Golan are not fighting units. They

64

aren't considered military outposts capable of blocking an attacking army. They have no anti-tank weapons with which to delay Syrian armor. In fact, they become a nuisance the moment war begins. The Army has to devote considerable time and facilities to evacuation of the settlers. This is an illustration of the long road Israel has traversed since 1948. In the War of Independence, the entire country was the frontline. Now, even border settlements are unprepared to repel enemy attack.

Their Own Kind

Near Ramat Magshimim, a Syrian armored column encounters an Israeli Beduin woman, Hasma abu Gadir, and her two daughters. Thirty year old Hasma took cover in a field during the heavy barrage, with her ten-year-old daughter and four-month-old baby. Syrian soldiers accuse her of spying for Israel. One grabs her by the throat and demands a confession. Her daughter rushes to her aid, and another soldier shoots and kills the child. After consultation, the Syrians decide to spare Hasma's life. They clamber back on their tanks, but not before shooting her in both legs.

In Central Golan, a young **kibbutznik,** Amos from Givat Yoav, avoids a similar fate. He went hunting this morning and was trapped by the Syrian bombardment. He takes cover under a bridge on the "Petroleum Road." A long wait, and then he hears the rumble of a Syrian tank. The firing persists and the tank is damaged. Two Syrian crewmen look for shelter at the other end of the bridge, without noticing Amos. A long time passes until other Syrian tanks arrive to extricate the two soldiers. As darkness falls, Amos slips away.

Overwhelming Odds

The Syrians assault with three divisions and other independent brigades. In all, some 800 tanks take part in the first wave. The mechanized divisions are to break

65

through the frontline and penetrate at least six miles, opening the way for two armored divisions to reach the Jordan River. The front is broached on two sectors. In the north, on the approaches to Quneitra, more than 200 tanks participate in the first wave. In the central sector by Rafid, the breakthrough is in two prongs. One Syrian force probes towards Nafah base camp and the Bnot Yaacov Bridge. The second turns south towards Ramat Magshimim and El Al, and then on to the Jordan estuary and Arik Bridge. The central and southern wave encompasses some 600 tanks; a staggering mass of armor compared with the small area in which it must operate.

Though another armored brigade climbed the Golan Heights on the eve of war, the total force is no more than 180 tanks — a part of that planned for defense against Syrian attack. The immense disparity between atacking and defending forces is immediately felt. The pace of attack is so fast that the Air Force has difficulty in supplying ground support. Syrian tanks approach very close to Israeli vehicles. The pilots can't differentiate, in this mountainous area, between the enemy and the IDF. Ground-to-air missiles add to their problems. The Air Force chooses to operate against missile batteries and other targets in depth.

Night Sight

As darkness falls, the Syrian tanks continue their forward thrust, aided by infra-red night-sight equipment. The Golan Heights Brigade has to face the main Syrian effort and is too thinly spread on the ground. As opposed to the force on the Quneitra approaches, which operates in greater concentrations, this brigade works in small groups. Its commanders are torn between blocking Syrian armor that flows like lava, and back-up defense to the IDF frontline positions. Either way, the brigade is slowly decimated.

The Syrian tanks relentlessly probe towards the Nafah command post. A little after midnight, they are a few thousand yards from Nafah, on the main Bnot Yaacov Bridge — Quneitra Road. At 02:00 hours, Hod suggests to the O.C. Northern Command that he leaves Nafah: "If you want to go on running this war, you must get out of here quickly. It's only a question of time until the communications installations stop functioning."

Haka Hofi takes the hint. Before leaving, he gives Brigadier Raful Eitan responsibility for the Golan Heights. Raful must now try to block until the reserve units arrive. Haka and Hod set out for the Northern Command bunker.

Ballistic Playground

In the middle of the night, the residents of Migdal Ha'emek close to Nazareth, awaken to a loud explosion, convinced that saboteurs are at work. In fact, it is the premiere of a new weapon, a ground-to-ground Frog missile fired from 55 miles away. The Syrians aim blindly at the Jezreel Valley settlements, but are apparently trying to hit Ramat David airfield. The Frogs will go on landing for three more days before the IDF Spokesman will be authorized to announce Syrian use of ground-to-ground missiles.

Waks III

Not long after Hofi and Hod leave Nafah, Captain Moshik Waks arrives at the foot of Golan with the first reserve company to reach the battlefield. In terms of time, the achievement is most impressive. Most of the men only reported for duty 12 hours ago. There is no time to wait for other companies of the battalion. Any force, however small, is sent straight up. Making up tank crews by their regular composition is not important right now.

If anybody deserves to be with the first reserve force on the battlefield, it is undoubtedly Moshik Waks. As a member of the Golan Heights Brigade, he knows the area like the palm of his hand. From the Six Day War till June

67

1971, when he was released from the IDF, he took part in almost every clash with the Syrians. His is a crack company, and a scoreboard in the battalion base notes that he and his crew have the largest tally of Syrian tanks.

The More — The Merrier

The assault on Suez is fundamentally different. Contrary to the Soviet doctrine, the Egyptians begin with only 15 minutes softening-up barrage that includes 240 millimeter heavy mortars. The first assault waves are infantrymen, who must seize a hold on the east bank and begin to consolidate bridgeheads; a mass assault of some 10,000 men. The Egyptians use high pressure water jets to break holes in the Israeli embankment. They cross in hundreds of rubber, wooden and metal boats along the entire length of the Suez Canal, with concerted efforts in at least seven places. They seem to expect heavy opposition, and therefore prefer multiple crossings, on the assumption that they must succeed somewhere. Twenty minutes after the barrage begins, amphibian tanks and armored personnel carriers cross the Great Bitter Lake, in Kibrit district, and are the first vehicles to penetrate Sinai.

The first assault wave is aimed at taking the places where the Egyptian Army engineers must erect bridges. Part of the force engages strongholds and other forward positions, to prevent the IDF activating installations to set the canal waters ablaze. The infantry climb the earthern embankment with the help of ladders, and spread like locusts. The strongpoint garrisons are most surprised, not at the heavy hail of fire, but by the hordes of men. The barrage prevents them from observing areas distant from their positions.

Combat Exercise

Egyptian engineers work alongside the bridges, assisted by frogmen. Trucks back up to the waterline and drop in lighters and bridge sections. The lighters are linked together, one after the other, and within half an hour – by the drill used in the Soviet Army – a foot bridge spans Suez. Three divisions of second-wave infantry race across; more than 40,000 men in a few hours. Then bridges for armor; heavier bridges, which according to the drill should take 4 hours to build but now take much longer – not because of IDF hindrance. The hitches are mainly technical.

The IDF is noticeably short of artillery. The few batteries are incapable of properly responding to the Egyptian fire. There are too many targets and too few guns. On Suez, as on the Golan Heights, the IDF's sparse forces have difficulty in stemming the deluge.

The assault force follows correct tactics. A few men attack the strongholds, supported by heavy artillery fire, while the masses bypass and continue on into Sinai. The fortresses are secondary. The primary Egyptian objective is to reach a depth of six to eight miles.

First Trauma

The scene opening up before the frontline garrisons is a nightmare. The quantities of shells and men, and the weakness of Israeli counter-fire is a shock to many of them. The first strongpoints to be attacked cope with anyone crossing within the range of light arms and mortar fire. But it is a drop in the ocean. Hordes of Egyptian vehicles cluster around the crossing areas, but Israeli aircraft don't appear in any real numbers. Those that do attack the Egyptians are not completely free agents; they encounter a barrage of missiles from the west bank.

Many of the fortresses are manned by reservists of the Jerusalem Division. This is their first tour of duty in the canalside strongholds. They reported on September 23, and are due to be released on October 25. Further south, the line is held by mostly religious **Nahal** men. For them the shock is greater, because the Day of Atonement has been desecrated. In one stronghold, the religious soldiers make no concession. During a lull between assault waves, a man

69

goes down to the main bunker to blow the blast that signals the end of the fast, on a **shofar** — a ceremonial ram's horn. .

When the barrage began, there were only three IDF tanks on the line between the strongholds. This is a small percentage of the number that should have been in position — if the defense plan had been activated in time. More tanks are racing from the **taozim** — the second line of strongpoints seven miles inland from the Suez Canal. Twenty tanks reach the canalside embankment within 30 minutes, but more than a third are immediately put out of action by anti-tank missiles and RPG Bazooka fire, emanating from Egyptian infantry on the embankment.

About 30 minutes after zero hour, two tanks reach the Pier Position at the southern end of the canal. At 14:45 hours, the entire first line armor is in battle. Reports of dead and wounded already pour into Sinai Force HQ. The rear unit has been moving fast for 30 minutes but the delay is great. Albert's command post already knows that the Egyptian attack is on a large-scale. Southern Command HQ also understands that it is a massive crossing but their battle picture is not clear enough. They know what is going on facing the strongholds, but little of what is happening inbetween. In the afternoon hours, the mood is still optimistic. Albert Mendler's command is ordered to prepare for a crossing to the west bank on Sunday night — tomorrow. By then, a considerable force of reserves should have arrived. The men who give the order cannot know that within a few hours, Albert's corps will have lost almost half of its tanks.

Agam II

Lieutenant Yitzhak Agam has been chasing around his reconnaissance unit store for an hour. The quartermasters are under heavy pressure. An order is finally given to issue equipment without obtaining signatures from the men. The problem is — not all the equipment is to be found. The armored personnel carriers allotted to Agam's company have plentiful ammunition, but no hand grenades and some machine guns are missing. Each APC has only one machine gun, with no barrel, and the tanks have no machine guns at all.

Agam is surprised to find that the field glasses are missing. Without binoculars, reconnaissance and armor actions will be very difficult. One man finds a pair of night-glasses with SLS starlight magnification in a neighboring store; the only one of its kind in the entire reconnaissance unit. The quartermaster tells Agam that he is out of Uzzi submachine guns. Yitzhak finally convinces a quartermaster of another unit to give him an Uzzi. There are enough shells in the tanks, but when they move out – the men discover that the gun sights have not been zeroed.

Button Undone

Ras el Ayish South stronghold on the northern sector is code-named "Button". As the crossing begins, it reports attacks by Egyptian soldiers. The sounds of battle can be heard over the radio. The fortress makes itself heard a few times, and then close to 16:00 hours, falls silent. There are no details of what happened. This is the first strongpoint to fall into Egyptian hands. The news from the more northerly "Tempo" strongpoint is also troublesome. The Egyptians seem to have penetrated its inner compound. All other strongpoints radio in regularly. The sea coast position reports an Egyptian force approaching along the coastal reef. The two Israeli tanks in the strongpoint compound hit six Egyptian tanks and five armored personnel carriers. Two Phantom aircraft, arriving at the right moment, assist in repelling the assault.

There is no good news from the men of the armored corps. Reports of disabled tanks mount by the hour. The brigade commanders alongside the Suez Canal report serious attrition of their vehicles. The shock is accompanied by surprise. The crossing force is known to be mostly infantry and the Israeli commanders are at first sure that IDF tanks will sweep them up easily. Approaching armor should send shock tremors through Egyptian ranks. But reports are that the infantry is standing fast in the face of tanks.

"They're firing thousands of missiles and bazooka shells at us," says report after report over the radios. The tank commanders charge the Egyptian infantry confidently and mow them down with their machine guns, but missiles fired from all quarters are hitting more and more tanks. At short range, the Egyptians are firing RPG7 Bazookas, while from further off, they shoot low-trajectory Sagger missiles. The hollow-headed bazooka shells penetrate tank armor and there is one launcher to every three Egyptian soldiers. Their infantry are far from helpless in long-range battle; Sagger missiles have a longer reach than tank machine guns. Firing shells at infantry is wasteful and inefficient.

During the afternoon, Maj.-General Gonen instructs his tank crews not to approach too close to the infantry. "If only I had more artillery," he says to the officers around him.

As darkness falls, the situation improves somewhat. Darkness gives cover both to Egyptian infantry, and Israeli tanks. Some tanks reach the strongholds and it would still be possible to evacuate most of the garrisons, but none of the senior commanders are thinking of it tonight. Such a suggestion would now sound like retreat. Moreover, according to the canal defense theories, there is as yet no need to evacuate strongpoints. The feeling is that the fortresses can still hold out; each has plentiful ammunition, food and water for a week of combat, and nobody entertains the thought that the IDF will not repel the Egyptians within a week. The larger strongholds have their own doctors and many of the wounded from the tanks are transferred to the fortresses rather than to the rear.

Mutual Surprise

Chief of Staff Lt.-General David Elazar, arrives at Southern Command HQ. Maj.-General Gonen reports on the situation and on the damage to the armor. The last report, just in, says that many of the front line tanks are out of commission, whether from missile and bazooka hits or because of technical faults. By any yardstick, the situation is bad.

The Egyptians are surprised at the ease with which they crossed the Suez Canal. The most optimistic Egyptian officers expected thousands of casualties. Their dead in the first wave were no more than 180 men.

At 18:00 hours, the War Minister reports the success of stage one – the crossing – to Sadat. "The Arab nation has crashed through the fear barrier!" – Sadat reacts happily.

Pleasure Cruise I

Israel's only good news today comes from the naval arena. At 16:00 hours, two hours after the outbreak of war, five missile ships weigh anchor and speed northwards towards Latakia on the Syrian coast. At 23:00 hours, the world's first ever battle between missile boats takes place. The Syrians are firing Soviet Styx missiles. The Israeli ships reply with Gabriel missiles produced by the Israel Aircraft Industries. The Russian missiles have 10 miles more effective range, but of the scores fired by the Syrians, not one Styx hits its target. Some are brought down by gunfire, but experts assess the main reason for their failure as being efficient Israeli electronic devices that tamper with the aim of the Russian-made missiles. The Gabriels' range may be shorter, however they fly low over the waves, making them difficult to spot and even harder to hit. The Syrians lose a torpedo boat, a mine-sweeper with its crew of 80, and 3 missile ships. One missile ship escapes, beaching itself at a spot where the Israeli boats pour forth their wrath on it.

INTERLUDE: THE FEAR BARRIER

Honor of a Nation

From the first moments of war, the Egyptian radio repeatedly broadcast: "The honor of our fathers, the honor of our children, the honor of the entire nation is in your hands. Stand fast! Be firm!" This slogan also appeared in the operation orders issued to Egyptian units. The war was, for the Arabs, more for Arab honor than for territory. The Egyptians and Syrians wanted to prove to themselves, and to the world, that they could fight. They didn't expect to defeat the IDF. They did hope to reinstate the Arab-Israeli dispute on the agenda of international debating tables but, above all, they wanted to restore their national, military and personal honor. A self-respect lost following repeated defeats.

At the height of the campaign, before the IDF established its own bridgehead across the Suez Canal, Egyptian Chief of Staff Saad a-Din Shazli wrote in an order of the day to his troops: "The war retrieved Arab honor. Even if we will be defeated now, no one can say that the Egyptian soldier is not a superior fighter." Egyptian War Minister Ahmad Ismail Ali visiting the front line, repeated the same concept: "Egypt is restoring her national pride. The armed forces are giving Egypt back her honor."

"Arab honor" was repeated everywhere. Civilians on the home front spoke of restored honor. A captured Egyptian lieutenant-colonel, commander of a ground-to-air missile battalion, told Lt.-General Haim Bar Lev: "We didn't achieve our military objectives, but we restored our honor; a great achievement, and the price was worthwhile."

Crescent of Frustration

The entire Arab world, from the Persian Gulf to Morocco, had been immersed deep in the "lost honor" dilemma since the Arab defeat of the Six Day War. The Arabs were mocked as warriors and their bitterness grew in direct proportion. Frustration made them speak of themselves contemptuously. Distant Arab countries, like Algeria and Libya, scorned the Egypt of 1967, which couldn't safeguard Arab honor in war. For Egypt the Six Day War was more than a simple military defeat. "Israel constantly degraded Egypt," said Hassanein Heikal, the editor of **el Aharam**.

Israel did not appreciate the degree to which frustration and bitterness could act as a stimulant for the Arabs. No one but an Arab could appreciate this. Israelis could only discern the tip of Arab feelings from their dealings with residents of the "occupied territories". The official Israeli attitude was that intensified frustration could only increase willingness for concessions. The Six Day War defeat did indeed convince many Arabs that the dispute with Israel could not be settled by military means; but this very defeat fortified their resolve to retrieve their pride by some kind of a victory. "It is enough to destroy two, or even one division of the IDF," Heikal wrote during the War of Attrition.

Unflexed Muscle

The Arabs hesitated. Fear of yet another failure — a bigger defeat — restrained both the Arab leaders and their armies. This was the Arab "fear barrier." Nasser made a half-hearted attempt to crash through it in 1969, when he started the War of Attrition. It was a contained and static war, with chances that were also limited. When a defeat appeared imminent, he hastily summoned the Kremlin to his aid. He was prepared to risk thousands of Russian soldiers in Egypt, solely to prevent a new debacle like that of the Six Days. Frustration ran so deep that Arabs could be heard saying nations must sometimes risk suicide to retrieve pride. Sadat said he was willing to sacrifice a million Egyptians in war against Israel.

The fear barrier was more than the indirect result of repeated defeats, and fear of additional failures. Israel deliberately and directly fostered the barrier, beginning in the early 1950s — the era of retaliation. The philosophy was based on two assumptions: **a.** The Arabs only understand and respect the language of force. Silence and restraint will be taken by them to be fear and weakness, inviting additional violence. **b.** If the Arabs use violence against Israel, ordinary punishment is insufficient. A double or triple price must be exacted. Thus and only thus will Arabs be compelled to reconsider the desirability of actions against Israel and her citizens. The then Chief of Staff, Moshe Dayan, was one of the fathers of this philosophy and Defense Minister David Ben Gurion approved it. Its chief agent was a young officer named Ariel Sharon.

Retaliation did perhaps retard peace. From a military viewpoint, it was only a deteriorating situation but it also created a new web of relationships between Israel and the Arabs. In this period which began at Kibya in late 1953, and ended in the 1956 Sinai Campaign, the IDF actively encouraged a fear barrier which would peak in the Six Day War. Still more layers were added when, in 1970, the Israeli Air Force bombed deep inside Egypt, and when senior **fedayin** leaders were killed in the heart of Beirut.

Nothing Ventured

Israel noticed the fear barrier rising. The IDF was aware of unprecedented Arab strength after the Six Day War, but wasn't ready to believe the Arabs would use it. Consequently, the IDF was always prepared to risk holding the line with minimal forces. The Israeli press frequently repeated the numbers of planes and tanks added to Arab armies, but the public reacted as though to share movements on the stock exchange. Egyptian Army commanders, led by President Sadat, said exactly what they would do, and described exactly how they would do it, but few Israelis payed any real attention. After all, the Arabs "wouldn't dare".

On October 6, 1973 — the Arabs did dare. Twenty years after the rise of the fear barrier, they crossed it for the first time. After two decades of stalemate, they could justifiably regard this war as a successful test of their own self-esteem. Egypt's greatest surprise was to discover how easy the transition really was. Their operational orders, seized by the IDF, clearly indicate their preparedness for hardships and considerable sacrifice.

OCTOBER 7, 1973

Blockade

Important news comes from far away, south of the Red Sea. From the bridge of a fuel-laden tanker, en route to the port of Eilat, the First Officer sees the wake of a torpedo approaching the ship. It misses its mark, passing behind the stern. The First Officer could perhaps have convinced himself that his eyes were playing tricks, but it was followed by a second torpedo. A heavily laden tanker has very slight chances of evading a torpedo but, luckily, the dispatchers are inexpert. It also passes under the stern, though somewhat closer. There can be no doubt that the torpedoes were fired by an Egyptian submarine. The tanker carries a foreign flag, but the Egyptians must have a list of ships that carry fuel to Israel.

Blockade of the Sharm e-Sheikh Straits in 1967 was a **causus belli** for Israel. The Egyptians now impose their blockade further away, close to the Straits of Bab el-Mandeb. The number of Egyptian Navy units remaining in the Red Sea ports since the Six Day War is small; three destroyers and two submarines. They were cut off from their main Mediterranean naval bases and had to sail to India for repairs and major overhaul. During the War of Attrition, Israeli Air Force planes sank a destroyer, while the Egyptians transferred torpedo boats and a number of missile ships overland to the Suez Gulf ports. The vessels were old, but enough to bar the transit of merchant shipping, and a far greater force than the puny Israeli "Red Sea Fleet". Unlike on the Mediterranean, Israel has no

77

modern missile ships in this arena; only small and fast, short-range boats.

The petroleum route to Eilat is closed, and it's no longer worth risking transport of oil from the Abu Rhodeis wells to Eilat. Israel must fall back on her emergency reserves, while ordering all tankers around the Cape of Good Hope and via Gibraltar into the Mediterranean. Defense Minister Dayan orders publication blackout on the Bab el-Mandab blockade — not the first information withheld from the public. Nothing has yet been said about the Egyptian Kelt missile fired at Tel Aviv. Maj.-General (Res.) Yariv who is at present responsible for information services, orders total screening of news about the fall of the Hermon Position. "There'll be enough problems when the time comes," says Yariv. This news blackout will only increase the shock, when the public are eventually told how bitter the battle really is.

Rhetorical Questions

At dawn, the Chief of Staff phones General Gonen: "Shmulik, there's a problem up north! In a few places, they've reached the Golan slopes. I must transfer most of the planes north. What's your opinion?" Though he asks, it's clear from his tone of voice that the decision has already been made. Gonen replies: "I'll manage. If they break through up north, they'll reach settlements. Here they'll penetrate desert. We can deal with them until the planes come."

The IDF forces are mostly deployed along the so-called "Artillery Road", five to six miles inland from the Suez Canal, though some units are even further to the east. The majority of the frontline strongholds are virtually surrounded and isolated. They must now stand by themselves, but for weak artillery or aircraft support. At this stage, the strongholds serve as observation posts, and are the only source of current reports on events near the Canal. But they cannot fill in the details of happenings in Sinai, nor indicate the depth and strength of Egyptian penetration.

The battle picture in Southern Command HQ is far from clear enough.

At 06:00 hours, Maj.-General (Res.) Ariel Sharon arrives at Refidim, travelling in a civilian tender mobilized in Ashkelon. His corps' reconnaissance force arrived earlier; Yitzhak Agam and his comrades approached Artillery Road at 04:00 hours. In Refidim, Sharon meets Maj.-General Mendler. Albert had been Arik's subordinate for two years. Arik knows him to be a thorough officer who always tends to adequate and sometimes even exaggerated preparedness in tense situations.

Sharon wonders: "Why didn't you deploy the tanks earlier?"

"I was ordered not to deploy," Albert explains in a choked voice.

Uninterrupted Flow

During the night, the Egyptians erect additional bridges across the canal. Egyptian Army engineers are doing good work, helped by the fact that Israeli artillery fire is not very heavy. They are using both sophisticated Soviet equipment and homemade infantry bridges. They also have English made pontoons and German floats. Eleven bridges have been erected, mostly on the central and southern sectors of the Suez Canal. By morning, five divisions of infantry have been transferred across these bridges. Now, they begin to transfer the vehicles and tanks of these divisions. While the infantry pushes forward, the vehicles and armor cross without interruption.

Close to noon, a hasty debate takes place in the Supreme Command War Room. Clearly the IDF situation along the canal is precarious. The Egyptians have obviously used the night to throw many bridges across Suez. There is talk of a new defense line, though nobody mentions "retreat". The operative word is "regrouping", and the reference is to the longitudinal road 20 miles east of the Suez Canal.

"It won't be for long," says O.C. Air Force, Benny Peled.

"We will destroy the bridges." This implies the transfer of Air Force effort from Golan. And so, at 14:00 hours, an order is given to redirect a considerable part of the aircraft southwards, at the bridges over Suez.

These are not easy targets. The Egyptians throw up smoke screens and have erected a number of dummy bridges. Their engineers exploit lulls between bombings to throw replacement pontoons into the water. As the hits on the bridges mount up, the Egyptians resort to another tactic. Between transfers of forces, they remove bridge sections to the east bank of the canal. This makes it difficult for the pilots to locate the bridges. To hit a section close to the east embankment, the aircraft must dive from the west side which is packed solid with missiles and anti-aircraft guns. When the planes depart, the Egyptians tow the bridges back into place.

Despite all difficulties, the pilots do hit bridges; nine sustain clear and unmistakeable hits. From the moment the Air Force begins to operate over Suez, the flow of Egyptian forces into Sinai is delayed. If the reserves can counter-attack tomorrow morning, then the Air Force activity is timely. Otherwise, it is doubtful whether these sorties can be kept up indefinitely. The Air Force is paying a heavy price. It attacks the bridges before dealing with missile batteries close to the canal. From the east side of the canal, scores of shoulder-aimed Strella missiles wing up at the planes. They fly like burning cigarettes towards the aircraft exhausts. From the strongholds, IDF soldiers see two Skyhawks hit. One blows up at a great altitude, while from the other, a parachute descends slowly over the west bank. Further north, in Port Said area, a Phantom is hit. A pilot parachutes down near an Egyptian village. The **fellahin** run from all directions and angrily beat him with spades and knives. Tomorrow the Air Force will, in cold fury, bomb the district where the pilot was murdered.

Two Camps

Now it is obvious that the main Egyptian effort is taking place south of the Great Bitter Lake. The Third Egyptian

80

Army commanded by General Abdul Munaim el-Vassel is operating here. His forces are trying to seep through to the roads that link up with the Mitle and Gidi arterials. The second great effort is in the central sector, in Ismailia District and facing the road to Refidim, where the Egyptian Second Army operates under the command of General Saad Mamoun. Smaller units have also penetrated Qantara District, where the Egyptians have immediate gains. Their forces have blocked the canalside road and gained control over the northern sector from Qantara to Port Said.

The armor under Albert Mendler's command is being decimated. Most losses are inflicted by Egyptian infantry. Whenever their tanks attempt to advance, they are hit. But the infantry dig in while some units advance, slowly and relentlessly chewing up the terrain. In front, they are defended by thousands of Sagger anti-tank missiles, some installed on personnel carriers, but most hand-carried in small suitcases. Two soldiers form a missile team. One positions the missile, tenses the wires and connects the detonators. The second, from a distance of a few dozen yards, guides the missile to target with the help of a telescopic sight. The Egyptian infantry slowly advances, and the IDF armor is pushed back. The lack of back-up artillery is critical. Tank losses are so heavy that in the afternoon hours, only a few dozen are still usable.

Sticky Situation

This morning, nineteen-year-old Ephraim Shulman from Jerusalem, a conscript tank driver, encounters Egyptian infantry by Timsach Lake. His company is supposed to push them back, but the Egyptians are well dug-in. Ephraim's tank commander, Yoram, is killed in one of the first encounters and the tank continues to advance with Yoram's body lying inside. Their machine gun mows down many Egyptians, but the remainder don't run. The tank sustains more direct hits. Its periscope is out of commission and contact between Ephraim and his two comrades in the turret is broken. A sudden jolt as they drop a track,

81

but the tanks of the company keep moving, not realizing that they are leaving Ephraim and his friends behind. Now the Egyptians turn on the tank. His comrades climb out through the turret with their hands up, but are mown down by two long machinegun bursts. A few minutes later, Egyptian soldiers enter the tank. Ephraim lies like dead. Some Egyptians take pieces of equipment, and other peer inside curiously.

Through the whole day, Ephraim lies without moving. At midnight, he gets out through the turret, after finding that the emergency flaps have been battened down from the outside. The Egyptians are dug-in close by. Ephraim stealthily creeps away, and at dawn hides in a clump of shrubbery, not far from the lake, where he stays all day. On the second night, he keeps moving till he reaches a stronghold. But it is empty and destroyed. He is close to despair but, after a short pause, decides to continue to the next fortress — and there he is in luck. The garrison hear his cries and open the gate.

Seventh Day

The Egyptians have virtually gained control over the Suez Canal. Most of the strongholds still hold fast but, the main IDF force has been pushed back. The home front isn't aware of it. Israeli civilians couldn't begin to conceive the possibility. The Government doesn't yet grasp the military significance of the Egyptian penetration and the losses sustained by Israeli armor. Ministers and citizens are sure that it's a question of a few hours before the Egyptians are swept out; after all, Israel is only in the "seventh day" of the Six Day War. The IDF Spokesman's communiques mention withdrawal from Suez in only general and cloudy terms: "Our forces have consolidated new defense lines facing the Egyptian bridgeheads." The reports of the Spokesman's 41 teams attached to the various units still only speak of victories. Any hint of problems or retreat is deleted by the censorship. Maj.-General Mendler's Order of the Day only mentions success and a rosy future: "Soldiers, you have stopped the Egyptian Army's main breakthrough. Our first objective has been achieved. The enemy is blocked. The stronghold line absorbed the first blow, and stood firm. Before a day is out, the full force of the IDF will be felt."

The reserves are indeed racing into Sinai, but it is a hasty rush of companies and individual tanks; not movement of a concentrated force ready to attack. The Egyptians interfere with the approach of reserve forces. Natke's forces, from Maj.-General Avraham "Bren" Adan's army corps, encounter Egyptian commandos on the northern road. At night, Natke's laden tank-transporters reach Romani district, some 20 miles from Qantara. Suddenly, heavy bazooka, machine gun and missile fire is opened on the convoy from the shrubs along the roadside. Tanks are hit, and a prolonged battle is waged against the Egyptians.

Double Jeopardy

At 06:00 hours, Brigadier Raful Eitan receives word in his command bunker at Nafah that Syrian tanks are closing in on him. He thinks about it for a few moments, and then orders his men to move out of Nafah. They drive a few miles down the road to the Bnot Yaakov Bridge, at the foot of Golan.

Raful and his staff wait an hour near the bridge, without news of any Syrian penetration into Nafah. Raful decides to return; the communications set-up in the bunker is too good to lose. There are few soldiers left in the camp. The bunker is cramped and steamy. The air-conditioning seems to have been damaged by the shellfire. Danny, a staff officer, ducks out for some fresh air and, with horror, notices two Syrian tanks by the camp fence — a few score yards away.

Danny was summoned from **Kibbutz** Hefzibah a few hours earlier, but didn't for a moment think that he was going to war. He went to his reserve unit to check on the situation, taking his 12-year-old son with him. While there,

Syrian shells began to fall not far away. A driver took the boy back to the **kibbutz**, while Danny accompanied Raful to Nafah.

Now he stands a few seconds, petrified by the sight of the Syrian tanks. He returns to the bunker and, in the quietest voice he can muster, says: "Raful, it's one minute to zero. We've got to leave. The Syrian tanks are on the fences!"

Raful answers, without looking at him: "According to what you say, it's one minute past zero!"

At that moment, a tank crewman with a belly wound is brought into the bunker. He had been sitting with his comrades in a tank that shed a track, when Syrians suddenly appeared. Their first shell hit a Syrian tank, but with no possibility of manoeuver — the other Syrians picked them off at their leisure.

Raful orders his men out of Nafah for the second time. They run to the vehicles, most preferring the better-protected armored personnel carriers. Raful and Danny head for a jeep. In the race out of the camp, a half-track sustains a direct hit. Another reserve officer suddenly decides to return to the bunker, telling Raful that he'll call down an air-strike on the camp, and the Syrians in it. As Zeevik, the reserve officer, enters the bunker, he grasps that his situation is desperate. He can call in the aircraft, but has little chance of getting away himself. Another Syrian tank is approaching the perimeter fence, followed by an APC loaded with Syrian infantry. The door of the bunker slams shut; there are 11 men inside, including the injured crewman. Syrian gunfire covers the entire area of the camp. Zeevik and his companions are trapped in the bunker for half an hour until a single Israeli tank arrives. It stops near the bunker and snipes at the Syrian armor. From the north, another three tanks come to their aid. The Syrians on the perimeter fence are hit, and the remainder of the enemy force withdraws.

Air Rescue

Moti Hod is now with Maj.-General Hofi at Northern Command HQ. Their main problem is the breakthrough of Syrian armor in the central and southern sector of Golan. Through the night, most of Golan Heights Force is ground down. In Quneitra District, to the north, one brigade stands fast. But how can the Syrians at the southern end of the Heights be blocked for eight to ten hours until the reserves can arrive? The only answer can be the Air Force.

Moshe Dayan arrives at Northern Command HQ early in the morning, and goes straight into conference with Hofi and Hod. All three know that there are no Israeli tanks to stop the Syrians on the southern heights. It is only a question of time till they pour down into the pastoral and unprepared Ginossar Valley, and on to Degania. "I will hold the south if I have enough planes," says Hod quietly. So far, he only has one squadron of aircraft at his disposal.

Dayan hears Hod out, and promises to work on the Chief of Staff and the O.C. Air Force. An hour after he leaves, Hofi and Hod are told they have another squadron. Moti Hod looks at Haka, and says: "I was born in Degania. The Syrians will not reach that far. I'll take care of that!"

Moti keeps his promise. Up to 15:00 hours, when larger reserve forces reach southern Golan, aircraft alone block the Syrians. When the reserves arrive, the Syrian spearpoint is a few miles from the Jordan estuary at the Sea of Galilee.

Tiger's Teeth

At the approaches to Quneitra, the situation is slightly better. The armored brigade is fighting a stubborn blocking action; it has sustained losses, but will not withdraw. For every damaged tank, it exacts a heavy price from the attacking Syrians. A 25-year-old company commander, Meir Zamir – nicknamed "Tiger" – performs exceptionally well. At 03:00 hours on Sunday morning, the brigade commander orders him to ambush a column of 40 odd

85

Syrian tanks. "When the brigade commander explained what I had to do, I panicked a little. I only had three tanks. I ordered two more to join me, and we set off. It wasn't pleasant telling the men that 40 tanks were about to descend on us.

"We fought at ranges of a few score yards. The first Syrian tank was set ablaze, and by the light of the flames, we hit the others. Suddenly, my driver shouted that a Syrian was bearing down on us. They were using starlight scopes (S.L.S.). My gunner couldn't swivel the gun fast enough. I ordered the driver to move forward and sideways. We came up on the Syrian from behind, and fired at a distance of one yard. There was a tremendous explosion and a flash. We closed the flaps to avoid being burnt. Within 45 minutes, we destroyed 20 Syrians. At dawn, we hunted down the remainder. I reported to the brigade commander that the mission had been carried out, and he replied: 'Tiger, I love you!' "

Tiger's company is outstanding; more than 130 destroyed Syrian tanks will be recorded to its credit, and yet the company loses not one tank nor one man dead. This is undoubtedly luck, but Tiger's men believe that thorough training and his cruel discipline contributed. At war, Tiger ruled them with an iron hand; for four days, he forbade them to get out of the tanks to avoid being hit in the bombardment. Nature's calls were answered, at his orders, in empty ammunition boxes within the tanks.

Fatal View

Since nightfall, battalions of a brigade on central Golan have been slowly pushed back and are being worn down hour by hour. The Syrians have seized Nafah and T55 tanks are crossing the main Bnot Yaakov Bridge – Quneitra Road, at a distance of six miles from the Jordan River. Brigadier Yitzhak Ben Shoham's problem is to predict the direction of Syrian advance and pull in from every direction his few tanks to block the thrust. At night, it's difficult to see the moves but, at dawn, Ben Shoham selects an elevated observation point. He leans over his tank turret, to study the area. As he spots Syrian tanks, he guides his forces across their path. While in this vantage point, his tank is hit by a shell, and Ben Shoham lies dead.

Waks IV

The first reserves to reach Golan sustain losses. They fight near **Kibbutz** Ein Zivan. Moshik Waks' company is struggling close to the Petroleum Road. He constantly encourages his men; from time to time, amid the shooting, he bursts into song into the microphone. One of his tanks bursts into flames and its turret flies skywards in a tremendous explosion. Moshik sings, but knows how serious the situation is. A few minutes before he dies, he calls into the microphone: "Boys, remember, we are fighting for our homes. If we move, they race on to Haifa!"

Back-up

Eyal Shaham's company fights further south behind a number of frontline positions which are in practice cut off. But his tanks keep on hitting at Syrian vehicles that approach the positions. Eyal is in constant contact with the Golani Brigade garrison commander of the position to his front. From Saheita Hill, Eyal can see every movement in the district. The Syrians located his force two hours ago and are raining artillery fire down on the hill. His tank was hit, and he sits in the turret of another while it is repaired. Eyal's driver is Moshe Nili and his companions in the turret are Amram Turgeman and David Golan. They shoot at distant Syrian tanks when a mortar bomb suddenly falls on the turret. Eyal, Amram and David are killed outright. Driver Moshe Nili remains alive and drives the tank to the rear in shock. "It was exactly eleven o'clock on Sunday," the position commander will later report. "I was speaking with Eyal by radio when his voice suddenly faded. This was a bad blow. He protected us from the rear during the hardest hours." Eyal Shaham's company paid a very heavy price. Of its 48 men, only eight remained at the end of the war.

Grand Prix

Other reserve units ascend the southern Golan road to Yehudia. The speed of their arrival on the line is critical. Many of the tanks come from Haifa on their own tracks. There is no time to wait for the whole force. Units go into battle as they arrive. Crews will be made up in the field. Two tank companies descend from Corazim to the Jordan estuary to meet the nearby Syrian armor spearpoint. Further east, there is a race between a Syrian column and an IDF armor battalion; a critical struggle likely to determine the fate of southern Golan. Both sides want the Gamla Pass, a ridge overlooking the Sea of Galilee and the Ginossar basin, which effectively controls the whole neighborhood. The first to seize the ridge will dictate the battlelines. Syrian T55 tanks climb from the east while, with the last effort of their engines, Centurions of the Golan Heights reserve battalion ascend from the west. From the nearby hills, Israelis — among them reservists who have just arrived — watch the race. The Centurions get to the top first. They turn their guns on the facing slopes and from a range of 100 yards, fire at the first enemy tanks. The Syrian armor is pushed back from Beit Gamla, but will not give way. Other Syrian tanks try to bypass and reach the Arik Bridge over Jordan.

Fallen Lair

The Syrians have a clear success on Mount Hermon. The Syrian commando seizes the extremities of the Hermon fortress. Some IDF men are driven out of the bunkers by thick smoke. Outside, they give themselves up. Others still fight from within the bunkers. They cluster in the inner rooms, and the Syrians make no attempt to follow. Last night, a group of five tried to break out, but were taken by the Syrians not far from the position. A second group of twenty goes out in the next stage. With a burst of covering fire, they crash through and put some distance between them and the fortress. Led by the garrison commander – a captain – they lope down the slope towards Israeli-held territory. At the upper cable-railway terminus, they come on the first of a series of Syrian ambushes. Most are killed, but four reach IDF lines.

Among the survivors is the garrison commander. He half-drags half-carries Doron Sharfman, a member of Moshav Yavniel. When the refugees arrive, they tell the O.C. Golani Brigade that a number refuse to surrender and, believing they will be rescued, remain in fortress bunkers. The excited Golani commander calls the O.C. Northern Command and demands permission to retake the position. Hofi hesitates. Military logic says – no! It's only a matter of time until the IDF opens a general offensive. The Hermon may possibly be taken from behind, with parts of the Syrian Hermon. But moral obligation to the remaining soldiers compels a response to O.C. Golani. Finally, Hofi approves the attack. Tomorrow at dawn, Golani will stage their assault.

Syrian commando prisoners taken from the Hermon position, will later relate that some Israelis did remain in the bunkers. One group stubbornly fights till the fifth day. Its five men are apparently convinced the IDF will rescue them but, on the fifth day, with water at an end, they decide to accept a Syrian surrender offer. They probably heard the echoes of battle when Golani attempted in vain to retake the position. They come out with their hands up. The Syrian commander angrily reviews them and orders their execution. This is also the fate of two others who surrender in the early stage of the battle. The Syrians evacuate the prisoners to their own nearby position including a number of wounded, one of whom is an officer. Two of the wounded find it difficult to walk, lag behind and are shot.

Execution of prisoners is not exclusive to the Hermon position. Alongside Hushniye, the Syrians take 11 Israeli

89

administrative personnel of the Golan Heights Force. They will later be found dead with blindfolded eyes and tied hands. All were shot at close range. At first the finders will be convinced that the Syrians shot them for convenience sake during an Israeli artillery bombardment, and while in flight, but then it will become clear that the method was used elsewhere. Seven manacled prisoners will be found in Hushniye village, and three more on Tel Zohar. Syrian prisoners will confirm that their comrades killed Israeli soldiers who fell in their hands. An IDF identity card and dogtags will come to light in the wallet of a Syrian commando taken captive on Hermon.

Treasure Trove

The Russians benefit from Syrian success on Hermon. A few hours after the entire position falls into Syrian hands, Soviet technicians and electronics specialists arrive. They inspect the mass of electronic equipment, item by item, and mark some as first priority for evacuation.

That same day, a helicopter will arrive to load the marked equipment. Other items, destined for evacuation on mule back, will be found packed and ready for dispatch when the IDF retakes the fortress.

Advise Without Consent

From the northern front, Moshe Dayan proceeds to Sinai, accompanied by Maj.-General (Res.) Rehavam Zeevi. Golan has made the Defense Minister more pessimistic than usual. In Southern Command War Room, Dayan tells General Gonen: "It's a tough war. Not an isolated incident! We must retreat to the second line, to the hills, and consolidate there!"

Dayan's exchange with Gonen and his offers is interrupted by a phone conversation with the Chief of Staff. Dayan asks: "What can you give Shmulik (Gonen)?" He refers to air support. Elazar tells him that there is almost no chance of increased air for the southern front. In the north, the Syrians have broken the Israeli lines, and the planes are desperately needed.

Dayan tells Gonen and his assistants: "It's clear that priority will be given to the Jordan Valley and Tiberias. Sinai isn't that important. Twenty miles more, forty less – it's less important than the north. You'll get more air support, but only tomorrow morning." Now Dayan returns to the need for retreat: "The water line must be abandoned, and everything transferred to the longitudinal axis. The armor that's there, and that will arrive must strike them. There's no point in building on the strongholds, and it's a pity to break through to them. It's not logical. I don't see that the situation will change. The men in the strongholds should try and break out by night."

"What about their wounded?" an officer asks.

"The healthy should try and cross the lines. The wounded? There's no alternative. Let them be taken captive."

A depressing silence falls on the room. The Defense Minister adds: "What I said was an advice at ministerial level. Of course, everything must be coordinated with Dado (General Elazar)."

When Dayan and his entourage leave, Gonen asks to speak with his corps commanders to issue his orders. He says nothing of retreat to a new line. Though he could have understood Dayan's proposal as approval, he doesn't even refer to it. In his opinion there can be no more retreat. Now the objective must be to hold 'Artillery Road'. The first commander to answer Gonen's call is Bren Adan.

Gonen: "Do you read me? We'll leave the wounded in the strongholds and try to break out. Bren! Bren, can you hear me?"

Adan (after a short silence and a few indistinct words): "That's a very painful step!"

To Sharon, Gonen says: "There's no chance of air. The situation on the sector is very tough. You ask about a counter attack? I assume southward and north-west. We won't get air for a long time, and certainly not in any

91

number. Arik, it isn't a matter of logic. It's no alternative. I told the Chief of Staff that I'll stand fast, even without the air force."

Double Check

From Sinai, the Defense Minister returns to the Supreme Command. In Tel Aviv he voices more horrifying comments: "This is a war for the 'Third Temple', not for Sinai. We must withdraw to Sharm e-Sheikh. Sharm e-Sheikh is the important thing. We must deploy on the second line, at the passes."

The Chief of Staff asks: "Even if we must deploy on the second line, why should we evacuate the Gulf?" "Perhaps not evacuation, but we must fight a delaying battle there," Dayan replies.

The Defense Minister's pessimism is contagious. With his powerful and dominant personality, his state of mind must affect those around him. Fortunately, Dayan doesn't issue orders in this spirit and the Chief of Staff's nerves prove much stronger; consequently the IDF doesn't beat a general retreat.

Dayan moves on to tell Golda Meir, Yigal Allon and Yisrael Galili that the situation is critical; there is no alternative to retreat down the lower slopes of Golan. The Prime Minister and her advisers are thunderstruck. Golda's Military Secretary, Yisrael Lior, leaves the room to seek encouragement elsewhere. Moments after the Defense Minister's departure, David Elazar enters the room. He knows what Dayan told the Prime Minister, but isn't that pessimistic: "The situation is bad, but doesn't necessitate retreat." He suggests that Haim Bar Lev should go north to see for himself, and he – Elazar – will go south. Dayan doesn't see Bar Lev's trip as bypassing his authority; he seems happy to share the burden of bearing bad tidings. A short while later, Commerce and Industry Minister Bar Lev appears wearing a uniform with the rank badges of lieutenant-general. Haka Hofi is informed that Bar Lev is coming to visit – without command authority, on a reconnaissance to gain impressions. Towards evening, Bar Lev calls Golda and, in his quiet monotone, says: "The situation is bad. Perhaps very bad, but not desperate." Retreat to the lower slopes is averted.

Dado Elazar flies south by helicopter with past-Chief of Staff Yitzhak Rabin. The Six Day War C.o.S. is not mobilized and is in civilian clothes.

While Dado and Rabin travel south, Dayan is talking to Mrs. Meir, this time on a different subject: "Golda, in all sincerity and friendship, if you think there is somebody more capable of handling the duties of defense minister, then give it to him. If I was Prime Minister and thought the defense minister had to be changed, I wouldn't hesitate a moment. It will be a mistake on your part if you don't do what you think right."

Golda replies: "God forbid!" For the time being this concludes the discussion.

Morale Gap

When the Chief of Staff arrives at Southern Command HQ, he finds a totally different feeling to that in the Supreme Command. The corps commanders don't mention withdrawal. Maj.-General Sharon is the only one who hasn't arrived by the beginning of the meeting. Two hours ago, Arik Sharon put the finishing touches to a plan for the rescue of garrisons from three strongholds in his sector. He spoke with the officers in command of two fortresses. In the third, all the officers were dead and his conversation was with the reservist radio operator, a Jerusalem waiter named Maman. As the planning session ended, Sharon contacted Gonen to ask approval for a rescue mission tonight.

"That is not something to be discussed by phone," Gonen tells him. "I suggest you come here. We'll go over the plans in a joint meeting of all the corps commanders. I'll send you a helicopter."

"But that way we'll lose the whole night," Sharon protests. The helicopter is two hours late. Meanwhile, the

Chief of Staff's conference begins without Sharon.

Adan recommends caution until sufficient artillery has accumulated. Gonen is bolder; he speaks of a need to cross the Suez Canal tomorrow. The Chief of Staff doesn't want to throw all available force into one counter-attack tomorrow morning. He insists on attack by stages; first, Adan's corps and only after its success — Sharon's corps. He doesn't approve the canal crossing, nor does he forbid it. Fording equipment has not yet been prepared. A crossing, if any, would have to be on the Egyptian bridges.

"Reach the bridges, and then we'll see," says Elazar. "I don't want to transfer a complete army over one bridge. If we seize a number, we'll move some tank platoons. In any case, a canal crossing will only be at my explicit order!"

Arik I

On the way back to his helicopter, the Chief of Staff meets Sharon coming in. Elazar reiterates the major points of tomorrow's plan. Sharon argues that he can cross the canal in the morning, while Elazar says the Egyptian bridgeheads must first be hit, and the IDF forces organized. After the war, Sharon will contend that, by today, he already has some 200 tanks. Other commanders will say that the main problem, after Mendler's losses, is lack of success in concentrating ample forces, and Sharon's corps isn't yet ready for a large-scale attack. Tomorrow morning, October 8, there will be some 260 tanks on the southern front.

Arik Sharon is much more concerned about rescue of the trapped men in the strongholds. The moral question bothers him. He repeats his plan to the Chief of Staff who, saying that it might cost 50 tanks, suggests that Sharon settles the matter with Gonen. Conversation with Gonen results in no change of the previously agreed plan. Gonen also stresses the dangers of a potentially costly rescue operation. Gonen was the one who mentioned a possible 50 tanks lost to Elazar. Sharon's idea of getting the men out of three strongholds tonight is rejected. There is still hope of reaching some strongholds in tomorrow's offensive.

Friend in Need I

The United States is today approached with an urgent request for weapons. It is now clear to the Government of Israel that this is an unanticipated kind of war – a new situation. Equipment is decimated so rapidly that the warehouses will soon be emptied, and much of the equipment will be unserviceable. Within two days, some 250 tanks are likely to be out of commission on both fronts, and dozens of planes will have been lost. The other side is also being worn down, but they have far greater quantities at their disposal – and the Soviet Union may be expected to assist the Arabs with more equipment. The request is passed on to the Americans, but Washington only listens without replying.

Professional Curiosity

An exotic conversation takes place in Washington this evening. Two senior officers from the Middle East are attending the U.S. Navy Staff and Command School. Shabetai, past-commander of the Israeli missile squadron, and the O.C. Lebanese Navy. The latter approaches the Israeli officer to ask for details about the fronts. Shabetai tells the Lebanese of the various moves, and about the first sea battle waged by Israeli missile ships off the Syrian coast. A number of American officers witness the conversation. Tomorrow, two American officers will approach Shabetai on a mission from the Lebanese. He will ask them to tell Shabetai not to harbor any personal hatred for him because of the Arab attack on Israel.

INTERLUDE: STRATEGY OF FIRE FIGHTING

Ego Earthquake

Analysis of Israel's actions on the Day of Atonement reveal the traumatic impact of the surprise achieved by the Arabs. Surprise was an immediate test for Israel's leadership, military machine and long-accepted strategic and operational assumptions. Trauma caused insecurity in both the political and military leadership. Politicians and senior commanders lost their self-confidence and few regained it during the war; even they only took hesitant steps. Henceforward most of their decisions were marked by exaggerated caution, atypical of Israel's usual strategic thinking. Shock also stripped the covers off old established weaknesses.

The weakness of the highest decision-making echelon first surfaced in the stage of preparation and anticipation. Something already known acquired new emphasis; the Government of Israel's decision-making process is basically faulty, and totally unsuited to a progressive country. The Cabinet, as a body, was not informed of tension on the borders, of enemy concentrations, of an IDF alert and of the possibility of war – until the very last minutes. Even before the alert, there was an accumulation of important data which should have been brought to the notice of the Cabinet. The Government certainly needed to be informed of the chain of events that culminated in a C Alert. In this case, the Prime Minister is to blame, together with the Defense Minister, who should have drawn her attention to the need for Cabinet concensus. The question is not what a minister remote from defense affairs can contribute to such discussions, but rather one of staff work. The Israeli Government still worked in "kitchens".

Too Few Cooks

The week preceding the outbreak of war again proved that, in vital and critical subjects, the Government relies on partisan improvisation for its decision-making process. In this Golda Meir did not differ from her predecessors, including Ben Gurion. She and Moshe Dayan continued a tradition typical of the pre-independence underground organizations, rather than of a state with a modern army. Important decisions were cooked and approved before reaching the Cabinet. The grounding of a Lebanese passenger aircraft in 1973, should have served as a warning signal, since the decision to go ahead – which was far from purely operational – was taken in a telephone conversation with a few ministers. This war again proved that the important thing is not who decides – but how. Moshe Dayan has considerable experience in security matters, but is no more immune to mistakes than any less experienced minister. Furthermore, in staff work, he does not differ from his predecessors.

Ben Gurion set the pattern for vital decision-making to which the cabinet is not party. The 1956 Sinai Campaign was his personal decision. He brought his decision to the Cabinet for approval only when the military machine was in high gear. The same was true for manufacture of modern armaments, essential security-scientific matters, procurement negotiations with various governments – and the decision to kidnap Adolph Eichmann from the Argentine. When Ben Gurion didn't want to decide, he brought the matter to a full cabinet session. It was only towards the end of his term of office that party criticism of this process was manifest.

On one occasion, the Ministerial Committee for Security Affairs decided, despite BG's objections, to discuss the presence of German scientists in Egypt and even invited Supervisor of Security Services Isser Harel, to a committee session for the purpose. But the Committee's move was more for personal reasons of its members than from desire to reform Ben-Gurion's decision-making process. His successor's willingness to bring more ministers into the security picture also derived from personal reasons; Levi Eshkol's weakness and desire to share the responsibility incumbent on him as Prime Minister and Defense Minister.

Golda Meir continued the pattern. She did not establish facts and did bring more ministers in on vital decisions, yet neither she nor her partners improved the staff work of government, or the process of decision-making. In the absence of routine and statutory procedures, it is no wonder that most of the cabinet heard of the possibility of war only two hours before it started. Till the war the Government did not operate as a brains trust, but as a feudal system. When war was inevitable, the Prime Minister tried to share responsibility with all her ministers.

Eyes Have They

Those whose duty it was to decide, were insensitive to enemy intentions, abilities and potential. There could be no better proof than the last minute argument over how many reservists to mobilize. The Defense Minister felt that a minimal force would suffice to swat away an enemy attack. This debate deteriorated into a squabble, adding to the already critical delay. The Defense Minister's confidence was not entirely for appearances' sake. Moshe Dayan believed it. Leadership evidently did not know what was happening "on the other side of the hill". The complacency was not of the nation, but primarily of the supposedly better informed leadership. As their suspicions grew, they looked north to Golan, and spared no thought to possible total war on both fronts simultaneously. Artillery was transferred from Sinai to Golan. Dayan was primarily worried about the Golan Heights' settlements. The feeling was that there would be one day of battle on Golan, or maybe local actions on Suez. Consequently, the alert order given the strongholds at the very last moment, spoke not of war, but only of preparation to face bombardment.

Spatial Logistics

Amazingly, everything was planned to prevent total surprise; whatever happened, there would be at least 48 hours warning. The war plans were based on this assumption and so were the underlying concepts. And this was leadership's psychological block. It's difficult to explain it any other way. The territories added to Israel by the Six Day War may have made her over-confident. With more extensive buffer areas, greater risks could be taken over mobilization of reserves in times of tension.

Eventually, these sentiments blurred the basic understanding of Israel's new geographic reality. The territories did indeed give Israel defensive depth, but also shortened time available for intelligence warning. Up to the 1967 Six Day War, the situation had been the very reverse. When Egyptians began to move into Sinai, red lights flashed on in the intelligence agencies. After the 1967 war, Egyptian forces were concentrated along the Suez Canal and would no longer require extensive movements to switch to the attack. Thus, it would be more difficult to predict events and the chances of sudden attack would be far greater. Moreover, the territories did indeed add defensive depth, but extended the IDF's traffic lanes; movement of reserve units to the front required more time.

The security inspired by the territories was undoubtedly a major reason for rejection of the Chief of Staff's proposal for a pre-emptive air strike. Fear of world opinion and United States reactions certainly underlay the Prime Minister and Defense Minister's decision. Nevertheless, this proposal would doubtfully have been rejected, had Israel been in the pre-Six Day War geographic situation. Then, she could not have taken unnecessary risks.

Hypothetical Questions

Historians will certainly debate the decision for many years but, militarily, such a pre-emptive strike would clearly not have prevented the war. From the Egyptian operation orders, it is obvious that they took this into account. The strike would certainly have caused heavy Arab losses, but would not have prevented their offensive. Since the General Staff were watching the north, the preventive air attack would certainly have been against Syria. The Air Force would probably have lashed out at missile batteries, headquarters and communications centers. This might have shortened the first stage of war, but would not have prevented it. The Air Force would probably not have sent its planes against Egypt at the same time. So, the canal crossing would have been carried out according to plan. A pre-emptive strike might have contributed to getting the tanks into position on the canal before the assault, and to placing the strongholds on a higher level alert. Whatever the case, the pre-emptive proposal raises another question. Preparations for the strike began on Friday, when the C Alert was declared in the standing army. In other words, the Chief of Staff's sense of impending war was strong even before the final information arrived, at 04:00 hours on Saturday. He took a logical step in ordering the Air Force to prepare, but it was a job only half done. Had he pressed for mobilization a day earlier, he would have closed the circle. He would probably have encountered the same if not more severe opposition as he did on Saturday morning, but he may just have succeeded in moving matters.

Uninformed Alert

The privilege of first innings was knowingly left to the enemy. Tragically, the alert was also faulty, or incomplete. Even if all the strongholds did receive the alert order — a far from certain assumption — they certainly didn't understand it as preparation against a canal crossing by thousands of Egyptians. Some believe the most tragic order of all to be the one given Maj.-General Albert Mendler; his tanks were not to be moved until two hours before "zero". The order was based on the mistaken assumption that the attack would undoubtedly begin exactly as predicted in the intelligence data. No one allowed for the possibility that this detail may be incorrect, mistaken or deliberately deceptive. Now, it is clear that all steps were taken, in error, based on war

100

beginning at 18:00 hours. Yet this assumption becomes even stranger in the light of earlier IDF thinking.

In 1969, the IDF held a General Staff war game that included a possible Egyptian afternoon offensive. Maj.-General Ezer Weizman was then responsible for the underlying assumptions, which held that the best time for an Egyptian crossing offensive would be between 14:00 and 15:00 hours. Such timing would allow the Egyptians a few hours of daylight, without over-exposing them time-wise to the Israeli Air Force.

The mistake was made, and no tanks were in their prepared positions when the offensive began. In hindsight, some contend that this was lucky, since the tanks would only have been trapped in an Egyptian deluge. This hypothetical contention is unacceptable. The decisive point is that the defense plan was not set in motion and Israel thereby assisted Egyptian attainment of tactical surprise.

When the first Egyptian shot was fired, Israel was obviously lagging behind schedule. The forward tank forces raced to the canal banks, but most were hit on the way to their positions. The greater bulk of the "armored first" in Central Sinai was ordered to move at 14:15 hours; it was only two hours later that the first elements of this force established battle contact – and that 12 miles inland from the Suez Canal. The Egyptian armored personnel carriers vanguard had already penetrated deep into Sinai.

Piecemeal Problem

The compulsion to make up lost time forced the units to go into battle in small groups – company by company, and sometimes not even that. Most of the armor counter blows in Sinai were therefore weaker.

No less serious was the paucity of Israeli fire power. The strongholds could only cover short sections of the canal with light fire. The tanks were compelled to struggle for their own existence some miles away. At the beginning of the Egyptian crossing, the lack of massive Israeli artillery

101

was immediately obvious. Some gun batteries were with the tanks in Central Sinai and received no order to move. It was Saturday night before all the Sinai batteries were in action. A few dozen IDF guns faced more than 1,000 Egyptian field pieces; a numerical gap that staggers the imagination. The dispersion of IDF artillery was so great that it was impossible to bring any two gun batteries to bear on any one Egyptian crossing point. This even surprised the Egyptians. A major premise of the entire 1973 war was now apparent — quantity and mass of armaments create their own quality. For those who face massive fire-power, it makes little difference whether the gunners are highly trained or not.

The real counter-fire of the first stage was provided by the Air Force, and even here the IDF was severely limited. At first, the Air Force had to cope with aerial interception. Many aircraft were compelled to drop their armament — loaded for the aborted pre-emptive strike — into the sea The Air Force flew a few hundred sorties over the Egyptians who were crossing the canal, but had no more than two hours till operational darkness — at 16:30 hours. As darkness fell, a bright moon rose, but night bombing was dangerous.

New Morality

The most obvious mistake of the war was apparently at the close of **Yom Kippur**. By dusk only two Suez strongholds had fallen. Apart from some points on the northern sector, it was still possible to reach most of the others. Tanks did indeed enter some fortresses to remove the wounded. These strongholds could have been evacuated and others could have been reached. When darkness fell, the strongholds had completed their primary role — of giving shelter during the heavy bombardment, and observing the enemy forces pouring into Sinai. The evacuation order wasn't issued. At dawn, the mistake was clear. From now on, it was a hard fight to rescue the garrisons. Analysis of battles on the Egyptian front reveals that rescue operations were among the most difficult and costly, both for the men in the strongholds, and for the paratroops ambushed near Ismailia and in Suez town.

The moral implications of men trapped behind enemy lines was repeatedly to bother commanders. In all Israel's wars, there had never been one like the Day of Atonement. The IDF knew similar situations in the War of Independence, but was then a young new army. Over the years, a sacred tradition was born; dead and wounded are never left in the field. To protect this sublime value, the IDF willingly paid a heavy price. Now, senior officers had to calculate how much they could afford to sacrifice for their distressed comrades. Some paid no heed to losses while others were more cautious. This was the first time since 1948 that the IDF left a large part of the battlefield in enemy hands, and this was one reason for the high toll in "missing" in this war.

Clarion Call

From the morning of the Day of Atonement, the method of reserve mobilization was on trial. It had been tried, improved and streamlined since its inception in the early 1950s, when Yigael Yadin was Chief of Staff. In the 1956 Sinai Campaign, mobilization was rapid, but not under enemy pressure. The problem was more one of concealing mobilization from enemy eyes. In the Six Day War, the reserves were mobilized in stages. October 1973 was the first time reserves were called out during a war that took Israel by surprise. Strategic depth and the Israel Air Force permitted mobilization without disturbance from aerial bombings, but there were totally different problems.

In general terms, as far as mobilization of men was concerned, the method was successful, though not without hitches in transportation. But there were many mishaps in the issue of equipment, after numerous innovations had reduced the time needed to send a reserve unit into battle to 24 hours, as against 72 hours 15 years ago. Men report and are registered, receive their weapons and personal equipment, and are assigned to a tank or half-track crew. They receive their ammunition elsewhere. They check gun sights, radio equipment and so on.

In the tense waiting period of 1967, days passed before reserve units were properly equipped; it didn't matter for they had three weeks in which to prepare for battle. In the **Yom Kippur** War, a week passed before the reserves were more-or-less equipped. General Sharon related that on his own initiative, he contacted a wealthy Jewish friend in New York and asked him to procure a few hundred pairs of field glasses.

Quartermaster Blues

Alongside weird disorganization and shortage of personal weapons and ammunition, even among front line units, there were additional reasons for the unpreparedness of men reaching the front lines. Some reserve units were undergoing transition and did not yet have all their new equipment. Stores of other units were being transferred to forward areas and men found their equipment in disorganized heaps on the floors. Some armored units received tanks without machine guns, since there was a decision to replace the existing guns with others. The exchange was incomplete when war began.

Many unprepared tanks were knowingly sent to the front line with bellies half-full of ammunition, or unzeroed gun sights. Some commanders argue that it was important for the tanks to reach the front line. This contention is easy to accept for the Syrian front where a small area was almost completely swamped by enemy tanks. The first reserves arrived quickly and were in combat within 24 hours of mobilization; an important and impressive achievement. It was these reserves who finally blocked the Syrians on southern Golan. Golan is easily accessible from populated areas of Israel, but Sinai is not; and many hours elapsed before reserve units reached the southern lines.

Part of the emergency warehouses have over the years

been moved forward. Yet the tanks still had to traverse hundreds of miles, and there were insufficient transporters. A considerable number were despatched on their own tracks. An order of priorities, by which the different units would receive tanks transporters, had to be set and this was done on Saturday morning by the General Staff. Artillery batteries were to receive a low priority, and some self-propelled guns were also sent on their own tracks. The last artillery units only reached Sinai on Tuesday morning, influencing the ability of Sinai Force to bring artillery fire to bear in the three most critical days.

Unlike the Six Day War, this was no mobile engagement, but a battle of fire power. Moreover, it was not a clash between tanks, but between Israeli armor and Egyptian infantry. The lack of artillery gave the Egyptian infantry an unexpected initial supremacy. With anti-tank missiles, they enjoyed a longer reach than did the tanks. They could hit armored vehicles from considerable distances, without taking unnecessary risks. Machine guns didn't bother them, even when the tanks were so equipped. More artillery could have struck harder at the Egyptian missile and bazooka-carrying infantry and, with smoke shells, could have covered the assault areas to hamper the Egyptian missile operators.

The situation of the armor brigades was aggravated by lack of 120 millimeter mortars. The elimination of mortar units proved a serious mistake, for they could have inflicted heavy losses on the Egyptian infantry, at long range. But more than 120 millimeter mortars were missing. The trend to break free of the use of mortar support had also extended to lighter weapons. Tank crews had armor-plate protection, but couldn't fight missile carriers with their own field pieces.

Slow Succor

The southward flow of reserve units lasted a few days. Roads were crammed with many thousands of vehicles, including tanks and personnel carriers. The operative concept called on the standing army to block the enemy till the reserves arrived, whereupon they would go straight over to a counter offensive. In the Day of Judgement War, this wasn't possible. The standing army was taken by surprise, and many of its units were decimated. The reserves had first to join the blocking battle, and continue the job of the standing army. O.C. Air Force Benny Peled described the situation as a great street brawl, occasionally joined by another man.

The pressure was so great that the General Staff reserve had to be committed to blocking the Syrian offensive on Golan. This contributed to the salvation of Golan, but prevented the General Staff from creating an immediate pressure point on either front. The distance between fronts and lack of armored reserve implied that the Air Force was the only possible tactical lever. Clearly, the use of the air arm alone could not justify a general offensive. The progression of events, and the way in which the reserves went into battle made it difficult for the General Staff to wage planned war. It was strategic fire fighting rather than strategic war.

OCTOBER 8, 1973

Enemy in Need I

This morning, Soviet Ambassador to Egypt Vladimir Vinogradov meets Sadat. The agenda is taken up with one question; supply of military equipment to Egypt and Syria. The Soviet Union can now show its full support for the Arabs, without over-endangering herself. The success of the first stage is not inconsiderable, and the Arabs must be allowed to hold fast and protect their achievements.

"Your weapons were in our hands when we crossed," Sadat says to the Soviet Ambassador, as they part. Vinogradov is radiantly happy: "I have served here three years as Ambassador, in good and bitter days, but this is the highlight of my work in Cairo."

At noon, news of a Soviet airlift arrives; Russian transport planes are approaching Syria, where there is a need for immediate assistance. The Syrian Army is already decimated, and continues to suffer heavy blows.

Friend in Need II

No final answer has yet been received from Washington, in response to Israel's request for arms. Tel Aviv maintains constant and anxious contact with Ambassador Dinitz and Military Attache Gur, who say that the Americans are still debating. The Head of the Defense Ministry Mission, Bondi Dror, has moved from New York to Washington and reports that considerable military equipment has accumulated. The main problem is in transferring it to Israel. El Al planes are insufficient and chartered aircraft can not close the gap.

The problem bothers the advisers of the U.S. President. Before Israel's request for immediate and considerable armaments, they had told her representatives that the Administration will supply the IDF with replacement equipment. When the request arrives, they are shocked by the numbers of weapons and quantities of ammunition lost in the first two days. The President's advisers realize that their suggestion to Israel to transfer the equipment herself was not practical. If the American Government wants it to reach Israel in time, the United States must take a more significant step; airlift the arms and equipment herself, implying deeper intervention in the war. Now the debates are on this point. The final decision will be taken in the U.S. President's office.

Ingathering of the Exiles

Israel does not for the moment receive the needed weapons but she has a flow of volunteers and immigrants. While the Soviet airlift bears armaments to Egypt and Syria, Russian immigrants are reaching Israel — and not only those who received exit visas before the war. The flow

107

of immigrants doesn't stop right through it.

Retired army officers are volunteering at Israeli representative offices throughout the world. An attractive non-Jewish girl reports to the Israeli Embassy in London, requesting espionage assignment anywhere in the Arab world. Most volunteers are Jews. In Florida, Meyer Lansky donates a million dollars to the Israel that deported him as a possible Mafia boss. Thousands of Israelis who were abroad when war broke out, including students and long-time residents, besiege El Al offices. The screening is thorough. Pilots, doctors and tank crew-men have first priority. Infantrymen are at the end of the list, even if they belong to elite combat units. At first, not even the paratroops enjoy special privileges.. The thinking is clear; like the Six Day War, this will primarily be a war of armor and the Air Force. As the planes reach Lydda, some arrivals are already inducted at the airport. Tank crewmen are sent directly to their units in the field. Some among them will fall in battle without their families even knowing they are home.

Nameless Line

The news from the northern front is not good. Though the Syrian armor has been stopped without reaching the River Jordan, the scales of battle have not yet tipped in favor of the IDF. The stamina of the front line positions is encouraging. The Syrians first poured down thousands of shells and bombs, and then brought up tanks to crack the forts with their guns. Few of the defenders were killed by the heavy fire. The waves of Syrian armor poured past the line, leaving the forward positions cut off and isolated.

Apart from the Hermon position there are 11 strongpoints along the cease-fire line with Syria. The distance from one to the next is considerable. This isn't a defense line designed to block general assault, but rather forward observation posts, designed to survey their surroundings and defend themselves. Many millions of Israel pounds were invested in the strongpoints. They comprise deep bunkers, fences and access roads paved with asphalt. Unlike Sinai, nobody debated the need for these positions, and so the line was not named after anyone.

So far, the Syrians haven't bothered overmuch with the forward positions. It is only now, in the second wave, that the Syrians assault some strongpoints, each of which is manned by from 12 to 25 soldiers. In two of them, Syrian tanks are stopped at the gateway and remain where they stand. In one, the attackers gain control of the extremities. In the bunker is a group of soldiers from Golani Brigade. Some are wounded and two are dead. The Syrians hesitate to charge in. They throw smoke grenades and scream curses. The garrison commander radios for artillery fire on his own position.

Of the 11 fortresses, not one falls. On the first night, the men abandon one strongpoint and sneak through the Syrian lines. Northwards near Quneitra, another is abandoned, but the garrison returns after a few hours. The remainder stand fast, surrounded, till the IDF reaches them. The siege of the last one will be relieved on the fifth day, as an armored column arrives on its way across the cease-fire line into Syrian territory. The garrison, led by a young platoon commander of Airborne **Nahal** are fit and well. They refuse evacuation and mount half-tracks to continue forward with the attack force.

Relief of Hermon I

Golani Brigade attempts to retake the Hermon but fails. For two days, the brigade commander has pressed the O.C. Northern Command and his staff for permission to assault the position. Haka Hofi feared heavy losses but four refugees from Hermon — among them the garrison commander — told of men still remaining in the bunkers. The brigade commander again approaches Maj.-General Hofi with an additional moral argument; the need to rescue the remaining men. One of Hofi's assistants supports him, and the O.C. finally consents.

The Golani units ascend to the position by two routes;

the main road, where they travel in tanks and half-tracks, and the mountain path. A recently arrived paratroop unit waits on the hills near Massada in case help is needed. The Syrian commandos are not in the Hermon fortress, but on the slopes leading to it; a correct tactical move, indicating their understanding of the terrain, and correct analysis of the possible attack. The assault is hampered by heavy mist over the mountain, making artillery and air support difficult. Golani Brigade doesn't reach the position. Thirty men fall, and eight remain on the battlefield.

Mounting Toll

The Syrian offensive has not yet lost its impetus. While additional IDF reserves race to the front, Ran's unit hangs on to the Yehudia road by its fingernails. Ran is lightly injured and evacuated, and his deputy takes command. Two days later, Ran's younger brother will fall on the Golan Heights. Close to noon, the situation on the road is defined as bad. Corps commander Dan Laner sends his deputy to the battle area. The road is strewn with Syrian tanks. In one section, 14 tanks snipe at his half-track as it races across in front of them like a carnival target, but the shells can't catch him. In the battle area, he finds some 20 of the brigade's tanks already unusable. One is lying on its side. Wounded are strewn around. He calls for the deputy brigade commander, and they talk over the radio, but in mid-conversation the voice suddenly vanishes. Silence on the set, until somebody else reports that the deputy brigade commander has just been killed. Giora, the brigade operations officer, takes over. Tank ammunition is running out. The only remaining possibility is to remove shells from the damaged tanks, and transfer them — under heavy bombardment — to those that continue fighting. In the afternoon, Giora leads a charge supported by aircraft and artillery and destroys seven Syrian tanks. The battle rages on through a whole day, without the brigade advancing one step.

Troubled Air

This is a hard day for the ground-support aircraft. Yesterday, they attacked frontline missile systems, but the Syrians brought up new batteries during the night, among them SA6s — which cause the most trouble. As opposed to the SA2 and SA3, they aren't positioned in permanent launching sites, vulnerable to planned attack. The pilots also have problems in spotting an approaching SA6. Other missiles leave a white contrail which serves as a warning flag; the SA6 approaches its prey without any telltale signs in the sky. It's fast and much more manoeuverable, with an as-yet-unknown electronic system, making tampering most difficult.

The Skyhawks play cat and mouse with the Syrian missile batteries as Moti Hod controls the battle. It is a cruel game which today will cost eight aircraft. In the afternoon, the Syrian rate of fire lessens; in place of bursts they only fire single missiles. There seems to be a missile shortage.

Quneitra's Turn

The Syrian now opens a major offensive near Quneitra; their second assault on the Golan Heights. The Syrians throw their last armored reserve — the 3rd Division, commanded by President Assad's brother — into this battle. Apart from one armored brigade stationed in Haleb District, the whole Syrian Army is already engaging the IDF. The attack begins at 16:00 hours, and a number of Syrian commando battalions operate with the armored division. The impetus of attack, concentrated as it is on a very narrow sector, is extremely intense. Apart from the first night, these will be the hardest hours experienced by the Golan Heights warriors. Considerable anxiety permeates Northern Command Staff. Having been repulsed in the central and southern sectors, the Syrians now throw their full force into the north. They are faced by a brigade, the soldiers of which have not slept in two days.

111

At the height of the offensive, Deputy Prime Minister Yigal Allon arrives at Command Headquarters. He scans the maps, and the blank faces of the commanders, hears conversations on the radio, and then takes Hofi into a corner. "Would heavy strategic bombing deep inside Syria make it easier on the front?" he asks.

"It may help. It will certainly hamper them," Haka answers. Allon contacts the Prime Minister's Office in Tel Aviv to talk with Golda. He reports on the offensive and his conversation with Haka Hofi, concluding: "I recommend it."

The Syrian attack lasts seven hours, without respite. Battalion after battalion are thrown into battle, as they seek ways through. Haka appears more worried than he did on the first night. He listens to the brigade commander knowing that if the latter says it's very difficult – then it must be critical. Close to 22:00 hours, the Chief of Staff calls. Haka wets his throat and says in a hoarse voice: "I'm not certain we will hold!" All ears prick to attention.

Brigadier Raful Eitan now has his HQ behind the brigade. His calmness contributes much. He is as stubborn as a mule: "We're not moving a yard! Not even one yard!"

At 23:00 hours, the brigade O.C.'s voice comes over the radio in Raful's half-track. "That's it!" he says, "I think that's it!" There's no need to explain what he means. He doesn't ask permission to retreat, nor waste any words about the force of attack. It's clear that the Syrians are breaking through the brigade.

"Five minutes more! Not more than that. Hold for another five minutes," Raful says in a softer voice. The O.C. doesn't answer, but another radio from one of the frontline positions, reports Syrian truck movement eastward – the first sign of a break in the Syrian offensive. The fire slowly wanes away, and the Syrian armor turns back.

Raful is by nature very economical on words. In the morning, he will tell one of his officers: "That was a terrible night. There were moments when it hung by a hair."

112

Desert Foxtrot

"It's not the Egyptian Army of 1967," Gonen tells his men in the War Room. In the Six Day War, Shmulik Gonen's brigade crossed swords with the densest section of the Egyptian defense, breaking through in one day, and being the first to reach the Suez Canal. This time, it's not that easy. This morning, Gonen receives aerial photographs taken at dawn; most of the bridges bombed by the Air Force yesterday have been rebuilt overnight. The Egyptians can renew the flow into Sinai. The Air Force doesn't return to the bridges today. It has other missions, and the IDF may well want to use the Egyptian bridges to cross to the west bank in today's Israeli offensive.

Gonen now adopts a tactic of "no retreat and no counter-attack." He is trying to achieve two things that are extremely difficult, simultaneously; to gain time, without losing territory. He orders his forces to operate in dance steps; back and forward, back and forward – a minor withdrawal followed by an assault back to the same hills from which the force had retreated earlier. Gonen is justifiably trying to husband his strength till all the reserve divisions arrive, but assault and withdrawal, time and again, must cost in attrition. Junior field commanders can't understand why they must attack a second and a third time, the same hill from which they were ordered to retreat yesterday.

Out of the Hat

The Egyptians also opt for preservation but only in one sphere, their air force. They are not at all considerate of their infantrymen, sending them into repeated assaults, wave after wave. However, the Egyptian General Staff acknowledges the Israeli Air Force's clear supremacy, and saves its pilots and planes for later. In the first two days, the bulk of Egyptian aircraft were on rear airfields. Now, they try a new tactic; mass aerial assault, apparently in the hope of losing less planes to aerial combat and reaching their

113

targets with at least some aircraft. The tactic doesn't work as planned. They approach various objectives across the expanses of Sinai, with 50 MiGs and Sukhois, but only 34 planes from this wave return to base. The second time, 60 aircraft assault in three waves, one after the other. Israeli fighter planes await them closer to the front line, and another 13 Egyptian aircraft crash to the ground.

Rebound

The first Israeli counter-attack of any size is developing on the Egyptian front. The general supposition was that the IDF would strike first on the northern sector. Yesterday afternoon, the Air Force heavily bombed Port Said area, and it seemed to be preparation for attack. But things develop otherwise.

A number of hours remain till the attack. Some of the men in the War Room and the corps lie down to sleep — to regain a little strength for the new test. The last details of coordination are being discussed, and final changes being made in plans to relieve the strongholds. Shortly after 04:00 hours Gonen warns Magen not to approach too close to the waterline because of anti-tank missiles positioned on the embankment, and then asks whether the breakthrough to the strongholds is possible — in Magen's opinion.

Magen: "There'll be no problem of crossing at **Matzmed** — but the strongholds are a different matter. Here it will be necessary to brief small forces." For some reason the briefing hasn't been given, or Magen doesn't know of it. And this will cause Gonen to transfer this task to Arik Sharon.

Gonen: "I intend to let Arik get to the strongholds and return. At this stage Adan will be held in reserve. When Arik returns — then Bren can begin."

At 04:20 hours, Bren's voice comes over the radio. Now he's told that Arik Sharon will proceed to the strongholds. Afterwards he, Adan, is to pour southwards without entering **Hezyon** — Firdan — and will cross at **Matzmed** with a

114

secondary unit to hold on an axis nine miles west of the Suez Canal. The Egyptian heavy armor divisions are still west of the canal, but Southern Command feels that penetration by an Israeli armored force — even if it's only one brigade — will throw the Egyptian High Command off balance.

Tack with the Wind

Shortly before 05:00 hours there is another change in the mission to relieve the Bar Lev Line strongholds. Intelligence officer David Gedalia reports to Gonen that Egyptian forces are penetrating the **Missouri** positions and the Chinese Farm. This is the sector where Sharon is planning on a breakthrough to the strongholds. Gonen now hesitates about leaving the mission to Sharon. He again contacts Bren Adan to ask whether he can take on the job. Bren promises an answer by morning. Sharon's mission isn't cancelled. Now two army corps have been alerted for a possible stronghold rescue mission. The final decision is taken at 06:17 hours. Gonen informs Sharon's staff chief that, because of the considerable enemy in the field, his corps will not attempt the rescue of the garrisons. The intention is to give Adan the job. But Bren Adan hasn't yet replied about whether he can do it, and apparently hasn't briefed secondary forces for the mission. The assumption is that he will succeed in this task in the course of his southward offensive.

It's already daylight and, at 06:05 hours, the Air Force begins to operate. It is to work freely over the whole front until 08:00 hours. The pilots' only instruction is not to damage the Egyptian bridges, and especially not at **Matzmed** and **Nissan**. Israeli forces are going to use these bridges to cross the canal. From 08:00 hours the aircraft will concentrate on supporting Bren's army corps.

A short while before Adan is to move, the War Room receives a report on the state of his forces. He is short of some tanks; a few only arrived on the front minutes ago. The Egyptian Second Army in Sinai, where Bren Adan is to attack, has 350 tanks. Two infantry divisions have crossed the canal so far in this sector. The Egyptian 18th Infantry Division, in the north, has a mechanised brigade and a brigade of T62 tanks. Southwards up to Ismailia sits the 2nd Infantry Division, with its own mechanised and tank brigades.

At 07:59 hours Gonen tells Bren: "Attack — and good luck!"

Bren replies: "I'm moving the lot." Then the War Room radios monitor his instructions to his brigade commanders.

Long Trek

To complete their mission, Bren Adan's forces must breakthrough and traverse a distance of 25-30 miles. This isn't easy, but an armored corps is entitled to assume that it's possible. The IDF has done tasks like it in the past, and the units are trained for it.

The first encounter with Egyptians takes place in Qantara district. This is perhaps the force's only successful action in the offensive. Natke's units strike at Egyptian tanks that sally forth from the direction of Qantara, and at missile-carrying infantry. Meanwhile, Egyptian aircraft are bombing Refidim. Three Migs are downed over the airfield. At Qantara, the difference in firepower between the Israelis and the Egyptians is felt almost immediately. The Egyptians have the advantage, and particularly so in artillery. IDF reserve artillery hasn't yet reached Sinai in full force. The terrible lack of mortars, especially in battle against the Egyptian infantry, is also hampering the forces. The missile teams can aim at the tanks from 3000 meters and are out of range for counter-fire. Bren's corps is getting support from Sharon's artillery.

Up to 09:00 hours everything proceeds more or less to plan. At 08:50 Bren orders Natke to prepare his forces for a link-up with the **Hezyon** and **Purkan** strongholds. IDF men are still holding in a stronghold in Qantara — but a link-up with them will be difficult. There is optimism in the War Room.

But Adan's army corps isn't yet in contact with the main forces of the Egyptian Second Army. His men have been told not to approach too closely the canalside embankment, because of missiles, but the restriction only applies to the last 3000 meters — and they are moving at much greater depth.

Bren: "We have no contacts yet."

Gonen: "Maybe it's worth looking for them more to the west."

Bren: "Till now we've avoided the west. Now I want to move in on **Hezyon**. We have already been in an ambush, but we're lacking infantry and artillery."

Wishful Thinking

Close to 09:30 hours, Gonen and Adan review the next move — the one where the troubles will begin.

Gonen: "What are your plans now?"

Bren: "I want to cross **Hezyon** from the north. I already have artillery. It's OK. (He refers to support from Sharon). I want to put a force inside. The question is what do you want in **Hezyon** — only to evacuate, or to cross to the other side?"

Gonen: "Before the crossing I want to destroy all the enemy forces that have crossed. I mean you to destroy all the enemy on the Qantara sector south to **Matzmed**. When you have done that, cross at one of the points. That's why it's important for the southward move to be a steady flow until you reach **Matzmed**.

Bren: "It will be alright. Do you want me to make contact with **Hezyon** and pull the men out?"

Gonen: "Positive! If it's possible to cross at **Hezyon**, then it would be good to do it with a small unit that will just stand fast on the west bank. In other words, two things are important: to seize one or two handholds on the west bank, and to move south fast, cross at **Matzmed** and hold on **Havit** (the code for an axis nine miles from the Suez Canal)."

117

Fairy Tale

Now, one of the strangest episodes of the war is about to take place. An operations sergeant listening to the command radio, in his excitement, records in the operations log: "Small reconnaissance units from Adan's army corps have crossed the canal in **Hezyon** (Firdan) and **Purkan** (Ismailia) districts." This important piece of news travels from ear to ear as far as the Supreme Command bunker. The hopes for good news have been so great, since the war started, that no attempt is made to confirm authenticity by a direct call to Gonen. Somebody passes the item to Major-General (Res.) Zeevi, who phones the Chief of Staff. General Elazar is participating in a Government session. He tells Mrs. Meir. Within the hour, the news leaks through to Sokolov House in Tel Aviv, where scores of foreign correspondents are sitting waiting for stories.

Censorship doesn't yet allow publication, but a *France Soir* correspondent succeeds in smuggling it out, and his paper appears, in Paris, with its main headline proclaiming that the IDF has crossed the Suez Canal.

Luckily the IDF Spokesman has not issued an official communique, but the news reaches the Military Attache's Office in Israel's Washington Embassy, and Major-General Gur passes it on to a few people.

Southern Command War Room is blissfully ignorant of the commotion on the home front. The command operations diary simply records receipt of Supreme Command approval to seize a couple of handholds on the other side.

Clean Sweep

The atmosphere in Gonen's command group is optimistic. And there is reason for this feeling. At 09:36 hours, they hear Natke, who is fighting on the northern sector facing and to the south of Qantara, report to the corps commander: "One force of mine is fighting against missiles and all sorts of infantry, crushing them and smashing them. A second force is in battle against tanks on the

118

central sector. Another made contact with tanks 15 minutes ago. It seems to me that we're slowly sweeping up the lot." Natke is an armor veteran who beat the Egyptians at Abu Ageila in the Six Day War. Now he sounds enthusiastic and confident. Bren tells him to be cautious, and not to advance too quickly. He is not to move over terrain without taking a good look at it first.

The battle in **Hezyon** district begins to develop after 10:00 hours. Bren Adan sends a force to relieve the stronghold, seize the bridge and put a small unit across. But first, a conversation with Gonen. Bren: "Can I also use *Akavish* (an east-west road)? "

Gonen: "I prefer you to approach **Missouri** from the north. It's faster. They're deployed towards the east, so you'll take them by surprise."

Bren: "Positive. I accept that. What I need is air support."

A C.O.'s Story

The attacking force in **Hezyon** district doesn't pay much attention to protecting the flank of the breakthrough. In place of this, it's busy with frontal penetration. One battalion is attacking, not without difficulty. The force is spread out. It is a reserve unit, and its commander has already been wounded in this offensive. After the war, he will relate: "We faced **Hezyon**, on an extensive dune about two miles away. I only took one company in with me, while two stayed behind. We were under accurate artillery fire all the time. I improved positions to avoid the fire, and asked the brigade commander for permission not to bring in two more companies — because we were being worn down for nothing. Nevertheless, I was under pressure to bring the two companies forward. We stood and fired in the direction of Firdan for almost an hour. I asked the brigadier for permission to pull back, for there was no point in letting the artillery decimate us, but I was ordered to advance and make contact. I started the battalion rolling towards **Hezyon**.

119

"The charge shocked the enemy at a certain stage. Up to 700 yards from the water, they didn't fire at us. That was between 10:00 and 10:30 hours. It tempted us into running for the waterline. And then, 700 yards from the canal, we took a terrible salvo; artillery, missiles – the lot. We reached infantry dug-outs. To the north, the infantry began to run, but in front of me – they stood fast in deep trenches. As I approached they began to fire RPG bazookas from all sides. Our most effective weapon was the tank commander's machine gun. The tanks zigzagged across, sweeping up the area. Meanwhile, tanks began to be hit from the other side of the canal. Most of the damage was done by missiles. I myself was hit by an RPG. My radio to brigade wasn't functioning, but I heard the front commander order seizure of the bridge with three tanks.

"Two things made me charge in. I was sure that I would get artillery and air support, and I thought that somebody would follow me. I hoped for artillery because when I asked the brigade commander, a number of times, the answer was positive. Quarter of an hour before the charge forward, there were a few artillery shells, and the hits were good. This gave me the confidence that there would be artillery. With its support, we would be able to take the embankment. Two tanks reached the ramp but were stuck there. I was also sure there would be air support. Before the charge, planes did come in and we thought they would continue.

"The nearer I got to the waterline, I could see more and more of what faced me. In hindsight, there was no point or possibility of stopping the charge. The battalion was spread over the whole area. It was impossible to stop the assault, because the losses would have been heavier, and there would have been chaos. Withdrawal only began after a large part of the battalion had been wiped out. Six of our tanks were destroyed, but many more were damaged. I was injured, and the command transferred to a company officer. Our losses in men were heavier. The men who succeeded in jumping from damaged tanks were picked up by the others.

"I had no mechanised infantry with me. I understood that this must be a larger scale action. The force could have seized a bridgehead, but somebody would have to come to race over the bridges. I know that there were other forces which the commander wanted to throw in to help me, but they didn't come."

Back to Square One

The attack fails. The remnants of the battalion pull back with torn tanks behind them. A nearby force can't come in to give help — it is out of ammunition. The force commander will later report: "When the force assaulting **Hezyon** began to be decimated, and the second force nearby was without ammunition, I asked corps for more force. I was ordered to pull out a unit from Sharon's corps, which was behind me, and take it under my command. I told its commander that I had been ordered to take him for missions, and he said: 'I have orders from the commander not to come.' I talked to his commander, and told him: 'This is a question of saving lives. They must come immediately, or it'll be too late.' He said: 'I have an order not to give.' I reported this to corps. Meanwhile another unit of mine arrived, but there was no longer need for aid."

The battered remnants of the battalion extricated themselves, leaving 17 dead and six burnt tanks behind on the battlefield.

While this battle is still raging, a very significant decision is brewing on the Sinai front. It relates to Arik Sharon's army corps. According to the operation orders, Sharon's corps — which is massed around Tassa — was supposed to be in reserve for Adan in case the counter-attack fails. When Bren completes his attack, the second stage will begin — Sharon's corps will work from north to south against the Egyptian Third Army, until it reaches north of Suez town, where it will cross the canal. The assumption is that this offensive will begin in the afternoon.

And yet, around 09:30 hours, it becomes clear that Gonen intends to order a move for Sharon's corps. While talking with Adan's staff chief, Gonen says: "I now intend to send Arik to the southern sector. One hour later, Brigadier Uri Benari — Gonen's assistant — contacts Sharon's chief of staff, and transmits new orders: "Prepare to move south. Line up the columns and be ready to move when ordered. Bren will take care of the sector. En route, you will destroy everything you meet, and carry out your mission at **Nissan** (a crossing)." A few minutes later the chief of staff in Sharon's corps asks whether it's alright to move immediately. Gonen takes the microphone to explain the order: "You can move as far as the Gidi road. Albert (Mendler) is now establishing contact and putting pressure on the forces facing him. Report to me when you reach Gidi. Only then will I know whether you're going into battle with the armor that's in the west, or whether you're going straight for **Nissan** to cross and take the town (Suez). Understood? That order I'll give you when you are in Gidi."

Staff chief: "Can we move now? "

Gonen: "Positive, but only as far as the Gidi road."

Why is Gonen issuing this order now? Last night, the Chief of Staff ordered no move for Sharon without a specific instruction. At 10:38, Gonen asks Assistant Chief of Staff Maj.- General Rehavam Zeevi for approval to move Sharon to the Gidi road. Two minutes later, Zeevi gives permission in the name of the Chief of Staff. General Elazar will later say that he shouldn't have been tempted, but was influenced by the optimistic reports that Adan's men had reached the bridges — and didn't yet know about the failure of the Israeli attack at **Hezyon**.

Southern Command War Room also isn't yet aware of the events near **Hezyon**. Gonen's decision is based on two considerations. All the reports from Adan's units in the field are good — so far. Everything seems to be going according to plan. There is a hitch in communications between Adan and his brigade commanders but, from the radio net, the main problem appears to be artillery bombardment from across the canal. Adan isn't the type of officer to complain quickly, or ask for help before he needs it.

Agam III

Yitzhak Agam and his comrades are experiencing their first baptism of fire in this war. It's morning, and more a chase than a real battle. It begins following a heavy Egyptian bombardment. The Egyptian guns are performing well; from the constantly changing firing missions, the artillery observer officers must be nearby. Agam's company patrols and quickly discovers tracks of three men in the sand dunes. They move rapidly down the tracks. Before long, three Egyptians suddenly rise from the shrubs. They saw the Israelis approaching, and apparently decided they have no chance. The haste of their surrender seems suspicious. They are tense as some of Agam's comrades search their equipment. Two are forward observation officers. The third is a commando lieutenant colonel who somehow got attached to them.

Their second action is south of Tasa, this time with the whole reconnaissance unit. Five minutes before it starts, Captain Rafi Bar Lev, Agam's company commander, arrives. Rafi reached Israel this morning. He is in civilian life a security officer on El Al aircraft. Rafi is considered a first-rate officer and is popular among his men. When his plane landed at Lydda International Airport, he thumbed a plane ride to Refidim and then hitch-hiked to Tasa.

While the tanks are taking defensive action against Egyptian armor, Yitzhak Agam's APC stands to one side. Yitzhak serves as spotter for the tank commanders, reporting the approach of Egyptian vehicles. The tank sights are not yet adjusted, so the crews prefer that Agam observes and presights for them. Meanwhile they hide behind a fold in the ground. As enemy armor appears, Agam informs them by radio, and they sally forth for

123

rapid action. The battle goes on until sundown. The unit has one man dead — its commander, Ben Zion Carmeli. Yoav Brom from **Kibbutz** Shefayim is appointed battalion commander on the spot.

Following the battle, Rafi Bar Lev reports to Brom that he is not ready for new assignments until the sights of his tanks have been adjusted. By moonlight, he makes the first adjustments with the tank crews. Now they are readier for battle.

Daylight Saving

In his situation appraisal, in the War Room, Gonen says that a few hours will pass before Sharon's corps goes in to attack. So he wants to save some time. The corps will traverse part of its route, as far as the Gidi road. This will guarantee against going into battle in darkness. One battalion will remain in the field until Bren Adan's forces arrive, but the rest of the corps will move a few score miles to the south.

In answer to a post-war question about fears of sudden complications on Adan's sector, Gonen will reply: "An army corps doesn't suddenly get involved in complications." And, at this moment, Gonen does have reason to be optimistic. He now asks Albert Mendler to apply more pressure on the Egyptians in his sector, and adds: "There are signs of retreat." Within minutes it becomes clear that this isn't retreat — but the reverse. On the southern sector, Egyptian tanks begin to move forwards towards Albert's men. For this reason Gonen tells Sharon that, approaching Gidi, he may first of all have to cope with Egyptian tanks.

The War Room receives the first unpleasant intimation at 11:45 hours. Bren asks Gonen: "Can we have air support in **Hezyon** area?   We're close to the water. We have a lot of casualties. A great many vehicles have been set on fire by missiles. I'm adding much more force, but we need the support."

Air support doesn't arrive, but Bren has little time in which to worry. At 12:05 he announces that six of his tanks are burning, and he needs fuel and ammunition. He doesn't ask for help from Sharon's corps. His announcement calms the atmosphere in the War Room, and the order to Sharon to move southwards isn't amended yet.

Sharon is apparently the only one who senses, at this stage, that the assault on **Hezyon** isn't developing properly. A few minutes before Adan's message, Sharon talks to Gonen about his move. While detailing the deployment of his brigades he suddenly interjects: "Just a moment, I wanted to tell you something. I've just come back from there – facing **Hezyon**. Bren's tanks aren't advancing. They've been standing under heavy artillery fire for an hour and a half. He has a lot of tanks that have remained behind, and didn't move with the forces."

Man Overboard

Amid all these moves, a struggle is in process to rescue a pilot who parachuted yesterday into the salt marshes on the northern sector. Albert Mendler joyfully announced an hour ago that he succeeded in saving a downed pilot in his sector. Now Gonen calls Kalman Magen, who has already been told to operate independently of Adan, and tells him: "One of our pilots has been in the marshes since yesterday without water, and with broken arms and legs. If you have to fight to get him out – do it! "

Kalman: "We're doing it now."

Gonen: "Nice work."

Despite Egyptian fire, a number of soldiers reached the pilot yesterday. When they tried to move him, he couldn't stand the pain and asked to be left. They finally gave up and decided to fetch a larger squad with a stretcher.

Gonen adds: "I'm bringing in air support for you – on Qantara."

Kalman: "Not yet. I first want the air to help the operation to get the pilot out. I'm sending the scouts in."

Gonen: "For the pilot – O.K. Afterwards move in towards Qantara and, if there's a bridge, send a tank platoon across to guard it."

The rescuers don't get their air support. In the afternoon, Kalman Magen reports: "Without air, they couldn't get near. We dropped 11 men with a platoon of tanks in a deep sweep. They ran into a missile ambush. We have a casualty and a hit on a tank. We're firing with the tanks. Without air, it's impossible to get the pilot."

Gonen: "Pull back but stay in sight of the place. Maybe we'll get him when it's dark."

Kalman: "Impossible. It's in the swamp."

The rescue attempt fails, and the pilot is taken prisoner by the Egyptians.

Take the Expressway

Around noon, Gonen decides to change the direction of Sharon's attack. In place of sweeping from north to south through the Egyptian Third Army, and then crossing the canal near Suez — Gonen now wants Sharon to move directly southwards without making contact with the enemy. Egyptian tanks are pressing hard on Albert's forces — and worrying Gonen: he fears a breakthrough southwards along the Gulf of Suez. Sharon can cross at Nissan — Suez town — and mop-up later, from south to north.

Gonen: "I would like you to get there as fast as you can, seize the Nissan bridge or another, and destroy their armor. In parallel — cross to the other side. How early can you be there."

Sharon: "I estimate around 16:00 hours."

Gonen: "I hope so. Start moving and lots of luck."

Missing Link

While Sharon is changing direction, Adan's forces are organizing for a second attack on Hezyon — Firdan district. A force from another brigade is now attacking, and the job is given to a battalion commanded by Assaf Yaguri. Time is running out and Yaguri isn't invited to any kind of orders group or briefing before the assault. He understands this to be a brigade plus operation for which his battalion is the spearpoint. He has no doubt that there will be significant artillery and air support. The relative absence of aircraft over the sector at this stage doesn't worry him.

Assaf will later say that he understood from his brigade commander that the mission was to link up with IDF units that had already crossed the canal: he was to sweep across the terrain and ford the canal. They, Yaguri and his brigadier, didn't know whether the units on the other side were from Sharon's corps or from the force that attacked in the morning. They didn't know that this force had failed and been thrown back.

Yaguri is moving when his brigade commander has a short radio conversation with Maj.-General Adan.

Brigadier: "Do we have forces on the other bank? "

Adan: "Negative."

Brigadier: "Till now, I thought we did."

Yaguri is of the same mind, and has already told his men that they are to link up with other units that have already crossed the Suez Canal.

His attack begins at 14:30 hours. He reports that his tanks are in good condition and are laden with fuel and ammunition. Twenty-two tanks enter the field. Ninety minutes later — four intact tanks are extricated with difficulty. The assault proceeds well at first, despite heavy missile and R.P.G. fire from the canalside embankment. But Yaguri is shocked by the absence of any artillery support. Some of the tanks approach the embankment, and Yaguri can already see the high arches of the Firdan Bridge, but nobody follows him. He calls repeatedly over the radio: "I can see nobody coming after us, and don't understand why."

The toll of hit tanks is mounting. Most fall prey to the R.P.G. bazookas. Yaguri's tank is hit and sheds a track. Now he orders his men to pull back while keeping up their fire. It's a retreat order, but few of his men can execute it. Yaguri's tank, which has meanwhile sustained another hit from a missile that sheered through the radio aerials, remains in the field. At 16:00 hours, Yaguri and some of his men are taken prisoner. Scores of Israeli bodies are strewn across the battlefield. Before the Egyptians pick him up, he counts at least 11 wrecked tanks of his battalion.

In the Dark

Because of communications problems, Corps HQ has only incomplete information on the situation. Southern Command still knows nothing about a second failure at Firdan, or about a battalion commander taken prisoner. They will only find out this evening. Adan's corps asks for a helicopter to evacuate wounded. It's now clear that the Egyptians are opening a parallel offensive on most sectors of the front. Gonen complains to Benny Peled that the air support so far is insufficient: with the Egyptians now attacking he must have more aircraft.

Gonen is considering a total change of mission for Sharon. He now wants to cancel the attack on the Egyptian Third Army in the south. He sends his chief of staff in a helicopter to check the exact deployment of Sharon's units. From the staff chief's reports he concludes that there is no chance of reaching the assigned area with the whole force before dark. Uri Benari issues an order to Sharon's forces to stop in their tracks.

Sharon's new mission is to take the Chinese Farm and **Missouri**, facing the northern expanse of the Great Bitter Lake. A large force of the Egyptian Second Army has concentrated here during the day. Sharon receives the order personally a little after 15:00 hours. Hours have passed since his units began their move and, because of changing circumstances, he hasn't yet succeeded in establishing battle contact with the enemy.

Interrupted Parley

The Egyptian counter-attack begins while Adan is in session with his brigade commanders to hear reports on the day's events and the current situation. The officers race back to their units.

128

Natke will later say: "I had a total of ten tanks fit for service. Gabi and I divided the area into two sectors. The sun was in our eyes. They attacked us with a great many tanks, and mechanised infantry. We set fire to a lot of tanks. It was twilight, and there was plenty of black smoke and flames. When their tanks halted, trucks and personnel carriers brought up infantry who began to charge on foot. This was the critical stage. They told us that Arik Sharon was moving in immediately to counter-attack. The situation was bad. We didn't know if we could hold them — with so few tanks."

The Egyptian assault on this sector is being staged by more than a hundred tanks, and thousands of infantry. Two of the Israeli commanders request permission for a partial withdrawal, but they don't succeed — the Egyptians are very close. A few score Egyptian vehicles are set ablaze, and their assault is finally broken on this sector.

Yo Yo

The concentrated attack around Firdan results in another change of mission for Sharon. Shortly after 17:00 hours, he is forbidden to attack **Missouri**. The heavy attrition on Adan's front leads Gonen to a preference to hold Sharon's forces in reserve. Even if he attacks **Missouri** successfully, he may not be able to break off contact. Sharon accepts the change with understanding, and says: "I think that's a serious consideration! "

As a result, Sharon's corps isn't put to use at this stage — or through the whole day. The only open option now is help from the Air Force, but this will also be a disappointment, as Gonen learns from O.C. Air Force Benny Peled.

It's getting dark and none of the objectives have been achieved. If anything — the situation has changed for the worse. The Egyptians have seized more terrain in Sinai, and have dug-in at greater depth. As the full picture becomes clear, Gonen begins to show greater caution about plans that he was previously prepared to approve. He agreed earlier with Kalman Magen on an attempt, aided by infantry, to link up with the strongholds on the north road. Kalman had even asked permission to raid the enemy armor in his sector. Gonen now tells him that, because of the worsening situation, the raid and the stronghold rescue mission must be cancelled.

Let's Annoy Them

At 18:26 hours, Maj.-General Sharon contacts Maj.--General Gonen.

Sharon: "Shmulik, I've been thinking about the situation. I think we have a way out of it. I think we should hold a consultation — perhaps invite the Chief of Staff and Moshe (Dayan). There is a possibility of getting out of this situation that we're stuck in."

Gonen: "What's the direction of your thought. Wait! Don't say it over the radio."

Sharon: "There's something else. An absurd situation has been created. These forces are annoying our tanks at night. We can drive them mad. After all, we are a thousand times better than them. I suggest that we sit and discuss it. I want to use those units, in company with . . . "

Gonen: "No, I don't agree, Arik."

Sharon: "I simply say that I would use them — so the Egyptians won't feel everything's for free."

Gonen: "We'll see. I'll suggest."

New Chapter

Close to midnight, the generals convene in Southern Command War Room. The Chief of Staff, accompanied by Maj.-General (Res.) Aharon Yariv, arrives at 00:45. Elazar has come from Tel Aviv where he has just told hundreds of newspapermen: "We will break the bones of the Arab armies." There is no atmosphere of failure, but this evening has clearly opened a new chapter on the southern front. There is also no reason any longer to rely on the Air Force achieving full freedom of action over the front-lines. The generals analyze the day's battles.

130

The most obvious fact is that the reports flowing in from the front were either too late, or didn't correctly describe the events. The Chief of Staff says in summing up: "I get an optimistic battle picture. As a result, decisions are taken that aren't appropriate to the real situation. Moves are made without contributing to the course of battle, and we waste forces and considerable time."

Another decisive and obvious fact from today's actions relates to the way in which forces were used. All the reserve units are not yet concentrated on the front, but a few hundred tanks are available. They are massed in three corps, and mostly with Sharon and Adan. The day's conclusions teach that the force was too dispersed. True, the support was little, and there is a shortage of weapons for infantry, but the hundreds of tanks weren't used properly either. The first assault only fielded 30 tanks, and the second — only 22. Such a force cannot carry out a mission that hasn't been clearly defined to commanders in the field.

Albert Mendler vigorously demands an attempt to reach the waterline as fast as possible. Gonen disagrees. He doesn't want to stage a new attack to cross the canal before massing more forces.

Desperate Quandary

The situation of the waterline strongholds has changed drastically for the worse. The front is now divided into four sectors, each commander being responsible for the strongholds on his sector. The officer commanding the northernmost force is Kalman Magen. Next to him, facing Qantara and the Firdan Bridge, is Bren Adan. Further south is Arik Sharon, and the southernmost is Albert Mendler. On each sector, some strongholds are evacuated, but others fall or surrender. One fortress on the sea coast will stand until the very end. Its garrison will repel every assault, including one from the sea using amphibian tanks. Egyptian vehicles are strewn all around, mostly hit by a tank that will remain intact to the very end.

131

On the canal banks, the situation is more complex. Efforts to rescue the garrisons are costing lives. Alongside the moral problem, an even more serious question; a danger that losses in rescue operations will seriously deplete the forces left to deal with the Egyptian bridge-heads. The rescue attemps near Firdan Bridge are a perfect example. The local stronghold commander is badly injured; his arm was shot off. His deputy is also wounded. The radio operator is in command. The brigade commander on the sector facing the stronghold sends in three companies, one after the other, but not one reaches its objective. Forty Israeli tanks are hit in this effort, and 50 men killed or wounded. Finally, the stronghold falls into Egyptian hands.

Democracy in Action

Further south, facing Ismailia, a garrison convenes for a hasty general meeting. The agenda, to continue fighting in the hope that the IDF will finally get through to them or to accept the Southern Command suggestion to evacuate and sneak through Egyptian lines. They vote to evacuate. As the moon goes down, they set off with one tank, to make their way through the Egyptian lines. An armored column moves out to meet them, but returns empty-handed. They make radio contact a second time, but again fail to find the men. In their third attempt, they fire a green flare, but this time encounter Egyptians. The column forces its way through hundreds of Egyptian infantrymen and dozens of tanks. Four APCs are hit and go up in flames. The men inside are wounded, and three are listed as missing. The tank on which the garrison are riding finally comes through, but the joy is mingled with grief.

The garrison commander near Qantara pressures HQ for permission to bring out the bodies of his dead men. The request is denied. They must travel a long and dangerous road. Carrying dead bodies will make it more difficult and dangerous. Forty-two men of the garrison, and others who have joined them, set out with the commander in the van.

132

From time to time, he has to support the garrison doctor who is in poor shape. They suddenly encounter an Egyptian ambush. The fire isn't heavy, but they make no attempt at charging their ambushers; their sole thought is to get beyond the line of encirclement. The column splits into two large groups. Two soldiers wounded in the ambush remain on the ground; their comrades don't notice that they are missing. One group comes through the lines via Qantara cemetery. The second group of 17 men, finds shelter in a house on the outskirts of Qantara town. In daylight, they are discovered by the Egyptians. After a short clash, the men decide to surrender. They have no more ammunition. Eight come out with their hands up; they will return home via an Egyptian prisoner-of-war cage. The fate of the nine who remain in the house is unknown; they will never be seen again.

In two other strongholds, the commanders prefer not to evacuate and both finally fall into Egyptian hands. The one, north of the Great Bitter Lake, is on the flank of the Egyptian Second Army. Amnon, responsible for rescue operations in this sector, suggests by radio to the garrison commander that he joins up with the men of the neighboring stronghold to sneak through Egyptian lines together. The commander has 30 men with a half-track, an armored personnel carrier and a tender. He thinks it over for quite a while and finally says that he prefers to remain. In the neighboring fortress the men pile on their one half-track and within the hour, reach IDF lines. On Albert Mendler's sector, Dan's tanks reach to within 400 yards of another stronghold. Dan radios the garrison commander to suggest that he comes out to the tanks. The officer consults his men and rejects the proposal.

Haunted Ether

Much depends on the garrison commanders. Some are prepared to take risks rather than remain in the Egyptian rear; they are finally extricated, but not without battles and losses. Other officers press HQ to act. Others again need to be encouraged. In one stronghold on the northern sector, a single soldier refuses to be evacuated. He will maintain radio contact for 48 hours before the set will fall silent. The fortress near Firdan provides a dramatic conversation between Arik Sharon and the radio operator.

Sharon introduces himself by the code name for O.C. Southern Command, saying: "The previous – – – is speaking to you." Finally he deciphers it. His clearly Yemenite voice takes on a ring of enthusiasm. He introduces himself as Yaakov Ben Nahum from Jerusalem: "I know who you are. I know you will come to save us."

He asks for artillery fire on his position, to repel the Egyptians. All attempts to rescue this stronghold will be in vain. Throughout, the voice of the Yemenite radio operator will be heard over the air. He talks incessantly. The communications instruments resound with his voice, which allows no rest. Towards evening on Monday, he will apparently understand that the end is near. Yaakov Ben Nahum will suddenly say: "Tell my mother I fought like a hero!" Thirty minutes later, he will report that bazooka rockets are bursting at the bunker door. The explosions will be clearly heard over the radio. And then – an endless silence.

Of the 16 manned strongholds, nine will fall or surrender; the last – the Pier Position – will only surrender after a week. Six strongholds are evacuated and the men are safe. The remaining one, on the coast, will hold to the end.

Pleasure Cruise II

Tonight, it becomes clear that the result of the first naval battle with the Syrians was no coincidence. A second battle takes place between Port Said and Alexandria. The Egyptian Navy is more self-confident than the Syrian. After the Six Day War, it registered a grand victory when it sank the Israeli destroyer "Eilat" by missile fire from Port Said Harbor. This time, their Russian missiles miss the mark. After a 45 minute battle, three Egyptian Ossa missile ships are sunk. Six crewmen are pulled out of the water and taken prisoner. The two battles suffice to convince the Syrian and Egyptian navies not to move out of port.

Public's Right

The home front doesn't yet know. The civilian population doesn't know that the Golan Heights are almost entirely in Syrian hands; that the Hermon position has been taken by Syrian commandos; that the Bar Lev Line no longer exists; that the Bab el-Mandab Straits are under sea blockade. Nobody bothers — or dares — give such bad news. Israel Radio still broadcasts reports of victories on the front lines. Newspaper editors and military correspondents receive regular briefings, but the papers are not permitted — by order of the censor — to publish anything of failures. Nobody will take responsibility for telling the public what is happening in realistic and frank terms.

This evening, the Chief of Staff appears at a mass televised press conference; one that will be long remembered. Elazar comes directly from a cabinet meeting. Yesterday, the Defense Minister appeared on television, saying that the Egyptians will be "smited hip and thigh," and he wouldn't want to be Egyptian at the end of the battle — but Dayan's face seemed unfamiliar. Many things have become clear in the last 24 hours, but there is nothing to be learnt from Elazar's remarks. He is applauded for saying that the IDF will continue to break enemy bones. Disillusion will come later, when the public will realize how serious the situation was when Elazar made this speech. The Chief of Staff is thinking — so he will say later — not of the public reaction, but of the men on the front line who must be encouraged, and of the best way to keep Jordan out of the war. Here and there, soldiers are encouraged by "We will break their bones", but for the public at large — this sentence will become a miserable symbol of misinformation during the war's most difficult days.

135

INTERLUDE: BAR LEV LINE

Changing Concepts

Defense and fortifications were never popular concepts in the Israeli Army. The IDF's very first doctrine of warfare was almost entirely based on offensive tactics and assault. Importance was not even attached to anti-aircraft defense for quite a few years.

A few days after the 1967 Six Day War, the IDF, on the east bank of Suez, came under a heavy Egyptian barrage from the other bank. Suddenly it was clear that if the army wanted to remain along the canal, and safeguard the lives of its men, it must consolidate. This was more "digging-in" than consolidation, about which IDF engineers then knew little.

In October 1968, the Egyptians opened a sudden bombardment along the whole canal front. Fifteen men died and dozens were injured. Bunkers were smashed as though they were card castles. O.C. Southern Command Yeshayahu Gavish then told me: "I was shocked by the force and effectiveness of the bombardment. The Egyptians activated 150 artillery batteries, and many of the shells had time fuses." The bombardment and another heavy one that followed, clearly indicated a need for basic change in the nature of canalside defense.

The bombardment heralded a stormy debate, which barely reached the public ken, on whether to base primarily on mobile defense, or fortifications along the waterline. The debate didn't end even when it was resolved by then Chief of Staff Haim Bar Lev. It gained force during the War of Attrition, and as conclusions were drawn from that war.

Contractor's Picnic

At the end of 1968, immediately following the bombardment, the IDF began a big consolidation operation. More than 100 heavy tractors were brought down to the line. Private contractors were assisted by some 2000 raw recruits, brought specially for the operation. It lasted four months, during which Israel refused to be provoked by the Egyptians. The new positions were given a new name — **maoz** — "stronghold" — to emphasize their strength and depth. The engineers mostly learnt from Red Army training manuals. Bunker roofs were covered by blast-proof levels, made of railway tracks taken from the Egyptian line that crossed Sinai. It was assumed that a shell, in penetrating, would explode on this layer of metal, instead of inside the bunker. Defense trenches were excavated, and the stronghold encircled in all directions by sharp barbed wire fences, mines and booby traps. Each fortress had its own electric system, drainage, kitchen and services. Vehicles and tanks, in differing numbers according to the size of the stronghold, could be brought into its compound.

The man made responsible for this operation was Maj.-General Bren Adan, who would later be O.C. IDF Armor. The planners entertained the thought — or hope — that the strongholds could prevent an Egyptian crossing. As evidence, each stronghold had loopholes facing the Suez Canal, with heavy machine guns and even anti-tank guns, installed in them. The opponents of the concept, led by Maj.-General Sharon, then-Head of Training Branch, mocked the concept of loopholes: "They will be blocked as soon as fire opens." When the War of Attrition began, it was indeed clear that the Egyptians had marked the loopholes; they were neutralized in the first incidents. Men were injured alongside the slits, and there was no alternative but to seal them.

Stormy Waters

There were two aspects to the argument; how to protect the line in a static war, and what would be the role of the **maoz** if the Egyptians would try a large-scale crossing. Maintenance of the line then meant repeated incidents, so much of the debate revolved around the first aspect, but

137

the problem of crossings was not ignored. Chief of Staff Haim Bar Lev represented the school of thought that favored strongpoints along the waterline. Its opponents were Majors-General Yisrael Tal — who then worked on weapon development in the Ministry of Defense — and Arik Sharon. Because of his stormy nature, Sharon played an outstanding role. He frequently consulted and exchanged opinions with Brigadier Abrasha Tamir, the present Head of General Staff Planning Branch. The debate was stormy enough to cause bad blood. It was orchestrated for slamming doors and strong epithets.

Tal and Sharon argued, **inter alia**, that there was no need to tie the IDF down to static fortifications. The strongpoints were good for shelter and concealment, but not for war, in which they would become unnecessary and dangerous. They would fulfill no real function in preventing an enemy crossing. The garrisons would be neutralized by heavy artillery fire, and could not create ample fire of their own. A more distant line of fortifications would be enough, together with a road network leading to the waterline. A static system so close to the enemy should be avoided. The line of containment should be much deeper, between Balusa in the north and Tasa in the south. Infantry should be moved back from the waterline and, in the space between the Suez Canal and the rear line, IDF armor will destroy any enemy who crosses.

Mobile Vulnerability

To say that Bar Lev thought solely of static defense would be an empty accusation. He saw the **maoz** as one component in an overall defense system, which was partly mobile and partly static. He didn't really believe that the strongholds would block a mass crossing, but opposed forward defense solely by mobile forces. He argued that mobile forces would be vulnerable to enemy ambush. The Egyptians would cross the canal and hold its bank. The IDF would repeatedly be called on to offer large-scale battle. Bar Lev's concept was that the armor would come

138

to the aid of strongholds, and rapidly field counter-attacks. Permanent presence on the forward line was of special importance, in his view.

As Chief of Staff, Bar Lev resolved the debate in favor of his own conception. His heir to be, David Elazar, didn't intervene in the debate, since he was fully occupied with current security on the Syrian, Lebanese and northern Jordanian frontiers. Though many senior IDF officers did support Bar Lev's approach, his obstinate attitude set a very personal seal on the subject. It was only natural that the line should be named for him.

Sitting Ducks

Debate was revived at the height of the War of Attrition. Despite the shelter that the strongholds offered, the number of casualties mounted; some from artillery fire, and others from Egyptian raids. Losses on the line finally caused the IDF to activate the Air Force against Egypt – beginning July 20, 1969. The northern sector commander told Defense Minister Dayan, during one of his visits to the Suez Canal, that he personally favoured withdrawal to the second line. He explained to Dayan that most of his dead were from bombs dropping inside the strongholds. "We sit too close to them," the sector commander – a veteran paratrooper – explained. "We are convenient targets for the Egyptian artillery."

At the end of the War of Attrition, Sharon prepared statistics to prove his point. Between January 1, 1970, when he took over Southern Command, and the cease-fire of July 8, 1970, there were 489 dead and wounded on the canal line. Though only 25 had been hit within the bunkers, 382 were around the strongholds. Most were service personnel who brought ice, came to repair generators, and so on. The maoz was a magnet that attracted considerable traffic.

Bar Lev did not withdraw, despite these contentions. He told me on the eve of his retirement from the post of Chief of Staff: "I see the decision to sit on the waterline as decisive in its importance. I personally resolved the debate. Were we not sitting there, the Egyptians would have gained a hand-hold in Sinai, and we would have been compelled to retake the line time and again. Of course it's difficult to prove, but the fact is that we are sitting there. They say the War of Attrition would have cost us less. Maybe yes and maybe no!"

As fate would have it, Bar Lev's bitter opponent, Ariel Sharon, became O.C. Southern Command. Bar Lev invited him to replace Maj.-General Gavish. Sharon arrived at his new command post and immediately set out to change the method of defense. The War of Attrition was still raging. Sharon repeatedly explained that the IDF must also contemplate a situation where it would not have aerial supremacy. Then it would not be easy to hold the line of strongholds. He pressed for a thinning-out of the strongholds; where there were a few on one sector, some would be transformed into mere observation posts. In parallel, he extended the second line. He intended to erect company strength positions four to six miles in from the canal, on the far slopes concealed from Egyptian observers. The positions were given a new Hebrew name – **taoz** – to differentiate from the canalside strongholds – **maoz**. Bar Lev also seemed to be taking into account the possibility of the IDF barely achieving aerial supremacy over the canal; such a possibility was mentioned to Defense Minister Moshe Dayan and Prime Minister Golda Meir. Bar Lev explained that if the first line couldn't be held, the force would be transferred to the second line and the armor would move forward.

Reduced Traffic

In his first weeks as O.C. Southern Command, Sharon proposed evacuation of 13 out of the 30 strongholds. The remainder were to be reinforced by another blast level, to include the corridors between bunkers, and to be of a much more fundamental form. At first, his proposal was rejected out of hand, but thinning-out did begin here and there while Bar Lev was still Chief of Staff. Two of the four strongholds in one sector, for example, were closed in Bar Lev's time. In seeking to down-grade the static Bar Lev Line, Sharon knowingly and deliberately extended it in another direction; the roads that were an organic part of the system. He paved hundreds of miles with special emphasis on roads at an angle to the canal, rather than along it. He sought to minimize the sections on which IDF forces must travel under Egyptian fire. Right-angle roads were also designed to permit rapid flow of armor to the strongholds and the canal. But this wasn't enough for Sharon; he claimed that the defended strongholds developed soldiers' natural tendencies to close themselves in. He issued aggressive orders for day and night patrols between and around the strongholds.

Beehive

The cease-fire of August 1970 was intended to last a month, with a possible extension for three more months. A decision was made to improve the strongholds, after 16 months of very heavy bombardment. One of the biggest construction operations in the history of Israel now began. The work in Sinai was directed by Maj.-General Dan Laner and his deputy, Kalman Magen. The existing **maoz** was to be converted into an even stronger fortress. Blast barriers of railway tracks were to be replaced by a new level of stone blocks, held between metal nets. Thousands of trucks carried rock to the Suez Canal. Druze from the Golan Heights were among the many laborers. The strongholds were prepared to withstand heavy artillery fire, and bombardment by Egypt's Soviet-made Frog missiles.

Ironically, Sharon was compelled to strengthen the very strongholds he wanted to eliminate. But one thing did make him happy; 250 new miles of road of which 150 were covered with asphalt. Plastic sheets were stretched below roads built in the northern swamps to prevent water seeping through to cover the freeway. Sharon paid special attention to roads running inland. Alternative alignments were laid around junctions. "Artillery Road", intended for rapid movement of gun batteries, was laid parallel with the canal. The front line fortifications alone cost IL.400 million. With the nearby net of roads, the front line expense reached half a billion Israel Pounds. Fortified strongpoints – of the **taoz** variety – were also built. Communications centers, war rooms and hospitals were installed at depth. Everything possible was installed underground, from piping and communications systems in the strongholds through to command posts.

False Impressions

Newspaper reports created the impression of a unified line along the Suez Canal; a sort of Maginot or Mannerheim. But it wasn't that way at all. From north to south, the Suez Canal extends 100 miles. Taking the lakes into account, the line held by the IDF was 62 miles long. Thirty strongholds were constructed on the waterline. In some places, they were built in adjoining chains. There were four in Qantara. On the northern sector by Ras el-Ayish, there were three. Three strongholds faced Ismailia. Where the IDF would cross the canal in the Day of Judgement War, north of the Great Bitter Lake, there were two adjacent strongholds.

The result was sectors of up to and over 10 miles without a stronghold. Observers were stationed in the gaps – during daylight. The Egyptians could operate in these sectors without fear of being spotted immediately. Some officers argued the possibility of daylight revealing that the Egyptians had transferred an infantry brigade to the east bank. Some hint of this could be found in the remarks of General Dan Laner, when he finished his tour of duty as O.C. Armored Forces Sinai: "We have, rather than a line, a depth. It is important to stress that this system must be managed in mobile and aggressive fashion.."

While the fortification work progressed, now on the authority of Arik Sharon, it seemed that his debating partner, Maj.-General Tal wasn't happy. In September 1970, Yisrael Tal, who was still working in the Defense Ministry, prepared a memorandum on the defense of Sinai. There was talk of possible partial agreement, in which Israel would withdraw, allowing Egyptian forces to cross the Suez. Tal repeatedly emphasized his opposition to strongholds that would impose strategic restrictions on the Israeli Supreme Command. Since the strongholds do exist, Tal said, they should only be held by a small force of mechanized infantry, which would maintain regular canal-side patrols; mobile defense, while the main force would remain outside Egyptian artillery range.

In January 1972, Bar Lev was replaced by David Elazar. Maj.-General Yisrael Tal was appointed Head of the General Staff Branch, and later also Deputy Chief of Staff. Maj.-General Sharon was still in command in the south. When Tal returned from "exile", a new team was created. It was to be expected that the two dissenters of yesterday, who now held key positions, would achieve what they had argued. Elazar, the new Chief of Staff, hadn't opposed them, and the Defense Minister was prepared to listen. But perhaps the dependence on the previous approach was so strong because the investment was so immense. At any rate, the Bar Lev concept was not changed – only weakened.

Indecisive Compromise

Sharon apparently remained uneasy. In his typical nibbling fashion, he began gradually to close strongholds. David Elazar agreed to thinning-out, but objected to closing all the strongholds. At the beginning of 1973, Sharon had in fact closed down 14 of the 30 frontline positions. He withdrew equipment from bunkers and sealed them. He suggested blocking communication trenches and removing barbed wire, but this was rejected; spotter teams used the "closed" strongholds in the daylight hours. Sharon wanted to close more but, when he left Southern Command in July 1973, there were still 16

143

manned strongholds, though the garrisons were small.

A compromise had been reached between Bar Lev's conception and the Tal-Sharon attitude; an unsuccessful one since it only related to the waterline. The defense system against Egyptian crossings remained an incongruous and undesirable mixture which would make its mark in the **Yom Kippur** War.

Theoretical Readiness

The IDF Supreme Command didn't believe that the Egyptians would succeed at a mass crossing of Suez, though repulsion of enemy incursions was frequently exercised. Each new unit reaching the line was put through the ropes. Junior commanders knew where their positions were, and what to do the moment the order was received. In case of full-scale war, the units were to hold fast pending arrival of the reserve armored divisions, which would immediately move in to attack, and cross into Egypt. The Bar Lev Line was initially intended not only for defensive purposes, but also as a jumping-off point to the west bank.

On October 6, 1973, the repulsion plan was disrupted and when one link in the plan snapped, all the others failed with it. Command did not know what was happening on most sectors. They hesitated, morally torn over the fate of the men in the strongholds. What was to be done first; repulsion of the Egyptians or rescue of the garrisons in virtually encircled strongholds.

In the final event, neither alternative succeeded properly. The Egyptians established sizeable bridgeheads in Sinai, surrounding most of the strongholds, which still served as good observation posts but only for their own narrow sectors. The bunkers gave good shelter, but not for long. The men who remained in the strongholds were compelled to rely on their own resources and their luck to extricate themselves from Egyptian encirclement.

144

Sleepy Tranquillity

The plan wasn't implemented because the alert order wasn't observed. Self-confidence led to a sleepy tranquillity. The IDF awaited a small battle, perhaps a new war of Attrition. The alert on the eve of the Day of Atonement, caused no forward movement of armor. The time the armored fist would take to go into action could be cut, but tanks waited at their peacetime stations. The General Staff transmitted the alert order to Southern Command, which relayed it to Armored Force HQ Sinai, but something went wrong **en route**. As a result, the IDF had lost the battle for the Suez Canal — five minutes before it began. In retrospect, not one of the IDF's concepts was put to use; not that of Bar Lev which should have been activated, nor that of Tal-Sharon. Whoever decided to keep the armor to the rear — missed the boat. The force that was, according to the Bar Lev plan, to take immediate containing action — didn't arrive in time. In the second stage, the IDF forces were compelled to fight, with no prior preparation, according to the Tal-Sharon concept, but without the rear line of infantry. As a result, the IDF lost the Suez Canal.

OCTOBER 9, 1973

Ministerial Earthquake

This is another very hard day for Moshe Dayan, who hasn't yet recovered from his fit of pessimism. He apparently sincerely believed that the IDF would easily repel the invader, and yesterday's lack of success in the south has strengthened his forebodings.

In the Supreme Command position, Dayan reverts to his remarks of the day before yesterday; the IDF must retreat to a second line on the hills. His hand drifts across the map, giving most of those present the feeling that he speaks of a line across the eastern third of Sinai Peninsula.

145

Nobody argues with the minister, nor do they order the forces to retreat. Dayan mentions that he intends to make the same remarks to the newspaper editors with whom he will shortly meet. He asks O.C. Air Force Benny Peled to join him for the meeting. Benny Peled's face wears a grim expression; he was told not long ago that his eldest son, a Phantom pilot, was shot down near the canal. He was seen parachuting into enemy territory. As Benny accompanies Dayan to the meeting, his son's comrades are trying to give air cover to him, and to a helicopter sent to rescue him and his navigator.

Dayan tells the surprised newspapermen: "Right now, we don't have the strength to throw the Egyptians back across Suez without almost-completely decimating our forces. If we try it, we will lose our army, and remain inside Israel without it. What we must do is deploy on other lines. And the same is true for southern Sinai. The Egyptians' road to Abu Rhodeis is open. I doubt whether our forces can close the gap. Somewhere between the canal and the mountain ridge, we must form a line that they won't be able to cross. They won't, if we deploy properly. All this is very significant. It's become clear to the whole world that we're no stronger than the Egyptians." He adds that at 21:00 hours, he will tell this to the nation in a television broadcast.

The editors are dumbfounded. Meanwhile, a secretary passes a note to Benny Peled: "The pilot and navigator who dropped in Sinai are fit and well. They are being flown back to their squadron."

Stop the Show

Within minutes, Golda Meir receives a report on Dayan's briefing session and his intention to broadcast to the nation. A newspaperman phones suggesting that she prevents the broadcast. Shortly after 20:00 hours, the Broadcasting Authority is informed that Dayan's appearance is cancelled.

In his place, the ex-Head of Intelligence Branch,

Maj.-General (Res.) Aharon Yariv, appears at a press conference. Without going into details, Yariv presents a balanced expose: "Let's not delude ourselves with rapid and elegant conquests. The situation is neither simple nor easy. The war is likely to go on, but let's not think in terms of danger to the population of Israel."

This is the first time that the Israeli public receives a blunt and frank evaluation and is given to understand that this is neither a continuation of the Six Day War, nor a blitzkrieg. Many begin to believe they were deceived and treated as immature till today. Yariv's frank remarks now grant him the status of a new leader.

Fall of an Idol

Dayan's status in the war leadership is entirely dissimilar to that of the Six Day War. In 1967, he came to a prepared army with ready plans which gained fresh impetus from his leadership. Within hours he then became the war leader, who led and enthused both the army and the nation.

Dayan of 1973 is not the same man. At critical moments he hesitates and avoids decision. He does not intervene in differences of opinions between commanders and when the difference is between him and a senior officer, he prefers for Golda to resolve it. This was even the case before the war, on the question of how many reserves to mobilize. Dayan only gives advice — emphasizing that it is "at ministerial level." He is not the same man who, one morning near the end of the Six Day War, on his own authority — and without first consulting the Prime Minister — ordered David Elazar to take the Golan Heights. When he visits the front, officers and men can again see that personal fear has no part of him. He reaches everywhere, with no consideration of danger, but is obviously satisfied to be a listener and onlooker, without commenting. His ever-present pessimism doesn't help the situation. Elazar and officers like Bar Lev and Benny Peled often have to balance the depressing and terrible effect of Dayan's presence.

Grandma Will Decide

Golda Meir almost unwillingly becomes the generalis-simo. It is strange to see a warrior of seven campaigns and brilliant past-Chief of Staff of the IDF bringing clearly operational subjects to a Jewish grandmother for decision. Golda doesn't shirk responsibility. Of itself, neither appointed nor elected, a "War Cabinet" arises alongside Golda; but not her famous "kitchen", which disbanded at the outbreak of war. Abba Eban is in the United States. Finance Minister Pinchas Sapir is also abroad to collect money. Agriculture Minister Haim Gvati is ill, while Justice Minister Shapira – Golda's friend and veteran adviser – is not at home in war consultations. Yigal Allon and Yisrael Galili remain by her side and, with Golda, form the regular War Cabinet.

Moshe Dayan oscillates between the Supreme Command, the war fronts, and the Cabinet Room. He reports to meetings where vital points are resolved but doesn't spend much time with the decision-makers. Dayan notice-ably prefers battlefield tours to conference rooms and command bunkers. It was the same in the 1956 Sinai Campaign, when he was Chief of Staff. Then he vanished for two days, but this time the IDF communications network is far more sophisticated and contact can be made anywhere within minutes.

Pressure Point

One of today's important decisions is to transfer the immediate pressure to the Syrian front. This is no easy decision. The IDF has become accustomed to successful switches of effort from front to front; a blow on one and a parry on others, and then a strike somewhere where the accent had been defensive. But in the past, first priority was usually given the Egyptian front, where the strongest Arab army stood. Then, and only then, were forces free to deal with other antagonists. The best example of this was the Six Day War. In the 1948 War of Independence, the

148

army behaved differently. At the stage when the Arab armies invaded, pressure was coming from all sides. As the first truce ended in the "Ten Days Battles," the pressure was transferred to the Arab Legion front because of its proximity to Israeli population centers and threat to vital objectives. In this war, the Syrian Army endangered the populated areas in the first stage. Yet when it's decided to transfer pressure to the Syrian front, the turning point has already come.

The Chief of Staff's suggestion isn't greeted with general accord but, after Dayan pitches in on Elazar's side and Yigal Allon gives enthusiastic support, the decision is clear. The debate actually began two days ago, with the question of where to send the tactical reserve — if at all. Deputy Chief of Staff Yisrael Tal suggested husbanding it for unexpected developments. Elazar decided to throw it on to the Syrian front. The force reached the Golan Heights at the most critical moment.

The failure of yesterday's counter-attack on the Egyptian front is undoubtedly a factor in the decision. Elazar presents additional reasons to Golda; it's not likely that the Arabs will ask for a cease-fire before they sustain heavy losses. Waging war without a clear-cut outcome will prolong it, and may well decimate the IDF. The most convenient place to unbalance the attacking forces is on the Syrian front.

Eyes on the East

The debate is not exclusively on military subjects. Eyes are also turned on Jordan and her king, Hussein. Traffic is crossing the Jordan bridges as usual, but no one doubts that Hussein must be seriously worried about his role in the war. The fact that he paid the heaviest price in the Six Days, which he joined only after assurances that Egypt was beating Israel, now deters him.

Three days ago, when the war began, a delegation of terrorist leaders came to Amman to meet Hussein's Prime Minister and demand permission for large groups to operate out of Jordanian territory. The Prime Minister told them that, contrary to the Six Day War, Jordan will not act this time – unless she is sure that the Syrians and Egyptians have won the first round; in other words, they have taken the Golan Heights and the Sinai Peninsula up to the Gidi and Mitle passes. Hussein tells his senior officers that Israel will quickly defeat Egypt and Syria, but it's clear that if this doesn't happen – their pressures on him will increase.

A third front will present terrible problems for Israel. And meanwhile, there is news of an Iraqi expeditionary force, numbering 16,000 men and 200 tanks, approaching Syria. Put all that together, and there is ample reason to give first priority to the Syrian front.

The feeling is of a race with time, but especially so on Golan. As far as the Egyptians are concerned, Israel behaves as though there is no hurry. In Washington, the Pentagon Spokesman tells military correspondents that the IDF seems to be behind its timetable and has lost more than 40 planes or about 10% of its air power.

Friend in Need III

President Nixon is well aware of Israel's losses. A special task force – composed of Kissinger, Defense Secretary Schlesinger, the Joint Chiefs and the Director of the CIA – receives current reports of Middle East events. Israel also reports regularly to the Americans, through the U.S. Military Attache in Tel Aviv, and the IDF Attache in Washington. Summaries are relayed daily to Nixon. Today, the President receives a telephone call from the Israeli Prime Minister. Golda clarifies the importance of rapid arms and equipment transfer. Nixon calms her, saying that Israel will receive the required arms, but the transportation question still remains to be solved.

The President already knows that the Soviet Union is pouring colossal quantities of armaments into Egypt and Syria. American intelligence agencies report that the greatest transportation operation in twenty years is going on at Black Sea ports, and airfields in Hungary and Yugoslavia. The first consignments primarily include anti-aircraft missiles — fired in their thousands by the Syrians and Egyptians — followed by ammunition for artillery and armor, but heavy tanks and aircraft are also in evidence. The quantities are so great that equipment has to be removed from the stores of regular Red Army units. In the second stage, a number of Warsaw Pact armies will also be asked to transfer arms and equipment from their depots. There is no time to remove Soviet insignia. Tanks painted in the green colors of the Red Army, are transferred to freighters. Identification markings of Russian units can clearly be seen on the boxes, together with the hammer and sickle. While trains transfer heavy equipment to the Black Sea ports, transport aircraft make their way to airfields in Hungary and Yugoslavia. One squadron of planes flies directly to Syria, passing — without prior permission — over Turkey. From Hungary, some heavy equipment is transferred overland to a Yugoslav port to be loaded on freighters for Alexandria and Latakia.

Waste Not

Syria is paying a very heavy price. The transfer of pressure to the Syrian front at first implies letting the Air Force loose. At 12:00 hours, Damascus gets the point. Before the sirens manage to warn against Israeli Phantoms, the planes are already in action. Bombs land on the Syrian Defense Ministry, and the Air Force Staff buildings. The nearby radio station is also hit, and its announcer's cries can be heard over radio sets. The luxurious quarter of Abu Ramana, location of many embassies, is struck by a stick of bombs. Other planes hit the city's power station and the large fuel reservoir near Homs. The strategic targets include the Lebanese radar station of el-Barik, halfway from Damascus to Beirut, which is transferring regular information to the Syrian Air Force. One Phantom is damaged over Damascus, and its two crewmen parachute down near the city. Flames burst from the tail of another, which

151

quickly turns towards the nearest Israeli airfield. The blaze in its tail burns the braking parachute and, in landing, the hook doesn't catch the cable on the runway. The plane rolls rapidly along on a punctured left wheel, and is only stopped by the crash net at the end of the airstrip.

Not all the planes manage to unload over Damascus. Moti Hod, in Northern Command HQ, overhears a radio conversation with a squadron commander who is returning with his load, and asks that his planes be directed at concentrations of Syrian armor in Hushniye area. Many tons of bombs drop over a small area where the Syrian tanks are clustered. The ground shakes from the explosions.

Regroup for Retreat

Today's major battle on the Golan Heights is in Hushniye district, where the only serious enemy force remains. Here the Syrians driven back from south and central Golan, have regrouped. The mistake of those officers who believed one armor corps enough to contain the Syrian Army, again becomes clear. It derives from faulty evaluation of the balance of forces. One of the two armored corps must now deal with a Syrian army concentrated in Hushniye and at the nearby military camp. IDF armored brigades, most composed of reservists, try to encircle the Syrian division, but do not succeed. Corps commanders Dan Laner and his deputy watch a long Syrian column escape through the gap between the IDF pincers. They do not allow a charge, for fear that Israeli forces will fire on each other.

To the north, where a division under the command of Syrian President Assad's brother made a heavy armor attack last night, the Syrians leave behind T62 tanks; the most modern and advanced tank of the Warsaw Pact armies. Here, the IDF plans a breakthrough and penetration into Syrian territory towards Damascus. In preparation, the area must be cleared of anti-aircraft missile batteries, so the aircraft can supply close support. The Air

Force concentrates its efforts into one of its heaviest sorties against the Syrian missile batteries. Ninety-five aircraft today attack the dense system. As in the Egyptian system, it is not the modern SA6s alone that decide efficacy. Russian advisers taught the Egyptians and Syrians that, apart from density of fire power, the important thing is to balance weaponry in such a way that they can cover all altitudes to endanger every aircraft. This is therefore no simple job for the Israeli pilots. They come in wave after wave. At the end of the day, heavy smoke billows over 15 missile batteries, but the operation has claimed five aircraft.

Aran III

Aran Zmora's unit loses 25 men in battle. Till today, 7th Brigade Reconnaissance hasn't fought a major action and this one is almost coincidental. Some men of Golani Brigade have been ambushed close to Bukata village. Their losses are heavy, and they radio for help. Eleven APCs from the reconnaissance unit are sent to their aid. Scores of wounded lie at the entrance to the village, with a single doctor tending them, assisted by a medical corpsman. The Golani unit indicates where the Syrians are concealed by hand signals.

Aran spots them immediately after the APC leaves the village. The Syrians are spread over a cultivated field, and many are dug-in. The armored personnel carriers charge, deploying over the field, and killing dozens of Syrians. A Syrian soldier straightens up and tries to hit an APC with a bazooka, but the driver is faster. He runs the Syrian down. The bazooka rocket grinds along the steel plate of the APC. A platoon commander in another APC is hit in the head and killed. The driver's legs are shot off by a bazooka shell. The assault goes on, and the Syrians begin to retreat but heavy artillery fire prevents a followthrough.

The reconnaissance unit now returns, via the village, to the main road. Golani wounded still lie at the entrance to the village. The doctor is having difficulty in handling the mass of wounded; they are loaded on APCs, which speed to a casualty receiving station. The sound of engines is drowned by the groans of the wounded and dying. As the vehicles race along the road, two RPG rockets are suddenly fired at them. The column goes on its way with the wounded, but two APCs — including the company commander's — leave the road to take care of the opposition.

While the Golani wounded are being unloaded at the casualty receiving station, the unit receives a cry for help; this time from their own men in the two APCs that stopped to deal with the bazookas. The company commander is dead, and the survivors are asking their comrades to rescue them.

The APCs race back without knowing exactly what happened to the company commander, and the two vehicles. As they descend from the road, they run into another Syrian ambush. Many score Syrian commandos are dug-in in a horseshoe between the terraces. On a higher terrace stands the company commander's APC, wreathed in heavy smoke. The second APC is motionless, lower down; it took a direct hit from a bazooka, and one of its occupants was thrown out.

The battle lasts a few moments. The problem is to get out of the ambush, and save the wounded. In Aran's APC, the platoon commander is killed by a bullet. Men jump from the vehicles, throw smoke grenades and fire at the Syrians. Others try to extricate the wounded, and are hit themselves. Wounded are loaded on an APC which reverses amid flames. As it reaches the road, fire engulfs it. Men jump out to remove the wounded seconds before the carrier explodes. Aran's APC pulls out of the ambush, still carrying their dead platoon commander. Later, armor will arrive to push back the Syrians.

Take the Helm

The possibility of appointing a new commander for the Egyptian front, over the head of the O.C. Southern

Command, Shmuel Gonen, arises today for the first time. Chief of Staff David Elazar, offers the job to his predecessor, Haim Bar Lev, who agrees, on condition that the Defense Minister and Prime Minister will approve. Meanwhile, he goes home to prepare. While at home, Moshe Dayan phones him having just heard of his agreement to take over as O.C. Egyptian front.

"Are you really prepared to go south and take command without any nonsense?" Dayan asks. Bar Lev answers in the affirmative and Dayan expresses satisfaction, adding: "I think there's no clear conception in the south. It's not clear to me what's happening there — and I don't know whether it's clear to anyone."

A few minutes later, Golda also phones to congratulate Bar Lev on his decision. She says she will announce it at tonight's Cabinet session.

Shmuel Gonen is far from content: "They didn't do it to Gavish in the Six Day War, when Dayan was prepared to take command in the south!" Finally it's decided that Bar Lev will go south as the Chief of Staff's personal representative. He will be the senior officer present, and as such will be able to exercise a veto. Gonen understands that he cannot reject this proposal.

At night, Dayan contacts Moti Hod at Northern Command HQ and asks whether he still has strength left for Southern Command. Moti agrees. Dayan believes that Bar Lev and Hod will strengthen the chain of command in the south.

Arik II

One reason for sending Bar Lev south is the conflict between Gonen and Sharon. Less than three months ago, Sharon was O.C. Southern Command. Naturally Arik feels like a "landlord" who has, one bright day, returned to his beloved old home to find it broken open with thieves running wild inside. His disappointment and shock is clearly noticeable; it finds expression in his comments to his corps staff from the moment he reaches Sinai. During his three years of command, he perfected plans to repel Egyptian canal crossings. He is a father of the theory that the Egyptians will be hard hit if they try to break in to Sinai. Now everything's upside down; the Egyptians crossed easily, the Southern Command plans are not put into effect and the invaders are not easily swept back.

When Arik Sharon left for civilian life, Maj.-General Gonen took his job. Now Gonen is General Officer Commanding while Sharon has Gonen's corps. Arik, a veteran general with extreme individualistic traits, finds himself under the command of a new and young general. As retired front commander, Sharon senses that a clash is unavoidable.

As Dayan and Elazar see it, Haim Bar Lev will save the situation. As Sharon's senior, they assume that his authority will be unquestioned. But the clashes only become sharper. Personality differences inevitably prescribe battlefield disputes between Bar Lev and Sharon. This isn't the first time that Sharon disagrees with Bar Lev; Sharon was an opponent of the Bar Lev Line and criticized Bar Lev's way of waging war on terrorists. When he was appointed O.C. Southern Command – by Bar Lev – Sharon criticized to newspaper editors the way in which the IDF was reacting to Egypt's War of Attrition.

No Monopoly on Dissent

A bitter and very similar argument rages on the other side. Egyptian War Minister Ahmad Ismail Ali is most cautious in his approach, and content with achievements to-date. He now prefers to consolidate. His opponent is Chief of Staff Saad a-Din Shazli, who argues that the first success must be exploited; Egyptian forces should break through to the Mitle and Gidi passes while the IDF is still suffering its first shocked surprise. Since Saturday night, when the crossing was well and easily performed, Shazli has been arguing for the immediate transfer of armor and a three-column thrust into Sinai and down the Gulf of Suez. This is the planned second stage of "Operation Granite

Two". Handsome and self confident 51-year-old Shazli is considered one of the best combat generals in the Egyptian Army. He, like Arik Sharon, began to attain prominence when he joined the paratroops in 1953. This was the year in which Sharon built Unit 101 and then took command of the paratroops. Shazli is very popular with field officers and men, and won publicity in commando actions as leader of a special force in the Yemen and in directing Egyptian raids across the canal during the War of Attrition. In the Six Day War, he commanded a special armored force in Quntilla District, where he evaded encirclement by Arik Sharon's corps.

Shazli's demand to break through to the Mitle and Gidi Passes is overruled, but he receives some compensation. The Third Army is ordered south towards Ras Sudar on the Gulf coast. Shazli thinks that this is too little and too late. He expresses himself frankly to Sadat, the General Staff and a number of newspapermen.

Meanwhile on the Israeli side, an IDF force commanded by Kalman Magen is succeeding in improving its position, and approaching the encircled coastline stronghold. The Egyptian thrust to Ras Sudar is faced by the IDF's standing army paratroop reserve, supported by a little armor. Most of the work is done by the Israel Air Force; planes pounce on the 50 Egyptian southbound tanks, which are helpless the moment they move out from under their missile umbrella. The Egyptians withdraw, but this is clearly not the end of the affair. Commando units operating in Ras Sudar and the Suez Gulf district are proof that the Egyptian Command wants this sector.

Make and Mend

The Egyptians are hastily consolidating on the canal and have already transferred 700 tanks into Sinai. The damaged bridges have been repaired and rebuilt. A steady stream of supplies crosses the canal; everything from benzedrine tablets through to generators and small water desalinators. Telephone cables, water and fuel pipes are laid under the canal. The supply system on the Israeli side is also stabilizing; long convoys loaded with equipment flow into Sinai to fill gaps and plug holes created by the hasty mobilization of hundreds of thousands of men.

The IDF's major problem is serviceable tanks; there are today about 450 on the front. Many are out of commission for purely technical reasons — not because of enemy-inflicted damage. Micky Bar Ilan, a reservist, is in charge of a technical team working on the battlefield itself. Micky's men chalk up a formidable record; they return 70% of the damaged tanks to service within four days.

Agam IV

In the afternoon, Arik Sharon's reconnaissance team goes on a scouting expedition which will have considerable influence on the IDF's canal crossing. Rafi Bar Lev and Yitzhak Agam's company spends hours observing the Egyptian dispositions north of the Great Bitter Lake. Further north, the Egyptian Second Army is dug-in. To the south, there is no significant movement in the direction where the Egyptian Third Army operates. This area is clearly the "seam" between the two armies. Yoav Brom, the unit commander, asks permission to penetrate deeper and check how far south the Second Army extends.

"We were surprised at the way Yoav directed the operation," Yitzhak Agam will later relate. "We moved towards the canal, keeping up a constant shooting match with the Egyptian positions to our north. This way we pinpointed their southernmost positions. We advanced over dunes to the Great Bitter Lake without any serious difficulty. It was by this route that we, a week later, guided the forces that established our bridgehead across the canal."

Yoav Brom's reconnaissance unit continues along the lake to its northern end, passing an IDF stronghold where the Israeli flag still flies. A tank is sent to the fortress' entrance but there is no sign of life. Yoav forbids entry for fear of mines or booby-traps. Darkness catches up with the scouts somewhere between the lifeless stronghold and the tip of the Great Bitter Lake. They organize for overnight camp at the only place where, on the fourth day of the war, an IDF force is on the water-line. "The Egyptians didn't attack, but it was a scary night," Yitzhak Agam will say. "We sat inside Egyptian lines. With starlight glasses, the only pair we had, we saw them moving around and could easily spot the silhouettes of their tanks."

Soldier's Farewell

At midnight, while Yoav's men are camped on the banks of the Bitter Lake, Maj.-General Albert Mendler completes the draft of his fourth "Battle Sheet". This will be his last "order of the day". He is soon to die, but neither he nor his men can know that this is his parting blessing: "I give my heartfelt thanks to the infantrymen in the strongholds for their very courageous combat and tribulations; I thank the tank companies who held fast, few against many, alone for countless hours in the inferno and who, by their fight, blocked the enemy, permitting IDF forces racing to their assistance to take position and attack; I thank the gunners who have worked wonderfully in difficult conditions. I am proud of all of you!"

INTERLUDE: THE IDF'S SURPRISES

Unappreciated Arsenal

The sudden Arab attack on Israel was not the IDF's only surprise. The Israeli forces experienced a series of tactical and technical surprises that should never have happened. There were only two weapons of which it can be said with certainty IDF Intelligence was not already aware: an unknown version of the Kelt air-to-ground missile that zeroes in on radar aerials, and a 180 millimeter gun with a range of 27 miles — the operative range of the American 175 millimeter is 20 miles. The gun also surprised American Intelligence.

There were other new, but known weapons, which were used for the first time, among them; ground-to-air SA-6 missiles, ground-to-ground Frog missiles, T62 tanks with its similarly new 115 millimeter gun and a Russian personnel carrier. The IDF's surprise was not the result of incomplete knowledge, but of inadequate thought. It simply didn't assess their effect on the battlefield, and hadn't planned for the eventuality of their use in action.

Deja Vue

The Egyptian crossing operation should have harbored no surprises. All the bridges, ferries, boats and pontoons had been seen before. Two years ago, the Russians sold — throughout Europe — an advertising film of a large-scale crossing operation on the Dnieper using all the equipment that the Egyptians received, and showing how it operated. The movie was purchased by the IDF and thousands of officers saw it.

Moreover many IDF men, including senior officers, actually witnessed Egyptian crossing exercises. The Egyptian Engineer Corps decided that the best model for a Suez Canal crossing is the Suez Canal. They staged a daylight crossing exercise near the island of Balah, where the canal splits in two, possibly with the intent of raising morale among their field forces. The exercise was filmed in detail so the critical stages could be studied. This movie was also shown to IDF personnel. The Army knew that the Egyptians intended to use powerful water cannons to breach the earthern embankment on the Israeli side; they practised with the pumps under the noses of men in the canalside strongholds. After one trial, Brigadier Raphael Eitan was asked for his opinion by the commander of a paratroop battalion that occupied the line. Without hesitation Eitan replied that the water cannon was good and would succeed.

The IDF knew, but made no preparations while the crossing operation was still in the planning stages. The army was relying on "smiting the crossing force hip and

160

thigh" in the second stage of mobile battle alongside the canal.

Tank Trap

The Egyptian and Syrian anti-tank weapons should not have been so surprising; the Sagger missile was an old acquaintance. The IDF even knew when the Russians initially refused to sell it to Egypt; they later gave in, and sold considerable quantities to both armies. Saggers had been fired at the IDF on both borders and Israeli tanks had even been hit by them on the northern sector of the Suez Canal. The missiles had been fired a few times on the Syrian border, but without hitting their targets. Intelligence even prepared a detailed brochure on the new missile.

At the beginning of the war, soldiers spoke of the RPG 7 Bazooka as though it was a new shoulder-fired missile, appearing for the first time. But the IDF had been acquainted with it previously. They knew it was a killer that could slice through any tank armor, and easily penetrate half-track walls. The terrorists often used it in the Jordan Rift Valley, and RPG 7s had fallen into IDF hands. Brigadier Emanuel Shaked, the Senior Paratroop Officer, who had been responsible for a Jordan Valley sector, long ago suggested that the IDF should manufacture its own RPG 7s.

Arterio-Sclerosis

The IDF knew — but was nevertheless surprised by the quantities in Arab hands, and especially available to the Egyptians. The lack of knowledge of such great quantities distributed among infantry units was an intelligence failure — but was it only that?

Technical knowledge of any weapon in enemy hands is insufficient. Translation of technical information into operational answers is more important. To command echelons, these weapons were known but the question is

161

rather whether men in the field were taught their significance. Knowing the effective range of a Sagger missile is not enough. The regular or reservist battalion or company commander has to be exercised in how to cope with it. The tank platoon commander has to learn how to avoid a Sagger.

The field command echelons and the rank and file of armored units were not exercised in countering missile attack. The only possible explanation for this lapse is hardened arteries following the IDF's great Six Day War victory. And for this, intelligence bears no responsibility; combat doctrine, unit structures and the types of weapons issued to the IDF are the exclusive domain of the operative echelon.

Garbled in Transmission

The Soviet doctrine of warfare, adopted by most Arab armies, has been studied and taught in the IDF for years. After the Six Day War, the IDF showed great interest in Soviet fording operations and bridgehead techniques. The details were known — but it again appears that their significance wasn't properly digested; there can be no other explanation for the lack of operational answers to the bridgeheads. Every Russian handbook on water crossings stated that a bridgehead is first seized by infantry, whose prime role is to parry counter-attack. It followed that the Egyptian transfer of infantry, equipped with thousands of bazookas and anti-tank missiles for their own defense, shouldn't have been at all surprising.

Had the Soviet doctrine been properly understood by all ranks, the IDF would have drawn different conclusions about the mortars organically attached to armored brigades, and artillery; the only weapons capable of dealing with masses of Egyptian infantry. The cut in artillery was the best evidence that the IDF was still preparing for mobile warfare on the Six Day War pattern. The artillery did make progress during the War of Attrition. However, its commanders had later to fight for every gun battalion.

Were it not for David Elazar, who supported the gunners, worse compromises would have been made. Respected and revered senior officers repeatedly contended that tank guns were all they needed. This war proved the poor success of tank guns against well-armed infantry.

Thrombosis

The IDF reacted to the Soviet water crossings and bridgehead doctrines exactly as the theory predicted. There were no prepared and brilliant counter-moves – only frontal attacks. The IDF banged its head against the wall; no vast movement over the expanses of Sinai – only clashes on a semi-static line. In place of the Egyptians being enticed into mobile warfare, at which the IDF excels, they were allowed to dictate confrontations between masses of fire-power where the IDF was weaker. The first stage created a situation in which one mass – the IDF – dwindled, while the other grew. It lasted a week and the IDF sustained heavy losses. Every brigade reaching the front repeated the mistakes of its predecessors. Each was in turn surprised by the anti-tank missiles, and paid a heavy price for its education. The IDF wasn't lacking in courage. Tank crews and mechanized infantry were outstanding in their bravery. Tanks charged missile-carrying Egyptian infantry and, suddenly, the simple charge – the race forward at any price – was no longer the answer to every situation. Luckily, the IDF could rely on the high standard of improvization common to its junior officers and NCOs. Commanders in the field quickly found tactical solutions for new situations, which should of course have been taught before the war.

Charges forward, no matter what the price, were not the sole prerogative of the Egyptian front. Golani Brigade's assault on Mount Hermon on the third day of the war, was frontal assault, in which unit prestige dictated the moves. It was not mountain clouds that defeated the Golani attack, but poor intelligence, and the fact that they did exactly what the enemy expected of them. Syrian prisoners, taken in the second Hermon attack, said they saw the Israeli soldiers advancing, and waited for them outside the captured Israeli position.

Bottom of the Barrel

The Supreme Command decisions of the second and third days – October 7 and 8 – were clearly dictated by lack of tactical reserve. The entire combatant strength was mobilized and the General Staff faced a constant danger of Jordan opening a third front. Were they to commit the armor reserve, or preserve it for unexpected developments? And if it was to be used, then on which front? Where the enemy was strongest, and where territorial achievement would change the political **status quo**? Or on the other front, closer to Israel's populated areas, where there was a greater chance of beating the enemy because of the initial balance of forces? The reserve was committed to the Syrian front.

Within 24 hours, it was clear that each front would have to manage with what it had; there could be no quick or large-scale reinforcements. There was virtually no hope of rapid unit transfer from one front to another, as had been done in previous wars. Officers who had thought that the new longer access lanes wouldn't hamper movements – were mistaken. Transfer of forces from Suez to Golan on roads choked with supply convoys, would take at least three days. Allocation of the tactical reserve to one front meant it remaining there for a considerable period of time.

He Who Doesn't Hesitate – May Be Lost

The Supreme Command adopted a more hesitant attitude to bold action on the Egyptian front; the borderline between "unsuccessful action" and "decisive failure" was very thin. The IDF was stronger than ever before, and was operating far from its old frontiers, but a local debacle might allow the Egyptian armor to race on towards the 1967 frontier.

Sharon's contention that concentration of forces for one effort would have allowed an immediate strike at the bridgehead, is justified by military logic. Some even argued that this would have been the best time to cross the canal and tackle the armored divisions which were isolated from infantry support. This would have disrupted the Egyptian lines and isolated the infantry divisions in Sinai.

However, there was another, more comprehensive logic; the proposal was a good one, but there were not enough tanks in Sinai and the bridging equipment wasn't ready. Approval of an operation based solely on the Egyptian bridges was not possible. If the plan failed, it wouldn't be a local failure -- but an immense defeat, endangering the entire southern front. In other conditions, the IDF might not have hesitated, however the surprise of **Yom Kippur** influenced the decision; the attack of Monday, October 8, had to be a scaled offensive. In other words; if Adan's corps succeeded, then − and only then − would Sharon's go into action. A canal crossing warranted special approval and was only permissible with small forces after success against the Egyptian bridgeheads. When the Chief of Staff made his decision, Lt.-General (Res.) Yitzhak Rabin who was present in the Southern Command War Room justified Elazar's approach.

Decisive Opportunities

Maj.-General Sharon is still convinced that the third day − October 8 − was the decisive one, and that the IDF lost an important opportunity. In any event, by nightfall on Monday, the IDF clearly didn't have sufficient force to cross and establish bridgeheads − however small. Bren Adan's men did reach the waterline, but lost dozens of tanks, withdrawing by the skin of their teeth.

On October 9, by command and government decision, the effort was transferred to the Syrian front. In practice, it only affected the Air Force. Yet it wasn't an easy decision to make. The choice wasn't between an offensive on the Syrian front and a new attempt to cross the canal.

165

Southern Command was only ready with a crossing plan on Thursday, October 11. The alternatives were a major offensive across the 1967 cease fire line on the Syrian front, or mere repulsion of the Syrians from Golan. The opponents of a northern offensive didn't suggest replacing it by an immediate crossing of the Suez Canal.

Gap in the Fence

Israel also had no immediate answer to the Egyptian sea blockade of the Bab el-Mandab Straits, through which her fuel came. The IDF had not completed a naval-air system capable of coping with this problem. While Egypt waged limited war against Israel, blockade of the Bab el-Mandab Straits could be prevented by the threat of total war, or reaction elsewhere; however this deterrent lost its meaning when the Egyptians risked total war. Egypt was prepared to block the straits precisely because she was well aware that the Israeli naval-air line-up in the Red Sea was incomplete.

Since this was the case, Sharm el-Sheikh was also of no use. Yet this should not lead to a conclusion that Sharm el-Sheikh is valueless as a guarantee of Israeli shipping in the Red Sea. A force in Eilat would certainly not safeguard Israeli shipping in Bab el-Mandab Straits, and doubtfully even at Sharm el-Sheikh. Yet the importance of territory lies not only in holding it, but also in the form in which it is used and prepared for eventualities.

OCTOBER 10, 1973

Pleasure Cruise III

The Navy's ships return to port after yet another night's operations. The ships can't win the war, but the sea is the only arena in which the IDF's success is total. The Navy is so far the only consistent bringer of glad tidings. In the Six Day War, it suffered many setbacks. This time, it was

166

prepared. The backbone of the fighting force is provided by 14 modern missile ships, of which the two largest were built in Israel. All are equipped with sea-to-sea Gabriel missiles. The tactic is to take war to the enemy. The Egyptian Navy has 24 missile ships, 12 submarines and 5 destroyers. The only way to prevent it approaching the Israeli coast is to do battle in Egyptian home ports.

This morning, the ships return from another mission in Syria. This time, the Navy joined the overall effort to strike at strategic targets – power stations and fuel installations at the ports of Latakia, Tartus and Baniass.

Blocked Pipeline

In parallel, the Israel Air Force strikes at airfield runways, to hamper the Russian transport planes that bring arms and ammunition. The I.A.F. checks which airfields can take the large Antonovs and blasts their landing strips. Some fields are far away in north Syria – at Haleb and Damir. One Russian plane is hit on the runway. Others turn back unable to land. Generally, the Israeli pilots carefully avoid Russian planes. The Syrians hasten to fill the bomb craters by stretching nets and casting asphalt. The giant Russian Antonov 22s are also bringing broken-down fighter planes, which Russian technicians assemble on the spot. Israel is fighting Arab enemies – and the massive logistic system of a Great Power. Russia's warehouses are only two hours flying time from Syria and the planes will soon be followed by sea freighters; dozens of which have already left Black Sea ports. The Syrians apparently realize that there is no limit to the available equipment. Their pilots, noticing that the runways from which they took off are decorated with bomb craters, make no attempt to save their aircraft. They circle till fuel runs out, and then parachute down, abandoning the planes.

Soviet involvement is growing day by day. Apart from the flow of arms and ammunition, the Russians are engaged in intensive espionage. On the Mediterranean,

Russian vessels listen in to Israeli ships and planes. During the war, the Soviet Union will launch five military satellites, and a Cosmos 603 which was orbiting before the war will be diverted to cross the battle area every day. The other spacecraft each spend six days in orbit, though they would normally return after twelve days. Thus, Soviet Intelligence receives a fairly current picture of events on the battlefield and the Kremlin reduces the possibility of being misled — as it was in the Six Day War — by inaccurate Arab information.

Friend in Need IV

The United States is also making herself more felt. Planes began to arrive last night to replace those lost in battle; Skyhawks, coming under their own power from American bases in Europe. Israeli Air Force insignia are painted on the planes before take-off, to enable them to go straight into battle upon arrival in Israel. Each warplane is now welcomed with open arms. Losses are great, and the end of the war is not in sight. Till today, the Air Force has lost 66 aircraft, and some pilots and navigators have been killed, or are listed as missing.

Washington is not at present interested in giving details of military assistance supplied to Israel. The decision on the airlift is still pending. Yet senior American officials tell Israeli representatives that it is most important for Israel to teach the Arabs a lesson. Defense Ministry representatives have submitted to the Pentagon a long list of weapons that Israel wants urgently, and it includes new types not yet in IDF hands. The Pentagon doesn't approve automatically, neither with regard to type nor quantity. The IDF urgently wants the new anti-tank Tow missile. Washington had refused in the past, though she agreed to sell to Iran and various European countries. Now, the Americans do approve the transaction, but there are not enough in the warehouses, or even with U.S. Army units. Apparently in peacetime, the United States is also incapable of keeping up with the great production demands of a modern war.

168

Even basic weapons, like the M16 carbine, do not come easy. In the past, the United States agreed to sell this new carbine to Jordan, but not to Israel.

Surplus Brass

The IDF doesn't lack retired veteran generals who want command roles. They almost arrive in groups at the Supreme Command post. Among them are officers with formidable reputations from past wars. Some get under foot, contribute nothing and even interfere. All want to be mobilized, and use the good offices of serving colleagues to remind the Chief of Staff of their existence. Lt.-General Elazar mobilizes three on his own initiative: Majors-General Rehavam Zeevi and Aharon Yariv assist him in special duties, while Maj.-General Yeshayahu Gavish – Six Day War O.C. Southern Front – is given command of Sharm el-Sheikh district. This sector was separated from Southern Command – which is fully occupied with the canal front, at the beginning of the war, in the belief that the Egyptian Army would make a special effort to isolate Sharm el-Sheikh.

Other reserve generals receive special assignments. The war is imposing an immense burden on senior officers; some have barely catnapped since it began. They need extra deputies and assistants. And there is another problem; the war came when the IDF was in the midst of a change-over in senior command. Many top positions are now held by officers who haven't yet acquired on-the-job experience. In Southern Command, the biggest in area and complexity, the Officer Commanding and his deputy were installed less than three months ago.

Takeover

Bar Lev sets off for the Egyptian front early this morning, after meeting Deputy-Chief of Staff Yisrael Tal to talk about bridging equipment. Tal notes where the various bridging tools are to be found in Sinai, and shows

169

Bar Lev a color movie on an IDF bridging exercise.

In the Southern Command War Room, Bar Lev tells Gonen: "I have no interest in hurting you. It doesn't bother me that Dado (Elazar), my ex-subordinate, is now my commander, and I hope it won't bother you that I am your commander." Bar Lev later tells Gonen's staff: "I am not the Officer Commanding. Those powers remain in Gonen's hands. I am the senior officer on the front, with full authority." Gonen listens with frozen features: "And so, I have my private Chief of Staff." In private, he tells Bar Lev: "I fear this will finish me after the war..."

While Bar Lev is on his way south, reserve general Shlomo Lahat, who was O.C. Sinai Armored Force during the War of Attrition, comes up from the peninsula. Since the outbreak of the war, Lahat has been with Sharon's corps. In the Supreme Command bunker, Lahat meets past chiefs of staff Yadin and Makleff, who have come to gather impressions. Yadin won't leave the place for many days. He hears from Lahat that morale is high in the south, and that the commanders cannot understand why no order has been given to cross the Suez Canal. Yadin remarks that there is no intimation of this in the Supreme Command, and suggests to Lahat that he repeat it to Moshe Dayan. Yisrael Tal joins the conversation, and asks: "How will the soldiers react if we decide not to attack?"

"There'll be mutiny," Lahat answers in his caustic style. Tal choses to ignore the sharp tone, and says: "I'm glad that you tell me this..."

A static battle is raging on the southern front. The daylight counter-attacks are no more than minor skirmishes with purely local achievements — and no battles take place at night. As darkness falls, both sides withdraw into night laagers to tend the day's wounds. The IDF never did this in the past. Something has changed.

Fulcrum

Gonen tells Bar Lev that today he senses the turning point for the first time. His feeling is based on the changing ratio in attrition of forces. The number of his tanks is continually growing, while the enemy is now losing more than the IDF. Till today, the ratio operated against the Israeli Army.

Arik Sharon isn't happy with the situation, and no stabilization in numbers of tanks can console him. When Bar Lev arrives at his HQ, Sharon explains that the situation is now a "war of attrition" in which the IDF's advantages in mobile battle and improvization are unexploited. Sharon's proposal is to attack the Third Army bridgehead as soon as possible with two armored brigades storming from north to south along the Great Bitter Lake. His plan is discussed with Southern Command staff, in the presence of Sharon himself and his brigade commanders, but rejected because the investment would be very great for small achievements. The memories of the failure of the second day and its tank bonfires are still fresh.

The attrition in tanks may have balanced out, but the losses in men continue at the same relentless rate. Static battles don't lessen the casualties. Marking time adds days under heavy artillery bombardment. The Egyptians preface every assault, however minor, with a heavy barrage, making use of courageous forward observation officers, who penetrate Israeli lines to direct the gun fire. IDF soldiers have learnt that sudden artillery fire often means a team of Egyptian observers hiding nearby; the search for artillery spotters starts while shells still fall.

Men of Steel

Losses among the tank crews are heavy. Junior commanders move up in rank as their officers are killed or wounded. There is no promotion, only added command responsibility. In one of Bren Adan's battalions, a young captain is appointed battalion commander on the battlefield. His flair is conspicuous, and he remains in this position.

Some tankmen haven't shut an eye since the war began. They fight from morning to night, with no knowledge

171

about nearby sectors. They know next to nothing of the war on Golan, and of the home front. After nightfall, some brigades use their communications sytems to broadcast items of news. There are plenty of rumors, including a story of a legendary brigade commander on the Golan Heights who is knocking at the gates of Damascus with his armor.

The battle flows so rapidly that many tank crews change their composition. Vehicles with wounded are evacuated to the rear, where an officer puts together new crews on the spot; a tank commander and gunner from another tank, a driver and wireless operator-loader from yet a third. Some men change vehicles three or more times. They're fighting with crewmen they never met before. In many cases, men are killed before their comrades, in the same crews, learn their names, and consequently, the list of men recorded as "unknown" or "missing" grows. In Adan's corps, one crew loses three commanders. First, the officer with whom they exercised and worked for years. When they bring his body to a collection station, a new commander – a reservist – climbs on the tank. Within an hour, he is also dead and they retrace their steps. The men at the collection station do not believe their own eyes when they see the tank come a third time with a body. This time the crew refuses to return to the tank. They are too shocked to fight. Adan gives instructions to leave them alone. He comes to chat with them a few hours later. It's a conversation more of facial expressions than words. Finally the crew returns to the tank – and to war.

This is the IDF's first war in which doctors have to treat numerous shock cases. Most of the combat fatigued men are the result of the initial blocking actions, when they lost contact with their units and fought surrounded by unknown faces. There are hundreds of them. Most only need a few hours sleep and a day to rest – and then return to battle. Some need psychiatric care, and others have forgotten their own names; they are transferred to base hospitals.

Ray of Light

Here and there, there is good news. The most important comes from the northern sector, where, after five days, Brigadier Kalman Magen's force breaks through to the isolated stronghold on the coast. This is the only one that will hold out to the very end, but another one in the south is still fighting though completely surrounded by the Egyptian Third Army. The coastline stronghold is encircled by hundreds of Egyptian commandos and Magen's armor cannot deploy properly since it must move along a narrow coastal strip. The tanks move into a commando ambush and paratroops must be called in to break the siege. The meeting with the stronghold garrison is one of the war's few happy moments. Soldiers embrace and kiss. The wounded are evacuated. However, this isn't the end for the garrison; the bombardments and ambushes on the coast road will continue.

Agam V

Yitzhak Agam and his comrades are having a better day. This morning, Yitzhak receives permission to enter the stronghold near last night's campsite. There is a condition; they are not to leave the APC for fear of mines and booby-traps. There are few signs of battle in the empty fortress; the mess hall is untouched, and the generator in the compound is in working order. The men in Agam's APC call out: "Are there any Israelis here? We've come to get you!" There's no sign of bodies.

The reconnaissance unit returns to IDF lines to re-equip. They receive hand grenades for the first time and their morale improves when they are also given machine guns. Up till now, Agam and his comrades have equipped themselves; every time they pass a damaged and abandoned Israeli tank or APC, they scoured it for machine guns and other combat equipment. Yitzhak was lucky. He found a telescope and is now the only platoon commander in his company to have one.

173

In the Net

The fate of some "missing" tank crews and garrisons becomes clear today. The Egyptian press publishes photographs of scores of Israelis, among them many who cannot be identified. It will later become clear that Egyptians in IDF uniforms were put in the ranks, before the photos were taken. A large group are shown on Egyptian TV, including soldiers from a stronghold that fell on the third day. The garrison were slowly pushed, in bitter and obstinate combat, into the central bunker without access to the ammunition stores. The supply of bullets dwindled hourly, and the bunker filled with heavy smoke. Finally, the men shouted that they were willing to surrender. When they capitulated only one of them was wounded. A little while later, there were five dead. They came out of the stronghold straight into a long burst of machinegun fire. The survivors were transferred amid blows and insults, to a military prison near Cairo, for interrogation punctuated by torture.

Meanwhile, the Southern Command newsletter — "Badarom" today writes: "A few dozen Egyptian prisoners, remnants of a commando unit, were brought at night to an IDF base in Sinai, and put into an improvised prisoner pen. They had to lie for the rest of the night on the ground, for lack of alternative housing. Each prisoner had been given one blanket, but a guard noticed that they were feeling the bitter cold. He took blankets from a nearby equipment store and passed from prisoner to prisoner, covering each with an additional blanket."

Return to Quneitra

On the Syrian front, this is nineteen year-old Second Lieutenant Yisrael Goldstein's big day. Yisrael belongs to an anti-aircraft unit. He was commissioned a year ago, and now commands batteries of 20 millimeter double-barrelled guns. He can cope with MiG aircraft, but is helpless against the Syrian artillery. Observer officers apparently spotted

174

his position at an early stage, and he has been under heavy bombardment ever since. Two guns have been hit, and a gunner killed. His men spend most of their time in a nearby bunker. Each time they receive warning of an approaching Syrian plane, Yisrael bursts out alone, to take his seat on the one remaining gun. When the planes leave, he loads fresh shells and returns to the bunker to wait for the next round. In this personal duel, Yisrael downs two MiGs.

Today, the last of the frontline positions are relieved after days in the Syrian rear. Hezi's paratroops retake Quneitra. The work is easy, and the men ask: "Where's the war they promised us?" The IDF has returned to the 1967 cease-fire line; where it was on the morning of the Day of Atonement — but the area isn't yet secure. Individual enemy soldiers and commando teams are still at large. The roads are periodically awash in shells, and katyusha rockets bark in bursts. On the Hushniye sector, the Syrians have left many tanks behind, mostly intact.

The roads to Golan are packed with convoys of ammunition and combat equipment. Tomorrow, the IDF will open an offensive in the direction of Damascus. The General Staff has decided to allow only one day for regrouping. Northern Command is ordered to complete its breakthrough plan within the day. An Iraqi division is known to be moving towards the front and has to be met. In the Six Day War, the Air Force located the Iraqis on their way to the front, but this time they move mostly by night.

Breathing Space

This is the first time that officers and men on the Syrian front have an opportunity to take personal stock. In the Golan HQ, Yissachar, a veteran reserve officer, says: "This is my fourth and worst war. Believe me, I'm fed up with it."

In the 1948 War of Independence, Yissachar commanded a Palmach company. In the Six Day War, he led an

175

armored brigade. His son is also serving as an officer in this war. In another week, Yissachar will be severely wounded on Hermon.

OCTOBER 11, 1973

Tally Ho

The IDF offensive on the Syrian front is opening with the objective of crossing the 1967 cease-fire lines, deep into Syrian territory. Raful Eitan and Dan Laner's army corps will break through, while Elad Peled's corps will hold fast on the line. Chief of Staff Elazar goes to Eitan's headquarters to hear details of the plan. This is David Elazar's first opportunity since the outbreak of war to meet brigade commanders in the field. Till today, he only managed to visit the command war rooms. This meeting takes place on the front line, north of Nafah. The officers cluster in Raful's armored personnel carrier. They are bleary-eyed and all sport a few days growth of beard. Ostensibly they have completed their job of pushing the Syrians back from Golan. Now, a new effort is demanded of them, and of their units that have already sustained hundreds of losses. It seems unfair, but there are no forces to relieve them. The IDF's manpower reservoirs are limited and Israel is fighting on two fronts. Elazar explains this as best he can.

Background Brief

At first he describes the position in Sinai. The Golan Heights officers don't know what is going on in the south. They caught occasional snatches of news from Israel Radio, but have no inkling of the exact situation: till now they were totally immersed in their war with the Syrians. The Chief of Staff explains that quick victory depends on the elimination of the Syrian Army as a fighting force. Only then will the IDF be free to transfer pressure to the

Egyptian front, and be less worried about the Jordanian frontier. Lt.-General Elazar adds: "It must be done! It is of supreme importance."

The preliminary stage has already begun. While Elazar is talking with Raful and the others, dozens of Air Force planes are operating on the sector where the IDF is to break through. The planes pass wave after wave, and the men in the APC periodically stop the discussion to let the heavy noise roll on. Suddenly, out of Syria comes a single plane, its tail on fire, limping back towards Israeli territory like a wounded animal struggling to return to its lair. Then a parachute can be seen in the sky. The abandoned plane spins down to crash nearby. While the parachute is still in the air, the Air Force radio operator in Raful's APC calls for a helicopter to rescue the pilot.

Happy Birthday

In another helicopter, Amos Gitai – who is 23 today – receives his life as a present. Amos, an architecture student, belongs to an air-rescue team. At the height of the attack, the Air Force is notified of a pilot who parachuted inside Syrian territory. A helicopter sent to get him returns empty-handed and out of fuel. While there is still hope of saving the pilot, no one will give up. A second helicopter is despatched, with a combat team, a doctor, a mechanic and two pilots. The lead pilot is experienced, and from a family with a flying traditiion. Amos Gitai is a member of the combat team.

The rescuers are again out of luck. On the way in, an anti-aircraft shell penetrates the floor, and explodes inside the helicopter. The craft rocks and shudders, but still flies. Machine gun bullets pass through it. The second pilot is killed in the explosion, the mechanic is badly injured and Amos is also wounded. The doctor treats the mechanic, though he was himself wounded in the explosion. Now, their objective is to save themselves. With difficulty they pull out of range of enemy fire and limp slowly back over Israeli territory. The hydraulic system is damaged and they make a crash landing. Instead of rescuing a pilot, they have brought back the dead body of another.

Twin Prongs

The decision for an offensive across the Syrian frontier doesn't evoke universal satisfaction. One senior General Staff officer believes that throwing the Syrian invaders out of Golan is sufficient; the pressure should now be transferred to the Egyptian front by the use of forces released from the north. However, the Chief of Staff first wants to take Syria out of the game. Dayan tells the Prime Minister that he hopes within 24 hours Syria won't have any force with which to continue the war. Damascus is also going to pay for Egyptian successes on the Suez Canal. The objective of the exercise is not conquest of territory, but the smashing of the Syrian Army, while bringing Damascus within range of Israeli artillery. If they face such a threat, the Syrians will prefer to stop the war.

The IDF moves in two prongs. Laner's corps forges along the main Quneitra-Damscus road in a frontal attack on the Syrian position at Khan Arnava. In parallel, Raful's forces plunge into the mountainous terrain on the northern sector of Golan. This is the Syrian weak link and the vanguard will swing around their flank, using the lower Hermon slopes to secure the Israeli left. It is also the shortest route to Damascus.

Raful's thrust is led by tanks that plow through minefields. In parallel, Golani Brigade invests two Syrian positions, followed up by tanks of the same armored brigade that held the Syrian offensive at Quneitra.

Tough Nut

Dan Laner's corps has to break through a dense disposition, erected around the village of Khan Arnava after the 1967 war. An extensive fortification straddles the main road at the entrance to the village, preventing the advance. While part of the armor tries to break through, other tanks supply heavy covering fire. The Syrian force is primarily based on anti-tank weapons. A number of tanks sit hull down in deep emplacements to serve as anti-tank guns, supported by very effective missile and recoilless rifle fire. Only three tanks of the spearhead remain intact by evening. The follow up column also loses 20 tanks in crossing the breach.

Hezi's paratroops mop up on both sides of the crack. The bombardment is heavy, and the battle bitter. "You asked where the war was," Hezi reminds his men over the radio. Yesterday's battle in Quneitra was incomparably easier. Bazooka rockets are fired from the houses of Khan Arnava at the tanks and half-tracks. A rocket hits an APC loaded with 100 kilograms of explosives. The explosion is immense, and a column of fire reaches skyward. Of the 13 paratroops and demolitions men in the carrier, not one survives. Teams of Syrian bazooka operators remain around the breakthrough point; they cannot stand for long, yet they continue to strike at the tank columns with exemplary courage. After nightfall, they exploit the cover of darkness to approach the tank laagers and fire their bazookas at point-blank range.

Aran IV

So far, some 500 Israelis have fallen in the battles for Golan. Many bodies still lie in the armored vehicles. The bodies of the reconnaissance men still await evacuation near Bukata. Aran Zmora and his comrades hear that their fallen friends have not been collected, and decide to carry out the task themselves. They load their 10 dead comrades on a command car, and drive to a casualty clearing station, but attention is only being paid to the living – the wounded. They don't want to abandon their friends' bodies, so they move on to the collection center for dead from this front. Aran and his comrades unload the bodies, one by one, and drive back in silence to the Golan Heights – to the front.

179

By evening, Raful's column is within 25 miles of Damascus. Defense Minister Dayan, who is on Golan, tells newsmen: "The distance to Damascus is the same as from Damascus to the Israeli border." A red light turns on in the Kremlin tonight. Israel is likely to threaten the Syrian capital. As opposed to the Six Day War, Israel is not now employing the principle of "fog of battle". The IDF has only just crossed the border, and is already talking of Damascus. Moshe Dayan, the man who in 1967 knew how to exploit the confusion of battle, no longer adheres to his own principle.

Dayan himself is showing signs of recovery from his depression. News that the United States in principle approves Israel's requests for equipment, and the fundamental change in the situation on the Syrian front are apparently the main factors in the Defense Minister's new frame of mind.

The breakthrough and advance on Damascus effect a change in style of Syrian communiques. When the first signs of failure can be seen, Damascus returns to its Six Day War type stories about American participation on Israel's side, contending that U.S. Air Force planes are attacking objectives in Syria, and that one has been brought down near Damascus. This isn't the only news bothering Washington; an item from Amman is more troublesome. King Hussein summons the United States Ambassador in Amman to announce that he cannot stand aside any longer. Till now, he has avoided involvement, but has found a formula that will perhaps save his country from IAF aircraft, and prevent total war. Rather than open fire on his frontier with Israel, he now sends the 40th Jordan Armored Brigade to the aid of Syria. This brigade, equipped with American Patton tanks, has already clashed with the IDF in the Six Day War, and its divisional standard, captured in Samaria, is a war trophy in the house of Dan Laner's deputy.

On the Egyptian front, there is an additional improvement in Yitzhak Agam's equipment. He and his comrades
now receive heavy machine guns. They feel better but still
lack binoculars, making life most difficult. After five days
of battle, logistics are beginning to look as they should.
The flow of fuel and food is satisfactory. The clothing
situation is also much improved. Personal small arms and
other combat equipment are still lacking. The supply of
ammunition is better, though a great quantity is held up
on the roads. Hours pass while the many traffic jams are
untangled. Many vehicles take the wrong route. As
opposed to Golan, trucks cannot leave the roads, from fear
of sinking in the sands.

Delayed Initiative

The IDF tonight stages the first raid behind Egyptian
lines, and the first night operation of this war. The men
involved are from airborne **Nahal**. They land from helicopters on Mount Ataka to the south of the canal, taking two
field guns with them. For 25 minutes, they bombard an
Egyptian HQ and ammunition stores on the plain below.
Not a large-scale operation — but it does contribute to
morale both of the paratroopers and the command. It is
the first of their operational plans to be approved.

On the Suez Canal, the Egyptian advance has virtually
been stopped. IDF forces are stationed along the length of
Artillery Road. The Egyptian Army hasn't yet completed
establishment of its bridgehead; according to plan, they
should by now have taken Artillery Road and the nearby
hills. Not one road junction is in Egyptian hands, and they
have crossed Artillery Road only at two places.

The fear is that the Egyptians will now make do with
their achievements to-date and forego the second stage of
their operation — breakthrough to the Mitle and Gidi
passes. They might continue the war, without agreeing to
cease-fire, and with five divisions in Sinai. Southern

Command is not prepared to make repeated frontal attacks on the bridgeheads, so something must be found to throw the Egyptian forces off balance. The only option is to cross the canal into the Egyptian rear.

Wet Feet

A canal crossing is no sudden brainwave of some officer during this war. The IDF has exercised it from General Staff level down to corps headquarters and units. Southern Command has detailed files, and has even held an exercise within its own area, during Sharon's tour of duty in Sinai.

The planning alternatives are many and varied, including a possible flanking operation in the Gulf of Suez – like the armored raid of September 1969 – or in the north. Now that preference is to be given to operations at the heart of the front, additional possibilities are also being discussed. Lacking tactical reserves, the IDF must concentrate on one major effort, and a single bridgehead. The decision, for various reasons, is in favour of a crossing on the central sector near the Bitter Lake. Wherever it takes place, the crossing must involve frontal breakthrough. The Bitter Lake sector was discovered, a week ago, to be the "seam" between the two Egyptian armies. The crossing point can be approached in such a way that the Great Bitter Lake will be on the Israeli flank. Terrain on the other bank also influences selection of the site. While in Qantara District, there are many sweet water canals and villages – by the Great Bitter Lake, there is only one canal on the other side of Suez. Beyond it a spacious plain extends westwards and southwards, providing room for the armor to develop impetus. This choice happens to coincide with an old Southern Command plan.

All that remains is to convince the Chief of Staff, the Defense Minister and the War Cabinet. Bar Lev plans, with Elazar, to come to the General Staff in Tel Aviv to present the crossing plan tomorrow morning.

INTERLUDE: NIGHT'S SLUMBER

Operational Cloak

"Night belongs to the IDF," so they said. Night operations have been an IDF trademark ever since the **Hagana** and the underground organizations that preceded the establishment of Israel. The IDF reached its zenith in night actions in the large-scale retaliation actions before the Sinai Campaign of 1956. The armor also developed techniques for the use of large units under cover of darkness, and the Air Force tried to keep up with the ground forces.

Most of the Six Day War was fought in daylight, but there were important night actions. One example was the breakthrough by Ariel Sharon's corps, which seized Um Katef on the Egyptian front; a brilliant set piece for infantry, armor, airborne infantry, engineers and artillery.

Night was first exploited as a means of bridging the quantitative gaps and reducing the effect of superior Arab fire power. The IDF persisted with night combat, though it gained strength, and it was conceivable that this development would continue. The sea-borne raid on terrorist camps near Tripoli in Lebanon, and the penetration of Beirut to strike at terrorist leaders and their headquarters, created an impression that this was indeed the case.

One Shift War

In the Day of Judgment War, the IDF strayed from its hallowed tradition. Major units were almost inactive at night and suggestions for large-scale night operations were usually turned down. The only units in action night after night, achieving operational surprise every time, were the ships of the Navy and their possession of modern weapon systems did not cause any feeling of over-confidence.

The Day of Atonement dawned on a confident army that believed it could solve all its problems, with its well-known enemy, by a direct frontal action in daylight, without need for the unconventional. Yet from the beginning to the end of the war, the Supreme Command had no alternative but to react to enemy moves. Throughout, the IDF never operated by the "indirect approach", which had been so successful in the past. The beautiful and brilliant plans remained in filing cabinets, even when the IDF took the initiative in a general offensive on the Syrian front, and in the Suez Canal crossing.

Silent Night

As darkness fell, the armored units were openly anxious to enter night laagers. The code sentence requesting permission to withdraw to night positions became one of the most used on frontline radios. The IDF Spokesman's morning communiques used a variety of phrases for this new situation: "Our forces passed a quiet night..." or "quiet prevailed during the night..." Why did quiet prevail during the night, and why did this situation elicit such satisfaction? Judging by past experience the IDF could have been expected to exploit its advantages in night fighting. Time was limited, so why weren't more hours of darkness used for big operations? Simply, night was no longer exclusive IDF property. The Arabs were prepared and the best proof was their considerable night sight equipment — infra-red and SLS. Starlight scopes, each costing about $2000, were attached to Kalachnikov carbines. Bridges were built over Suez, commandos landed and operated, and considerable quantities of armor were transported, especially on the Syrian front, in the dark. The IDF tank crews were virtually blind in the face of Syrian tanks, and it was only their resource and courage that decided the battle.

The few night actions that did take place confirm that better use of units could be made in initiated attacks in the dark. Two operations on the Syrian front were good examples of this; the brilliant seizures of Syrian Hermon and of Tel Shams, after the armor pushed through its foothills in daylight.

Unexploited Talent

The paucity of raids in the enemy's rear, and especially in his own territory, seems strange. Since the War of Attrition, paratroops and reconnaissance units had staged raids that stunned the enemy, from Naga Hamdi in Upper Egypt to Beirut in Lebanon. The paratroops trained for years at striking deep within enemy territory, to pin down his forces and upset his balance. Why were they almost unused this time? The paratroops and scouts fought bravely, but alongside or in support of armor. They were used as elite infantry, but not as commandos and raiders. Apart from a raid near Mount Ataka in Egypt, and a penetration north of Damascus to blow a bridge and delay Iraqi convoys, there were no night missions. The raid in Syria was ample proof that the units still possessed the capability, though there seemed to be no desire to use them. Their talents and years of training were ignored.

The paratroops at first served as a General Staff reserve. They could easily have operated, though hesitancy, and the tendency to concentrate on the heart of the front, prevented it. Raids would not have decided the war, but would have contributed no less than the naval actions. War must be seen as one campaign of many and varied moves in and from different directions. Accumulated impact finally determines whether an enemy stands or falls. The Egyptians, for example, barely felt the war anywhere but on the front line, while they didn't hesitate to blockade Bab el-Mandab or fire a Kelt missile at Tel Aviv.

Poor Relative

The Israeli infantry had been disregarded for years. All the other arms received relatively bigger slices of the cake. The Air Force got a superior weapon system, among the best in the world, the Phantom aircraft. The Navy after years of neglect, owned sophisticated systems — rapid missile boats, electronic equipment and highly efficient Gabriel missiles. On land the emphasis was —justifiably —

185

on armor; everything centered around the tank. The number was increased — to 2000 or more, according to professional publications — and most underwent significant improvement; diesel engines and 105 millimeter guns.

So far so good, but the war proved that focus on the tank alone had created an imbalance. The success of the tank in the primarily mobile Six Day War instilled the fallacial belief that it could solve everything, day and night, both in open and built-up areas. Yet, the tank often remained helpless, because its partners in the mechanized team weren't there, or were too weak. In the first stage, armor stood alone facing Egyptian infantry, and was too exposed without self-propelled artillery, mechanized infantry and combat engineers.

The gunners were best off of all, though they were far from satisfied. In the 1956 Sinai Campaign, their failure had been absolute. In the Six Day War, IDF artillery for the first time passed the test of rapid armored movement. But the gunners did not receive recognition until the primarily static War of Attrition, when the General Staff was compelled to procure additional guns quickly. The artillery were given long-range 175 millimeter guns, and sophisticated electronic systems to assist in laying precise fire. After that war, the gunners had to stuggle for their place, not only because of budgets.

The combat engineers were worse off. The best evidence of this was the IDF fording equipment which couldn't even be compared with the Egyptian; Russian fording equipment is at least one grade above its Western counterparts. The guiding Soviet principle is highly-mobile bridging equipment designed to delay movement of units as little as possible. Their PMP floating bridge, already existant in 1963, is still ten years ahead of parallel U.S. and European equipment. The Egyptians also purchased floating bridges from West Germany and England, and assault boats from France. The IDF did not even have the best of Western fording equipment. In the Six Day War, there were no bridges except for World War II surplus. In 1968, the IDF began to explore the aspects of fording,

186

with Defense Minister Moshe Dayan supplying the stimulus. The subject was developed, the long-range plans were many, but war still caught the IDF with inferior and inadequate equipment.

The last partners in the team, the infantrymen, were in the worst position; they gained no benefit at all from the growing IDF powers. Infantry brigades were transformed into mechanized units, but became strictly second league, especially in the allocation of resources. Their half-tracks were from World War II — and the American APC 113 was only purchased in very small quantities. Some even contended that mechanized infantry were a degradation, because they were infantry who had forgotten how to fight on foot.

Unarmed Footsloggers

Other infantry — the paratroops,.Golani and reconnaissance units — were bottom of the list for allocation of combat tools and modern weapons. In the Six Day War, it was decided that the Israeli-made Belgian FN rifle was obsolete, and prone to blockages; a modern Israeli carbine had to be developed. Three years were wasted in a delay that was strange by any standard. Finally, the Galil rifle was chosen. On Independence Day 1973, paratroop units marched in the IDF parade with Galil rifles, but these were only first samples. So the IDF fought the Day of Judgement War with an obsolete rifle as its standard weapon and crack units looked like a partisan army, equipped with enemy arms taken as war booty. The Russian Kalachnikov carbine was the most desired object among Israeli infantrymen. But the Egyptians didn't rest on their laurels; the 1973 Kalachnikov was better than its Six Day War sister. It was lighter in weight — with plastic magazines — and mostly equipped with snipers' scopes and night sights. The Uzzi submachinegun and the FN could not compete.

Another item on Israeli soldiers' most coveted list was the Russian RPG 7 bazooka; an anti-tank weapon every

IDF man was happy to be equipped with, because their regular issue was obsolete. And the reason; the Armor Corps tacticians believed the tank would solve the problem of enemy tanks.

The Egyptian infantry were prepared for war, while — during October — Israel had to plead urgently for modern anti-tank weapons.

There was no comparison between the land and air mobility of Egyptian infantry, and their Israeli counterparts. The Egyptians were equipped with personal anti-aircraft missiles. The only aspect in which Israeli infantry had better equipment than the Arabs, was in communications. Nevertheless, the 1973 Russian communications equipment was not the crude and simple stuff possessed by the Arabs in 1967; not were the Egyptians satisfied with Russian communications equipment alone; their commandos used Japanese radio receivers.

OCTOBER 12, 1973

Last Stand

The completely encircled Pier Position, facing Port Ibrahim and Suez town, is the last but one stronghold left on the Bar Lev Line. It has fought since **Yom Kippur**, under the command of 21-year-old Lieutenant Shlomo Ardinest, assisted by a 27-year-old doctor, Lieutenant Nahum Verbin. There are 37 men in the bunkers, and many of them are wounded. Five of the garrison are dead. Lieutenant Shlomo's deep religious faith helps him stand up to the heavy pressure. Yesterday evening, HQ decided to make a last effort to rescue the garrison. The mission is now entrusted to a naval commando unit, commanded by a young lieutenant. The plan is to come in by boat, and evacuate the men by the same route. This is their last chance. A few moments after being assigned the mission, and studying maps, the commandos are on their way. The sea is tranquil, and the moon full; dangerous light for the commandos. After hours of slow progress, the men in the boats can see the pier in front of them — a dark block. Suddenly, the night silence is broken by radar-directed 130 millimeter guns. Explosions all around and high columns of water. Shrapnel strikes the boats, and they ship water. The commandos radio HQ to report that the Egyptians have discovered the boats; they are ordered to give up the mission and return to base.

Following this failure, there is serious talk of surrender. During the first two days, it would have been possible to evacuate the men, but thousands of soldiers of the Egyptian Third Army now stand between the IDF and the stronghold. Much command thought is being devoted to this problem. On the one hand, for 37 members of the garrison to fight till they fall would be pointless. On the other hand, nobody wants to order the men to surrender. Such an order would have a detrimental effect on IDF morale and educational values. Nevertheless, negotiation begins with the International Red Cross.

Agam VII

Today Yitzhak Agam and his comrades finally receive field glasses. This particularly delights the tank commanders who have found it difficult to sight their guns at ranges greater than a thousand yards. The glasses arrive at the end of a chase in which 25 Egyptian commandos are captured. The men have been repeatedly warned that the Egyptians are likely to drop commandos in the IDF rear, prior to a large-scale armored offensive. This morning, tracks of a large group are discovered between Tasa and the Gidi Pass. Agam's company is alerted to give chase. They pass wreckage of two Egyptian helicopters, with dead strewn alongside. These were the craft that landed the Egyptian commandos. Suddenly they see a strange sight: two tanks, with a number of crewmen clustered around and, not far away, 25 Egyptian commandos sitting on the ground, with two tankmen guarding them. It seems that the two tanks remained in the field overnight, after one lost a track. At dawn, while waiting for mechanics to arrive, a group of Egyptian commandos approached. The Egyptians didn't open fire — they gave themselves up.

The prisoners are now stripped for hidden hand grenades or revolvers. The ease with which the commandos gave themselves up is reassuring to Yitzhak Agam. When he and his friends arrived at the front, they were told that the Egyptians are fighting differently — not like 1967 or the War of Attrition. They shoot till hit, or until crushed under tank tracks. Now Agam concludes that the devil is not that terrible. He ponders whether there has indeed been a revolutionary change in the Egyptian soldier's willingness to fight to the bitter end. The men of his platoon can't all compare the Egyptian of 1973 with his brother of 1967; half of them have no previous combat experience whatsoever.

Parley

While Agam is chasing commandos, Bar Lev arrives at the General Staff, bringing with him general outlines of the crossing plan. Fording the canal needs approval both from the General Staff, and from the Defense Minister and the Cabinet, because of its danger and political implications.

Bar Lev first talks with the Chief of Staff who then asks him to present the plan to the Defense Minister. While they wait for Dayan, Elazar contacts the Prime Minister's Military Secretary — Yisrael Lior — to ask for a session of the War Cabinet to discuss the proposal for a Suez crossing.

Dayan's Military Secretary, Brigadier Yeshayahu Raviv, attends the meeting together with the Defense Minister. "What's the purpose?" Dayan wants to know, apparently referring to the direction the forces will take on the west bank.

Bar Lev for a moment infers that the Defense Minister is questioning the entire operation. He says: "It's the only move that can tip the scales of war. The only way we can

190

defeat the Egyptians. Without a crossing, there will be no cease-fire, for the Egyptians are under no pressure, not even political." Dayan retorts: "Leave the political question alone. You must discuss it in military terms, if you decide that it can be done."

Command Quandary

Dayan leaves without making his views clear. Bar Lev and Elazar are in a quandary. Elazar must decide whether to bring the proposal to the Prime Minister and War Cabinet, without knowing whether Dayan will oppose it. Meanwhile, the time of the Cabinet session has already been set.

Elazar again contacts the Defense Minister's Military Secretary: "Without the Defense Minister, I will not go to Golda. If the Minister opposes the plan, there's no point in talking about it. He must decide on his position."

A few minutes later, Raviv calls back to announce that Dayan will participate in the meeting with Golda.

Pros and Cons

Four ministers attend the Cabinet session; Prime Minister Meir, Defense Minister Dayan, Deputy Prime Minister Yigal Allon and Yisrael Galili. Most of the staff generals join Elazar and Bar Lev. Bar Lev presents the ratio of forces on the front, the main details of the operation and its chances of success. The Chief of Staff and the O.C. Air Force, Benny Peled, are his most enthusiastic supporters. Elazar wants a crossing as soon as possible, for he senses that the sands of time are running out . Washington hasn't yet decided on an airlift of military equipment for Israel. Israeli planes are shouldering the whole burden and the Quartermaster's Branch is receiving worrisome reports on the stock levels of certain types of ammunition.

There are contrary opinions. The reasons for delay are offered by a general who makes a fiery presentation based on military reasoning; fording a water barrier is the most difficult and risky kind of battle, and though the IDF has exercised crossings, the main burden must now fall on reserve units. He adds that an army usually crosses from a river or canal bank in its hands to the enemy bank, but in this case, both banks are in enemy hands.

In his opinion, the IDF's strength is in armor-armor battles — so better wait for the Egyptian Army to attack, and they must! He doesn't say what will be the alternative if they don't attack.

Postponement

The ministers ask for clarifications. Moshe Dayan now supports the crossing plan. Yigal Allon, on the other hand, says that he cannot take a stand on the question before going to the front and talking with commanders, adding: "Better let them attack first! Our turn will come and then — the decisive battle." In this situation, there is clearly no point in bringing the proposal to a full Government session. Without concensus in the War Cabinet, the Government can't reach a unanimous decision.

Meanwhile from Sinai there is news that the Egyptians have begun to transfer their heavy armor — the 4th and the 21st divisions, plus a mechanized division — across the bridges. Clearly they intend to renew the offensive. Within a day, 1200 Egyptian tanks will be concentrated in the narrow belt of bridgeheads and a relatively armor-free vacuum will remain west of Suez. The participants in the meeting now agree to defer the crossing until after the Egyptian offensive. The proposal will not be brought to the Government this evening.

Lost Army

Dan Laner's corps, operating on the central sector of Golan, finds itself surprised, not by the Syrians but by the Iraqis. Some days ago, it was known that the Iraqis had sent a mechanized division of some 200 tanks to the Syrian front. Arab newsmen announced their coming, but till this morning, Israel had no clear news on their exact location, route of advance and destination.

They appear on the flank of a brigade of Sherman tanks. The surprise is complete. For a day the Syrians have been in retreat towards Damascus and now, suddenly, a new force is coming from the east. The first thought is — it must be an Israeli force that has lost its way; better not open fire yet! Then, a report that the advancing column contains Centurion tanks, the standard equipment of Israeli armored brigades. Luckily, an officer notices that the advancing Centurions carry a different gun. Israeli Centurions are armed with a long-barreled 105 millimeter gun that has a highly visible flash eliminator. The older model Iraqi Centurions carry an 83.7 millimeter artillery piece.

By radio, HQ confirms that the approaching force may be the Iraqis. They come from the direction of Kfar Shams in two columns and seem unaware of nearby Israeli forces and unfamiliar with the terrain. The Iraqis apparently want to fill the gap on the line left by the retreating Syrians, but haven't been properly briefed. This is the luck of the Israeli force, for otherwise the encounter would end differently.

The Iraqis arrive while a large part of Laner's corps are refuelling and making repairs. Many tanks lack ammunition after the day's battles and haven't yet been re-equipped. News of the Iraqis arrives at Corps HQ while the staff are in conference. A young subaltern rushes in, shouting: "They're on us!" The surprised officers send the youngster back to a good vantage point to take a better look — perhaps things will seem different. He returns after a few minutes with the same news: "They're coming in masses!" Laner's deputy goes out again with him. The young officer is right. An enemy is approaching from the east.

Interrupted Nap

There is no alternative but to straighten the lines and choose good positions. The chaos is great. The tanks pull back quickly, but the order doesn't reach everybody. The surprise among Hezi's paratroopers is even greater. Hezi has just woken from a few minutes nap in his APC. He wouldn't permit himself the luxury if he didn't believe the day's batles done. He wakes to a babel of anxious calls over the radio. There's no vehicle to be seen anywhere around. It's strange. He contacts Corps HQ and is told of the order to move to a new line, beyond the main road. If he doesn't rush, the Israeli tanks will take him for an Iraqi.

The first battle with the Iraqis will last till noon tomorrow. After straightening the line and transferring non-combatant echelons to the rear, Laner's deputy, Moshe, orders two armored brigades into a deep swing around both flanks of the oncoming Iraqis. The first gunfire is exchanged at dawn, while the Iraqi Centurions are 200 yards from IDF Shermans. As the Israeli tanks come out from folds in the ground, it is the turn of the Iraqis to be surprised. The sniping continues for hours until 50 Iraqi tanks lie smoking on the field. The remainder retreat eastwards under cover of heavy artillery fire.

Further north, on Raful Eitan's sector, IDF units encounter another force — the Moroccan Expeditionary Force which till now has been held as a tactical reserve. As Raful's forces break through, the Moroccans retreat in panic-stricken surprise. The rear guard is under Israeli tank fire, and they leave 30 intact tanks and other equipment behind them.

Sacrificial Lamb

Rafiq Helwai, commander of the 68th Syrian Brigade in the 7th Division, has been ordered to transfer command over the remnants of his brigade, and report to the General Staff in Damascus this morning. Helwai was entrusted with the defence of the Quneitra-Damascus road at a point close to the frontier. His brigade stood for hours in the face of Laner's forces. When the front line crumbled, he ordered a retreat in the hope of saving his men and regrouping. In

Damascus, he finds that the summons is to stand trial for ordering retreat without prior approval. He now bears the brunt of anger at the IDF success. Helwai, the sacrificial lamb, is given a quick hearing and sentenced to death. His execution is immediate. Rafiq Helwai is a Druze, and the whole Syrian relationship with the Druze community is one of mixed feelings. It is common knowledge that Israeli Druze serve in the IDF and are now on the Lebanese frontier. The Syrians are venting their anger on the Golan Heights Druze villages, which have been pounded by aircraft and gunfire since the beginning of the war.

Syrian amazement at the disintegration of the front line and the IDF advance on Damascus is immense. The General Staff orders units in the field not to retreat, but to continue fighting despite the IDF thrust. They hope to gain a respite in which to erect a new defense line south of Damascus. The Syrian Engineer Corps is working feverishly on fortifications and tank barriers, making use of the Avag River tributaries. The Syrian Air Force is now thrown into battle, and the Israeli pilots tear it apart; 29 Syrian planes are downed in battle today. At this rate, the Syrian Air Force will be decimated within a few days. Even if they receive additional planes by the Russian airlift, there will be no pilots to fly them; 30% of pilots whose planes have been shot down, died. North Korean pilots, in Syria and Egypt, have apparently been ordered not to seek aerial combat. The Israeli pilots are eager to fight them, but the Koreans evade clashes.

Cook's Tour

An attempt is being made tonight to do what wasn't done previously – hamper the Iraqi approach to the front line. The chosen objective is a big bridge 60 miles north-east of Damascus, and the task force is a regular paratroop brigade reconnaissance unit. A helicopter flies them, under cover of darkness and at low altitude, straight into Syrian territory. The biggest problem is accurate navigation in total darkness. At first, the big undefended

195

bridge is bombed. The Syrians don't seem to be prepared against deep raids. Their eyes are on the coastline, where two brigades are pinned down. The bridge is demolished, and then the reconnaissance unit lays an ambush around its wreckage. Military vehicles soon begin to cluster close to the destroyed spans; an Iraqi Army convoy mostly of tank transporters. The paratroopers open fire hitting most of the Iraqi vehicles. This will be the only raid in the Syrian rear.

OCTOBER 13, 1973

Mother Russia

The Kremlin now bares its fangs in its first threat of direct intervention. Yesterday, the Russians began to grasp that the Syrian front was collapsing, and that far from taking the Golan Heights, the Syrians now faced a threat to Damascus, the nest of Arab nationalism. The Soviet communications media gave voice to the Kremlin's fury: "The Soviet Union will not be able to remain indifferent, in the light of the criminal acts of the Israeli Army."

Russian Ambassador Dobrynin now relays the warning to American Secretary of State Kissinger. Dobrynin tells the Secretary of State that the Red Army has alerted two airborne divisions. Dobrynin doesn't tell Henry Kissinger that part of the HQ staff of a division is already housed in a wing of the Syrian General Staff in Damascus. This division is permanently stationed in Tula in the Soviet Union, but is now en route to a military airfield near Belgrade, where it will embark on planes destined for Syria.

Dr. Kissinger replies that the United States wouldn't want the Soviet Union to do anything irresponsible in the Middle East. A short while later, Moscow's announcement and Washington's retort are brought to Israel's notice. In parallel, additional units of the U.S. Atlantic Fleet are ordered to join the Sixth Fleet in the Mediterranean.

The Kremlin isn't satisfied yet. Last night, a Russian freighter was sunk in Tartus Port, during a battle between Israeli missile craft and Syrian warships. Nearby Latakia is the main gateway for Russian military supplies reaching Syria. Russian missile boats converge on Latakia while their comrades install SA6 missile batteries on the quaysides. Israel learns of the Russian intervention in Latakia; the Navy is ordered to avoid Latakia and Tartus, because Israel has no desire to give the Soviet Union justification for direct involvement. From now on, the Israeli Navy will only stage two more actions on the Syrian coastline — at Banias Port and a coastal bombardment of a bridge.

Join the Club

The Kremlin also prods other Arab countries into fighting. The Soviet Union asks King Hussein and President Bourguiba to support Egypt and Syria, and sends part of the military shipments from Rijeka in Yugoslavia to the Algerians who have expressed willingness to give an armored brigade to Egypt. Even without this prod there are inter-Arab armies on the Egyptian and Syrian fronts.

The Jordanian armored brigade, with its 80 Patton tanks, today takes position 10 miles from IDF units. Saudian armored vehicles, of French manufacture, are moving across Jordan towards Syria, and Libya is loading an armored brigade onto ships for Egypt. The Moroccans are sending an additional unit, this time to Egypt. Kuwait has decided to dispatch a small armored brigade to the Egyptian front. The Kremlin believes that Arab mass must eventually make its mark on the battlefield.

Friend in Need V

Washington lags a few days behind the Russians. The White House only today decides on an American airlift for Israel. Maj.-General Casey, Director of Logistic Operations in the Pentagon, will be responsible for it. The name of the operation: "Nickel Grass". The U.S. Air Transport Command is ordered to send Galaxy C5 and C141 aircraft to military bases, where equipment will be urgently loaded for Israel. The Pentagon is making preparations to transfer war planes. The commanding officer of a South Carolina air force base is instructed to prepare 18 Phantoms for a long flight. The officer is told that U.S. Air Force identification insignia must be removed before take off. The planes will be refuelled either in flight over the Atlantic, or on U.S. fleet carriers. In parallel, Pace Air Base in New Hampshire is ordered to dispatch three KC135 tankers to three points over the ocean.

Paper Pact

The Pentagon would prefer to refuel the Phantoms, and transport planes, in Europe, but problems have arisen with America's NATO partners. Europe's fear of an Arab oil embargo is stronger than community of interest. Spain and Britain are the first to inform Washington of their refusal to refuel American planes en route to Israel. They are followed by a Greek announcement of closed air routes to the Middle East. One after the other, NATO members refuse even indirectly to assist the United States. Refuelling facilities at NATO military airfields are all closed; the only exception is Portugal. One other country offers encouragement; South Africa announces the grant of economic assistance to Israel in her battle against the Arab states and Communist encroachment. It is a lonely voice. For Britain, a ban on refuelling of American planes is not enough. She also declares an embargo on arms shipments to the Middle East; a one-sided embargo, since her transaction with Kuwait continues. Britain also delays shipments of drugs contributed by British Jews for Israeli wounded.

Strangers in the Air

The Great Power involvement is more and more evident. A warning siren sounds throughout Israel at noon. At a speed of more than mach 3, the unidentified plane passes over Syria, Israel and Sinai, on to Cairo and the Aswan Dam. Israeli aircraft scramble to meet it, but its speed and altitude allow no approach. Egyptian planes also try in vain. A few hours later, it will become clear that this is an American SR 71 espionage plane.

The Russian airlift is also gaining ground. Yesterday and the day before, the Syrians were suffering from shortage of ground-to-air missiles, making life much easier for the Air Force during the breakthrough operation. The Syrian batteries are again firing dozens of missiles today. Six Israeli aircraft fall, all hit by missiles. The Israeli pilots take revenge on the Syrians in aerial combat. Arab lack of coordination finds expression in the air, as elsewhere. The Iraqis have put planes up to support their ground forces. A quartet of Iraqi Sukhois by mistake attacks Syrian positions, and are downed by four Syrian aircraft. Israel completes the job by claiming two of the Syrian craft.

Political Implications

Damascus suburbs have been within Israeli artillery range since last night. The IDF wouldn't win the war by such a bombardment but the fact is of potential psychological and political significance. Israel could also cause real damage to Damascus by intensive bombing, if she wanted — but both possibilities are unexploited. The Government has already rejected proposals for heavy bombing of strategic targets in and around Damascus, except for one raid on strictly military targets. Now the ministers won't agree to artillery bombardment — not only because of the Russian threat, though it is a factor. The new orders only permit fire on military targets outside Damascus, including Maza airfield and army camps to the south of the city.

The IDF isn't going to continue its advance on Damascus for reasons both of physical ability and politics. The army could seize additional territory and destroy more Syrian units but deep penetration into Syria implies sinking in "Napoleonic snow". The main military objective now is to improve the new front lines.

There is another possibility — a move to the south-east, in the direction of Mount Druze; an old plan in the minds of some Israeli politicians. After the Six Day War, Deputy Prime Minister Yigal Allon contended that Israel made a mistake by not reaching Mount Druze and assisting in the establishment of an independent Druze state on the Golan Heights — to serve as an additional buffer between Syria and Israel, and Syria and Jordan. The suggestion now surfaces again, but Moshe Dayan vigorously opposes it as an unnecessary burden on the IDF; anyway he isn't at all certain that the Druze are really interested.

Agam VIII

The anticipated Egyptian armored offensive doesn't materialize. Apparently they haven't completed transfer of the armored division from the west bank. Egyptian action is still limited to heavy bombardment and local armor battles; meanwhile, for the IDF, it's an additional day in which to regroup. Today, one week after the outbreak of war, Yitzhak Agam's unit is finally completely equipped. Day by day, more accessories and ammunition have been added, some of it by the unit's own salvage operations in IDF armored vehicles hit in battle. The final item is welding of machine gun bipods. Till now, the guns have been fired without firm attachment; they were simply laid on the sides of an APC. As the unit returns from a patrol on the Egyptian Third Army Front, a team of reservist welders arrives, and works quickly under bombardment.

Nuclear Age

The Air Force makes another heavy bombing raid on Port Said District. The dropping of thousands of bombs on this ostensibly marginal sector is no coincidence. There are fears that the Egyptians intend to position Scud missiles here to fire at Tel Aviv from the closest place within their

200

reach. The operative range of Scud missiles is almost 190 miles. The Russians transferred Scuds to Egypt on the eve of war and are now manning batteries themselves. This is a more advanced missile than the Frog — and has the capacity to carry atomic warheads.

In Southern Command War Room, the defense plans against the Egyptian armored offensive are being re-examined; where will the Egyptians attack? On what sector will they concentrate their major effort? The Israeli commanders are trying to put themselves in Egyptian shoes. There are weak points in the Israeli line, and one is the "seam" between Arik Sharon and Albert Mendler. Egyptian Intelligence must have discovered it during a week of battle.

Their Decision

Everyone expects a large armored battle, but the atmosphere is oppressive and atypical of an army waiting for action; the reason — the fate of the Pier Position has been sealed. Red Cross representatives have already made contact with the Egyptians who are prepared to accept the stronghold's capitulation. A few days ago, the Israeli Command refused to contemplate the possibility, but as the situation of the wounded deteriorated, the garrison asked for the Red Cross to arrange surrender. This morning, though arrangements are already made, there are second thoughts in the General Staff and Southern Front Command. Moshe Dayan says, in Supreme Command War Room: "You don't tell IDF soldiers to surrender. They must decide alone." Radio contact with the stronghold is maintained directly by southern front HQ, but the Supreme Command can intervene in the conversations. At 09:50 hours, Southern Command radios:

HQ: "Are you prepared to stand fast?"

Garrison commander: "I fear not! Our situation is very tough. I want to surrender."

HQ: "I amend the previous order. You aren't compelled to surrender. It's still up to you."

Garrison: (after a pause) "How long must we hold?"

HQ: "I can't make any guarantees."

Garrison: "Hold on!" (again a long pause) "Isn't it too late to change the decision?"

HQ: "It's up to the judgment of the garrison!"

Garrison: "The question is how long?"

HQ: "That's up to you. If you decide to hold on, we'll help as much as we can."

Garrison: "That's not enough."

HQ: "Those are the conditions. You decide!"

Garrison: "I fear I can't hold any longer. It's decided to surrender!"

The garrison officers are in a quandary. The change of orders and the transfer of decision to them is a heavy load to bear. They would prefer a direct order. Now they feel they are abandoning the fight. "They shouldn't do it to us," says a member of the garrison.

The stronghold radio operator, Amos Segal, reads the garrison roll, noting the wounded among them and giving the condition of each, followed by a list of dead. There are occasional breaks as the Egyptians interfere in the transmission. Across the lines, in HQ, the conversation is now being monitored by Marco, a signaller who knows some of the dead. At the end of the conversation, he says: "Stay cool!" Then he gets up from the radio set, moves to a corner of the room, turns his back and bursts into tears.

Then There Were None

In the stronghold, Lieutenant Shlomo Ardinest and Dr. Nahum Verbin make the last preparations for surrender. They burn documents, the doctor changes dressings on wounds, and Shlomo asks his men to shave, change clothes and go out as proud soldiers. One man is ordered to take the Scroll of the Holy Law with him. Each IDF stronghold has one. The Scroll in the Pier Position is a gift from the Jewish community of Rumania.

Shlomo Ardinest and Nahum Verbin negotiate with the Egyptian sector commander, who has come to the west

202

bank accompanied by newspapermen and television came-
ramen. Shlomo asks and receives permission to collect the
bodies of his dead. He returns to his men. The wounded
cross in the first boat, followed by a group with the Scroll
of the Law. Meanwhile, Shlomo holds his last conversation
with HQ:

Garrison: "I've got to leave. My regards to home."
HQ: "Do you want anything?"
Garrison: "To go home!"
HQ: "Are you aware of our situation?"
Garrison: "Negative!"
HQ: "Our situation is good." (a pause) "It was done
because by the time we reach you ... it might be late."
Garrison: "We've accepted it all in good spirit. Other-
wise this would be a second Massada."
HQ: "We'll see you on the tv screens with your heads
up. Tell them to keep their heads up. Let's see a smile!
You want to add anything?"
Garrison: "Inform the families. Console the parents.
Ask the boys to look after them. It's all because of the
wounded. They're transferring the wounded and dead.
They promised to observe the Geneva Convention."

Death of a General

With the surrender of the Pier Position, the story of the
Bar Lev Line is at an end. But it isn't the last of today's
casualties. The corps commanders are to meet around
noon in Tasa. The Chief of Staff wants to analyze
tomorrow's moves with them. He flies to Tasa by
helicopter, together with Bar Lev. Gonen is with Ezer
Weizman in another helicopter, and is talking by radio
with Albert Mendler who returned a few minutes ago from
a tour of the line. Suddenly, Albert's voice vanishes, and
there is nothing but atmospherics. Gonen tells Weizman:
"Something's happened to Albert!" A shell has exploded
in Albert's half-track, killing four occupants. Albert is still
breathing as they reach him, but he dies in the helicopter
on the way to hospital.

At Tasa, Elazar and the other senior officers are told of Albert's death. He was to have completed his tour of duty in Sinai six days ago, and to be appointed O.C. Armored Branch. This is the end of the road for a boy from Austria, who fled from the Nazis with his mother, reaching Palestine as an illegal immigrant on the eve of World War II. He joined the IDF during the 1948 War of Independence, and steadily climbed the ladder of rank.

Kalman Magen, who was to have taken command of Sinai forces, is now given Albert's corps. When the war began, he took command of the northern canal sector. Now, he is flown to Corps HQ on the southern sector.

"I didn't expect to take command this way," Magen tells the corps staff, and then: "Operations Officer, give me a situation report!"

INTERLUDE: TIMETABLE

Damocles Clock

The IDF only opened the offensive in which it crossed the Suez Canal on the tenth night of war. Was Israel fighting with no consideration for a political timetable, or for the clock hung over her head like a sword? If so, was the delay the result of tactical mistakes and bad decisions or of faulty strategic conceptions that pre-dated the Day of Judgement War? Could the IDF have achieved an earlier decision over the Arab armies and, if so, where could the war have been shortened?

The IDF spent years preparing for a blitzkrieg, and the intentions were good; Israel's strategists knew that short wars save lives, lessen the burden on the reserve army and the economy, and partially alleviate political dictates from abroad, or military intervention by the Great Powers. Strategic planning was based on ability to defeat the Arab armies rapidly, and make substantial battlefield achievements in the first stage. The Six Day War was a model of the concept.

The Six Day War and the War of Attrition were the bases for computation of ammunition and equipment stock levels. The planners allowed a safety factor, assuming that the next war would last longer than the 1967 war; a few more days were added to reach the stock figure that should be maintained. Sadat himself noted, at the beginning of the 1973 war, that Israel had ammunition for only ten days of combat.

Since decision would be reached reasonably quickly, it was assumed there would be no need to maintain the entire reserve army for a long time. Consequently there was no need to prepare a modern carbine for every soldier, or immense quantities of blankets and underwear. After the war, it did indeed become clear that the IDF had expended less of some types of ammunition than the Supreme Command had estimated. Empty warehouses weren't always an accurate indication, since immense quantities were on the roads, en route to units. However, stocks of some types of ammunition — for example artillery shells — were almost completely exhausted. Moshe Dayan admitted this to the Knesset in justifying Israel's acquiescence to a U.S. request for transfer of food and water to the besieged Egyptian Third Army.

The Day of Judgement War also exposed a serious default in U.S. ammunition and equipment stocks. The Pentagon disclosed that ammunition supply to Israel had depleted more than 30% of its stocks. In fact, a relatively small army had thinned out the warehouses of a Great Power to danger point.

All on One Card

America's problems were of no consolation to Israel. The fact remained that the possibility of prolonged total war was barely discussed — if at all — and could only be conceived in terms of the War of Attrition experience. A war in which the timetable would be upset because

Intelligence couldn't warn of enemy attack in time, wasn't taken into account. The absurd reliance on the sole possibility of blitzkrieg was a major cause of delay in the timetable. Egypt had correctly concluded apparently with Soviet assistance, that she must base on the IDF being unable to wage blitzkrieg. The Arabs opened war on two fronts simultaneously and planned on the use of vast quantities of manpower and weapons to force the IDF into diffusing its effort, and dispersing its forces. The IDF's operative conception was shown to be incomplete, while the Soviet-Arab theory proved well founded this time. The conclusion must be that delay in the timetable to no small extent derived from conceptual and planning mistakes.

The assumption of rapid victory in the coming war was undoubtedly rooted in mistaken evaluation of the balance of power and of the efficacy of certain weapons. Intelligence Branch knew numbers and quantities, but IDF operative echelons didn't interpret the information properly. Senior Israeli officers claimed that, in the event of an IDF canal crossing, the Egyptian Army would be defeated within four days, assuming that war on the west bank of Suez would be waged in the format of the Six Day War. The protagonists still argue that, but for Soviet involvement, the IDF could have defeated the Egyptian Army within four to six days. Yet this argumentation is indicative of the faulty strategic-political conception which initially contributed to the delayed timetable. Militarily, the IDF might have achieved rapid victory, had other factors not intervened in the course of battle, but this calculation could have no place in serious planning. Countries cannot live in a strategic vacuum. Nowadays, the Great Powers do intervene in one form or another whenever a war takes place and the Arabs took this into account.

Refereed Match

The idea that the IDF could win an almost absolute victory over the Egyptian Army proved fallacious. Even assuming the military balance of power to be favorable, political conditions would doubtfully have permitted it. Following the Six Day War and the War of Attrition, it should have been clear that the Soviet Union wouldn't allow Israel to achieve a decisive victory. In 1967, the IDF won a brilliant victory, yet Israel didn't harvest the real fruits. A month after the 1967 war, the Arab states decided, at the Khartoum Conference, that they wouldn't negotiate with Israel, wouldn't recognize her and wouldn't make peace with her. While the battlefield was still smoking, the Soviet Union began to rehabilitate the Arab armies.

If this truth wasn't learnt in the Six Day War, the War of Attrition taught even more clearly that the Soviet Union could not allow Israel to defeat the Arabs. In early 1970, the Israeli Air Force began to tip the scales of war by deep bombing within Egypt. Israel was on the threshold of victory — when the Soviet Union sent pilots and modern missile batteries to Egypt. The Israeli Air Force was compelled to stop bombing Egypt. Soviet intervention surprised both Israel and the United States; had America understood that Russian intervention would reach such dimensions, she wouldn't have given her tacit agreement to the Israeli bombing. When Russian intervention in the War of Attrition intensified, Washington increased pressures on Israel to make her accept a cease-fire and, in parallel, initiated the "Rogers Plan" for solution of the Israeli-Arab dispute.

The lesson that should have been learnt was a double one: The Soviet Union wouldn't allow Egypt to be defeated, even if it didn't imply conquest of Cairo; Washington would activate pressure on Israel the moment that Russian military involvement would increase. For the Egyptians; Egypt had failed to force the U.S. into making Israel withdraw. So, if Egypt would again resort to military means, she probably wouldn't do so in the partial and unsuccessful fashion of the War of Attrition, but in total war.

Empty Victory

Israel won the War of Attrition but, because of the Soviet Union, didn't achieve a tangible decision. The IDF's main failure manifested itself in that it neither understood the significance of the way in which the war ended, nor did it adapt its strategic thinking to the new lessons. The IDF could also have drawn conclusions from what had meanwhile happened in Vietnam; the United States hadn't reached an absolute decision, solely because another great power backed her adversary. U.S. military power was more than sufficient but strategic limitations wouldn't permit victory without involvement with the People's Republic of China. American entanglement in Vietnam grew as long as Washington didn't change her war objectives. Nixon and Kissinger finally decided to seek disengagement of U.S. forces. If this could happen to the United States in Vietnam, Israel could be expected to face an even more serious problem, when the Soviet Union backed her enemy. But Israel didn't learn.

Strategic concepts prior to the Six Day War were clear, but this was not the case after 1967. The IDF didn't know exactly what it wanted to achieve in a new total war. Defense Minister Dayan offered no guidance, and the many generals rotating through the General Staff didn't change this state of affairs. The IDF still concentrated on a "war of decision", with no consideration for the fact that it must imply burying eighteen years of Soviet labor in the Middle East.

Status Quo

The 1970 civil war in Jordan inspired a new partnership between Israel and the U.S. Washington saw Syria's invasion of Jordan as a breach of contract by the Kremlin. Henceforward, the U.S. was prepared to support regional **status quo**, until Egypt would agree to negotiate. In practical terms, the support was expressed in military assistance for Israel, and in deterring the Soviet Union from military involvement in the Middle East. Israel's role in the partnership was in military preservation of the **status quo** in the field; in other words, at any price to prevent the Egyptians from crossing the Suez Canal. Israel failed and undermined the partnership – which was so essential for her. The IDF planned for the Egyptian Army to be defeated in the second stage, instead of preventing tangible Egyptian achievements in the first stage. The Suez Canal line was held by sparse forces, on the assumption that matters would be sorted out later, or that Cairo would refrain from total war, out of fear of deep air-strikes within Egypt.

The timetable, dislocated by faulty strategic concepts, was further aggravated by hitches close to the outbreak of war and on the battlefield; the intelligence failure to warn of an impending Arab offensive, delayed mobilization of the reserve, the failure of the canal defense plan and the location of the regular army blocking forces to the rear.

A schedule isn't solely a function of hours or days, but primarily of the nature of events. If we start from Soviet unwillingness to permit decisive defeat of the Arab armies, then the sands of time run out when there is a tangible threat to the integrity of the Egyptian Army, or of an IDF approach to Cairo or Damascus. Then the Soviet Union must move to achieve immediate cease-fire by the threat of military intervention that limits the IDF's manoeuvering space.

What If?

What would have happened if Intelligence Branch warned in time, and the reserve had been mobilized substantially before the Arabs intended to open fire? One possibility is that the Arabs would have sensed it, and refrained from opening fire; a reasonable but eventually unworkable assumption, if they were indeed resolved to smash the **status quo** by total war.

A second possibility is that the Egyptians would have in any case opened their offensive and succeeding in crossing

209

the Suez Canal, though not on such a large scale. Their bridgeheads would have been smaller, and there would have been a reasonable chance of dislodging them. The reserves would have gone into battle earlier. The IDF crossing would have taken place on the third or fourth day. The Soviet Union would have suggested a cease-fire, and threatened military intervention. But, it would have happened earlier — not on the eighteenth day. In other words, war could have been shorter, and the losses incomparably smaller. Other Arab armies, such as the Iraqi, wouldn't have reached the point of intervention, and the Arab political campaign couldn't have gained such impetus.

None of this happened, because Israel's timetable was dislocated. Some officers, led by Maj.-General Arik Sharon, contend that much lost time could have been regained had the IDF advanced the timing of its crossing operation. Yet, the counter-attack of the third day, raises doubts whether the IDF would have been capable. The attack was possibly a poor one, but the fact remains that the IDF did not reach the canal bridges, let alone move over them. Because of the course of the blocking action and the delay in reserve mobilization, the IDF had insufficient force to cross the Suez Canal before the fifth day.

The only option open to the IDF Supreme Command was repulsion of the Syrians from Golan without a later move into Syrian territory. The effort might then have been transferred to the Egyptian front, thereby allowing for an earlier canal crossing; a possibility, but it would have implied a crossing before the Egyptian heavy armored divisions moved into Sinai. The task force would have encountered this armor on the west bank. The danger would have been greater, but with the possible chance of destroying large Egyptian armored forces, undefended by their infantry which was already in Sinai.

However, between the fourth and seventh days, emphasis was on the Syrian front. Only King Hussein can say whether the IDF offensive actually prevented him from opening a third front. On October 13, the eighth day, the IDF offensive on the Syrian front drew to a close. It would be a mistake to think that much more could have been done in Syria. I believe that the offensive petered out because the IDF had exploited all its potential. Even if the Supreme Command decided to take Damascus, it is doubtful whether this would have been immediately possible. The number of tanks then available was insufficient to renew the offensive. The Iraqi division that suddenly appeared was indeed mauled, but it did delay the IDF even more. The presence of a Jordanian armored division, with another already on its way to Syria, also dictated cessation of the offensive.

Slow Motion

An additional delay of some 24 to 30 hours duration was undoubtedly caused at the IDF's Suez Canal bridgehead. Because the bridges weren't built on time, and with the approval of the Chief of Staff and agreement of the Defense Minister, Southern Command ordered a halt in the transfer of additional tanks to the west bank. Maj.-General Bren Adan's army corps was held up, and Sharon contends that this blocked the IDF offensive. According to him, additional tanks and other equipment could have been transferred on the same ferries that carried the initial force, and valuable time would have been saved.

His critics claim that the delay was caused because Sharon didn't extend the bridgehead, or bring the bridges to the canal banks in time. They say that basing an offensive on the narrow bridgehead of this stage, and transferring additional armored forces before it had been expanded, involved immense risk. The initial decision was to risk a limited task force. When problems arose, Defense Minister Dayan raised the possibility of halting the entire operation. One way or another, this delay was the last and not necessarily the most important or decisive delay in the series.

OCTOBER 14, 1973

Wound-up Spring

Southern Command War Room waits for the Egyptian armored offensive. The atmosphere is of a giant spring, wound-up and ready to unleash. All believe there is no question that the Egyptian attack must come. Some officers still indulge in the thought that the Egyptians should have been pre-empted by an Israeli offensive to split the Second and Third Armies down the center, and cross the Suez before the enemy armor goes into action — but it's no longer realistic. All effort must now be devoted to smashing the Egyptian offensive expected at any minute. Deputy Chief of Staff Yisrael Tal, who arrived with Elazar before dawn, paces the long room like a caged lion: "This will be the decisive battle. Five hundred Egyptian tanks will go up in flames!"

On the Syrian front, the IDF offensive is in fact over. During the night, the line has moved closer to Damascus and stabilized. The IDF now stands at the entrance to the Laja lava rock regions that prevent armor movement, except by road. The two Syrian divisions on the sector have been smashed and are in retreat. To lessen the Israeli pressure, Damascus calls on Cairo to open an offensive as soon as possible. Egypt believes that now is the time, but doesn't know that the Israeli offensive in Syria is petering out. The Israeli Air Force is still thought to be busy on Golan. The Egyptian Army is to open the second round with 1200 tanks and 14 batteries of anti-aircraft missiles assembled in Sinai.

The offensive begins at 06:00 hours with a heavy 45 minute barrage by hundreds of guns and mortars. The Egyptian Air Force also tries to flex its muscles, but its effort is less concentrated. Among the attacking aircraft are Mirages transferred by Libya to Egypt. In one place, the Mirages surprise IDF soldiers, who hold their fire, believing the aircraft to be Israeli; the error costs a few casualties.

212

After the bombardment, the armor attacks along the entire length of the front; 800 to 1000 tanks move in unison into the largest tank battle since World War II. The Egyptians now demonstrate poor operational control; there is no concentration of effort, but rather diffusion of forces over scores of miles in five thrusts. The only losses inflicted on the IDF are in a sector where the Israeli line is held by Russian T55 tanks – booty from the Six Day War. The Russian armament has been replaced by a standard 105 millimeter IDF gun. The clash is between Russian tanks on both sides. Egyptian armor and infantry come close to the Israeli tanks, hitting a few of them, but are forced to withdraw.

The Egyptians make one unexpected move in the south, where Magen's corps is operating. The Egyptian 4th Armored Division attempts a deep flanking movement, but with only one armored brigade that penetrates a **wadi** on the edge of the front, in a south-to-northeast movement. The **wadi** ends near Bir Gafgafa in Central Sinai, and is the only place where the Egyptians penetrate more than 12 miles – to the Mitle–Ras Sudar road. Most of these tanks will not return. While Air Force planes pound them from above, Magen's tanks give battle along the penetration route. At the end of the encounter, 51 hit and abandoned tanks can be counted. Only 30 Egyptian vehicles return to their starting-point. Two Israeli tanks are damaged. The son of Uri Benari, Deputy Southern Front Commander, is one of the commanders in this action.

The Egyptians are losing tanks everywhere. Paratroops hold up the column that is trying to break through to Ras Sudar, while the Israeli Air Force destroys them. In the north, near Qantara, Sharon's men set a few dozen tanks ablaze. The Egyptian attack begins to wane at 14:00 hours, and peters out by 15:00 hours. Reports arriving from all sectors show a record number of tanks destroyed. Cautious counts indicate some 260 damaged or wrecked,

213

and many are beyond repair. This is a considerable number, even in terms of the vast quantity at the Egyptians' disposal.

The achievement is doubly impressive since less than ten Israeli tanks are damaged and most of these are Russian made. A few more battles like this, and the balance of forces will change beyond all recognition. The results already erase a number of question marks. Till today, the Egyptian infantry had shown surprising capability, but it wasn't clear whether the Egyptian armor had also improved. Now, the level of Israel's mostly reservist tank crews has proven considerably higher than that of their Egyptian counterparts.

Revert to Pattern

Until this morning, there had been a noticeable improvement in reports submitted by Egyptian field commanders. In previous wars, Egyptian officers frequently lied to higher echelons, thereby hampering compilation of a reliable picture of events. They recorded fake victories and false reports of successful missions, confusing and delaying command reactions. Field commanders were sceptical about the orders they received, knowing them to be based on their own false reports.

This time, the Egyptians have so far been careful in their official announcements, and field officers have more or less reported exact situation pictures – up to the first big failure; today's armored battle. The Egyptian officers now begin to report accomplishment of missions, though they are still far from it. Their Supreme Command is taken in by these reports and believes that it can use the magnificent but non-existing results to exhort other officers. Egyptian victory communiques are so proliferous that David Elazar calls Haim Bar Lev to ask whether the Mitle Pass is really in enemy hands.

This is one reason why Bar Lev this evening allows himself to tell the Prime Minister: "They have reverted to their old form, so has the IDF!" Golda Meir is in a cabinet

214

session when Bar Lev phones. When she's told that he is calling from the south to report on today's armored battle, she leaves the Cabinet Room to chat with him. The conversation ends with Bar Lev's remark: "And I strongly recommend approving the crossing operation!"

The crossing is now an obvious step, and the units have already been ordered to prepare. Some believe that the Egyptians will try their luck again tomorrow, so the conclusion is – come what may – the operation will begin tomorrow night. This time, the proposal is brought to a full Government session. There are no opponents to the plan as presented by the Chief of Staff. The Minister of Religions only raises the possibility of a raid on the west bank, rather than a drive to encircle and break the Egyptian Army.

Agam IX

Rafi Bar Lev, Haim's nephew, today finds himself and his reconnaissance company in a number of tough unplanned actions to help other units extricate themselves from the terrain. The first cry for help is early in the morning. The company is summoned north, towards an IDF position facing the area north of the Great Bitter Lake. Yitzhak Agam is the first to arrive with his platoon. From the high ground, he can see two tank platoons and a number of APCs trapped below. Smoke is pouring from one of the tanks and two armored personnel carriers that were hit by anti-tank missiles. Agam can clearly see the smoke contrails left by missiles in flight. A few miles further north, towards Chinese Farm, another battle rages. From the distance, Israeli tanks can be seen charging, while Air Force planes give close support.

Rescuing of the trapped tanks and APCs, already laden with dead and wounded, is no easy matter. Agam's platoon has no support weapons to cover retreat. The Egyptians are out of machine gun range, and the lack of 81 millimeter mortars is especially felt. The only possible way to the trapped force is by some route that isn't exposed to the Egyptian missile operators — Agam finds a roundabout route. By radio, he suggests that they follow him back up the track by which he descended. The APCs and two tanks fall in behind. Another tank remains on the field. Its commander decides to wait for dusk to avoid the missiles. A fourth tank climbs by another path entirely exposed to the Egyptian infantry. Halfway up, a Sagger missile sets it ablaze.

Rafi to the Rescue

Meanwhile, Rafi takes the rest of the company further north towards another force which is calling for help. The unit that attacked here has withdrawn, leaving five tanks exposed to Egyptian fire. Somebody is calling for help from one of these tanks. They have been hit by armor-piercing shells, but seem intact; apart from the holes by which the warheads entered.

While two tanks give cover from the rear, Rafi takes another into the field. The Egyptians notice it, and bring down artillery fire. Rafi descends from his tank, and climbs into one of the abandoned vehicles. Inside lies a barely conscious wounded man — the one who radioed for help. Rafi tends to him and then starts the engine and drives the tank back off the field. He retraces his steps to climb into the second tank. Its gear-box is wrecked, and the tank can only travel backwards. A number of manoeuvers, with shells falling all around, and this tank is also out of danger.

The shell fire gains in intensity as Rafi tows the third tank. Two badly injured crewmen are inside. On the deck of the fourth tank lies the body of a crewman. While Rafi is removing the tank from the field, the body falls off. The fire is now so bitter that Rafi's men try to convince him to leave the fifth vehicle, and the dead body that fell off: "It isn't worth it! There are only dead, and we're likely to pay with more dead."

"They are dead, but Jewish dead..." Rafi replies.

While the argument goes on, Egyptian tanks approach

216

and one of Rafi's rearguard vehicles is hit by an armor-piercing shell. Its crew, all in good shape, jump out and run to the rear. Rafi, in anger, shouts after them: "Is your tank on fire?" "No!", a soldier replies, looking back at the tank he has just abandoned, with the terror of his recent experience still in his eyes.

"Then go back and keep fighting!" Rafi orders.

The company withdraws without Rafi getting the remaining tank, and the dead bodies. At dusk, the unit commander, Yoav Brom, arrives. He heard about the company's battles, and the rescue operation. "You've done well!" he says. When he leaves, Rafi tells his men: "I don't agree with Yoav. There were some blunders. Men abandoned tanks. The second battalion left five vehicles with wounded. Tanks we could fight with. Some of us also abandoned a damaged tank."

Friend in Need VI

At 18:30 hours, the first plane of the American airlift lands at Lydda Airport; a giant Galaxy capable of carrying 120 tons over 3500 miles. From now on, the airlift will work round the clock. Up to now, the equipment has been brought by El Al passenger planes from which the seats have been removed. Twelve planes, loaded with boxes to the cabin roof, have already landed at Lydda. El Al will still continue, but the Americans are taking over the bulk of the burden. Twenty-five will land over the next day. While the first plane is still at sea, 100 miles off the Israeli coastline, fighter planes meet them and escort them in to Lydda. Joy and relief can clearly be seen in the faces of those waiting on the field.

Two soldier girls present flowers to the crewmen. The first to arrive is Colonel Doppler Strobau from New Jersey, at the head of a team of 30 men who will supervise the operation. The reception by soldier girls with flowers will become a custom with all the crews that follow. Later, Golda Meir arrives at Lydda. She hugs and kisses two pilots who are presented to her. The surprised airmen are asked if

217

they would like anything special in their few hours in Israel. One of them says he would be happy to tour Jerusalem. "Organize a car for them," Golda tells her entourage.

Part of the arriving equipment is urgently needed on the front. IDF forces are expending more ammunition than the planners had thought possible. Stocks of artillery shells are especially low, and the greatest demand is for the long range 175 millimeter American cannon; these shells are transferred directly from the planes at Lydda to the front. Other ammunition is sent first to the warehouses.

Ammunition to continue the war is now a high priority. There is no sign of impending cease-fire, the Arabs aren't even talking of it, and nobody has yet brought a proposal to the United Nations. "The family of nations doesn't want to embarrass the Arabs from fear that they aren't yet ready for cease-fire," says the Defense Minister during a visit to Southern Command War Room. "Anyway, cease-fire won't help us at this point." Moshe Dayan doesn't know that U.S. Secretary of State Henry Kissinger is mentioning for the first time to Soviet Ambassador Dobrynin, that battles should end, with each party remaining where it now stands. Dobrynin makes no response, yet a proposal for a solution in this spirit has clearly been raised for the first time. The Russians will accept it when it seems the most appropriate move. Washington understands Dobrynin's silence. So, American officials urge Israel to speed up, and show a more offensive spirit.

Preview Price

The joy generated by the airlift is still only shared by few. Nothing is yet said about it in public. The whole nation is in mourning tonight. For the first time, an IDF communique speaks of 656 dead on both fronts. The true number is greater, but this will only become clear later. In the Six Day War, and the 1956 Sinai Campaign — the number of fallen was only published at the end. Now, the

218

Government decides not to wait. Rumors have become a plague, and the silence of spokesmen only increases the question marks.

OCTOBER 15, 1973

Pleasure Cruise IV

Dawn, and the Egyptians neither open fire, nor repeat yesterday's attempt at an armored breakthrough. During the night, their hopes of smashing through to the Gulf of Suez and its oilfields were dashed. The Egyptian plan was for an armored column to thrust along the coastline, while helicopter-borne commandos would land in the IDF rear. Both the armor and commandos would receive their equipment and ammunition by sea. For this purpose, the Egyptians loaded a large fleet of fishing vessels, and installed machine guns. The Egyptian armor and commandos were blocked yesterday by IDF tank crews, air force and paratroops. The rest of the job is done during the night by the Navy. The tiny Israeli boats encounter the loaded fishing vessels in the Ras A'reb basin of the Bay of Suez. The battle is short and sharp, and 18 Egyptian ships are set ablaze.

If at First

At the other end of the canal, on the Mediterranean coast, the IDF is taking a heavy blow. The siege of the coastal position, facing Port Fuad, was raised a few days ago, but the Egyptians haven't given up. During the night, they land a seaborne commando of a few hundred men, with the intention of renewing the siege. The commandos dig-in on a reef alongside the road to the stronghold. A convoy, accompanied by tanks, runs straight into the Egyptian ambush. The first salvos include dozens of RPG rockets and anti-tank missiles fired at close range. The

219

narrowness of the coastal road prevents the tanks from turning. The blood-soaked battle rages five hours as help is rushed from the rear — more tanks and paratroops. At the end of the battle, there are 30 dead bodies among the convoy. The retreating Egyptians leave dozens of dead and 60 prisoners.

Unwanted Victory

On the Syrian front, where the fires of battle are dying down, Hussein's army comes into action for the first time today. Patton tanks of the Jordanian armored brigade attack from the south. The crews know their business, but are in an inferior position on the terrain. Of the brigade's 80 tanks, 22 are damaged. Israel isn't looking for this victory, and does not publish anything about the battle, which takes place a few miles from the main road from southern Golan to Damascus. Amman reports the armor clash apparently with the objective of emphasizing Jordan's part in the war against Israel. The Jordanian Government even announces that it is sending another armored brigade to the Syrian front.

Better Late

This evening, the IDF will begin crossing the Suez Canal; an operation postponed from the first week of the war. The moment it becomes clear that the Egyptians are not staging another attack today, a green light is lit to signal the crossing.

In the Southern Command War Room, the crossing plan is explained to the corps commanders and dozens of officers. Sharon's corps is entrusted with the hardest task — establishment of the bridgehead. The choice is a successful one. Sharon is the most experienced in knowledge of the terrain, and the most senior corps officer. As O.C. Southern Command, Arik Sharon carried out crossing operation exercises, and prepared operational dossiers for HQ.

Sharon's corps is to transfer paratroops and armor to the other side and to erect three bridges. The bridgehead will be expanded north of the northernmost bridge. The bridge parts are to move over two parallel roads to the crossing area. These roads will be maintained clear and open for Adan's corps, which will pass down them and cross by the bridges that Sharon will erect. When Adan's tank crews have passed through, Sharon will send an armored brigade after them. Then part of Magen's forces will also cross, while his other units remain in Sinai to pin down the Egyptians.

As the corps commander who is to open the operation, Sharon now details the tasks of his units. While one brigade applies pressure from east to west, in the area north of the Great Bitter Lake, another will penetrate to the designated bridgehead. The first brigade will distract Egyptian attention as the second creeps through the sand dunes, at the "seam" which corps' reconnaissance discovered last week. The scouts will lead the column, followed by the paratroop battalions who are to be the first across. Then the breakthrough brigade, destined to secure the bridgehead, together with an armored battalion which will cross with the paratroops. This battalion will tow the parts of the first bridge with it.

The axes of attack on the west bank are also decided. The first armored battalion to penetrate will move in the direction of the agricultural strip, paying special attention to anti-aircraft missile batteries. Bren Adan's forces will strike out in another direction; first westwards and then, at a distance of 15 miles from the canal, south towards Mount Jenifa. The operational order doesn't mention the Egyptian capital. The corps commanders are only told to be prepared for advance westwards.

The crossing equipment has already been prepared in Sinai. On the northern sector, complete pontoons, built by the IDF, are ready. More pontoons and bridge parts are located near Refidim in Central Sinai, and at Tasa. The crossing and engineer units have been standing-by in Sinai since the third day, and are now ordered up to the front line. Everything converges on Tasa, ready to move along the two roads to the northern tip of the Great Bitter Lake.

Main Street

At 17:00 hours, the units begin to roll out of Tasa. Apart from the crossing battalions, with their bridges, Adan's forces are hastening from the north, and Sharon's rearguard units are on the roads through the central sector. From the south come the paratroops who must meet up with the engineers to receive the rubber boats in which they will cross the canal. A mass movement on narrow paths and dirt tracks causes an almost unavoidable traffic jam in less than one hour. Approaching darkness adds to the confusion, and the military police are helpless. There are no traffic lights, and the only illumination is the flash of artillery fire. IDF guns have already begun a heavy bombardment along the whole front, with the hope of distracting Egyptian attention from the sector where action is to develop.

The traffic jam grows by the minute. Few pontoons reach Tasa from the northern sector. Another nine come from the south, from another crossing battalion. The bridge parts are delayed 12 miles from the canal. This is the bridge that should be first in the water and it is towed by a number of tank crews with no previous experience. The men trained for this task were crews of an armored brigade that was worn down on the first line, on Yom Kippur and the following day. The crews now entrusted with the towing operation haven't slept properly since they arrived at the front. Movement is slow and soporific. The driver of the lead tank falls asleep, and the edge of the bridge jams into another tank. Half an hour elapses before the two are separated. Then a tank swerves out of line and a towing cable breaks. Another hour passes without movement. Meanwhile, the road ahead is choked.

The pontoons for the other bridges enjoy no better luck. They are also towed by tanks down a 15 ft. wide asphalt road, without firm shoulders. Each pontoon is long

222

and wide, with edges jutting out on either side of the road. Had it been empty, the pontoons could pass, but thousands of vehicles are jammed together three and four deep. In addition, vehicles carrying casualties are coming in the opposite direction, from the canal. The blockage is total. There is no way to transfer the bridge parts and pontoons. The only ones who pass are Danny's paratroop battalion, who break through by sheer force, shoving with their half-tracks at other vehicles, and descending from the road into the dunes. The engineers have been waiting for them by Tasa, with the large rubber boats, since the early hours of afternoon. They only arrive close to 20:00 hours, and each half-track receives a rubber boat as it passes the crossroads.

Arik III

The blockage on the roads is arousing considerable anxiety in the Southern Command HQ. Some believe the whole operation should be postponed. They ask Sharon's opinion as the man responsible for the bridgehead. Some officers in his HQ would also like to postpone the operation. After a few moments to himself, Sharon decides to continue, despite everything! He fears that a delay in the offensive will result in the closing of the Egyptian "seam" and necessitate bitter breakthrough battles. His corps will go ahead with its offensive, but will transfer forces to the west bank in two thrusts rather than one. The tanks will cross on lighters and the officer in charge of ferry craft is now ordered to follow the breakthrough brigade.

Stop Pushing

The reconnaissance force is in the lead. First Rafi Bar Lev's company. Before moving out, Rafi collects his men, gives his last orders and asks his officers to repeat the details out loud. They must reach the Great Bitter Lake by the same route they took last week. Rafi concludes his briefing: "I hope we'll meet again!" The armored personnel carrier that leads the column towards the canal, is that of Ami Freedman, a member of **Kibbutz** Shfayim. Movement is slow. The scouts want to bypass the canals close to the Bitter Lake, and must pause occasionally. From the rear, the breakthrough brigade commander is pushing, but Rafi replies impatiently: "When we find the road — we'll tell you!"

An hour passes before Ami reports that he is out of the dunes, and has reached the Bitter Lake. It is now almost 21:00 hours. They turn north to the end of the lake and movement is easier. Rafi now heads the column, followed by a tank platoon. The scouts are followed by an armored battalion and then paratroopers. So far, the Egyptians have sensed nothing. Not one shot has been fired.

A reconnaissance company takes over the empty stronghold north of the Great Bitter Lake close to its junction with the canal. The crossing force assembles near the stronghold in a large compound surrounded by an embankment. The paratroops drop their rubber boats into the water. As they cross, the tension is electric. The first men climb the steep west bank. There are no Egyptians. Flashing lights from the other bank and a voice over the radio: "We've taken hold! We're in Africa!" Now the others come. Boats ferry more paratroops across the canal.

Mistaken Identity

Rafi's company moves north from the crossing point to mop up. The area is crawling with Egyptians; trucks in deep dug-outs, gun positions and tanks. At first, the Egyptians apparently believe this to be a column of theirs. The moment shooting begins — they panic. Vehicles go up in flames and, in the light of the blaze, Egyptian soldiers can be seen bolting. The fear is that the Egyptians will open fire, from the rear, at the west bank. Towards midnight, tracer bullets can be seen on the west bank as the paratroops mop up the bridgehead. The feeling in Rafi's company is a good one. The operation is developing as it should. The Egyptians haven't yet shown any serious opposition, and the only casualty is Ami Freedman's APC; a soldier was killed by shrapnel, and Ami has been wounded in the eye.

After midnight, the Egyptian fire gains intensity. The first self-propelled ferry craft reach the compound but, further north in the direction of the Chinese Farm, the armored battalion that is trying to enlarge the bridgehead encounters serious opposition. The Egyptians have called many tanks into action, together with teams of anti-tank missile operators. The full moon helps the Egyptian defenders, and the bonfires around their vehicles illuminate the terrain. Egyptian fire covers the two roads leading west to the Bitter Lake. The track across the dunes is the only open route out of their range.

Rafi Bar Lev's company is now summoned to help the armor battalion south of the Chinese Farm. At 03:00 hours, the reconnaissance company is already deployed alongside the armor, when there is tank fire from behind. Rafi ponders whether to answer it. For a moment, he believes that it comes from another IDF unit. The first to be hit is Ami Freedman's APC, the one that led Sharon's corps towards the canal. The fuel tank is hit, and the APC ignites in a tremendous flash. Two of the crew jump out – Ami and his platoon sergeant. Six dead remain within, among them the corpsman who tended Ami's wounded eye. Yitzhak Agam jumps from his vehicle to help the wounded, but the burning APC explodes. Ami and the sergeant lie nearby, both suffering from burns.

Routine Check

At 03:07 hours, Maj.-General Gonen makes radio contact from the War Room to Danny, the bearded paratroop officer who is now on the west bank of Suez. Chief of Staff Elazar is standing next to Gonen, and all present in the room are eager to hear what's happening on the other side. Danny's radio operator, a veteran of the unit's Six Day War battle for Jerusalem, hands the receiver to his commander.

Gonen: "This is the General. What is your situation?"

Danny: "I'm ashamed to tell you, but everything's O.K. No casualties apart from one scratched by a fence."

Gonen: "Congratulations! O.K. so far. Now talk with my commander."

Elazar: "This is Dado. Over."

Danny: "Roger, over."

Elazar: "How do you feel there? Over "

Danny: "Truthfully, it feel great."

Elazar: "Congratulations. Congratulations. Over and out."

Agam X

On the other side, in Sinai, the whole area is now a vast battlefield. The Egyptians are trying to close the roads through which the forces are pushing towards the Suez Canal. Suddenly Yitzhak Agam hears the battalion operations officer calling Rafi on the radio. Further south, close to an empty stronghold, the battalion commander's tank has just been hit. Yoav Brom, who took command to replace an officer killed in the first days of the war, is now dead himself. The operations officer wants to transfer command to Rafi, but he doesn't respond. "Rafi isn't answering," Yitzhak Agam says to his neighbor. The soldier, without a word, points at Rafi's tank going up in flames a few score yards away. While the operations officer still calls for Rafi, a shell has penetrated the tank turret, killing Rafi and two others instantaneously. The tank driver is safe, but in shock.

In the Southern Command War Room, Haim Bar Lev stays close to the radio, listening to the battle orders given the breakthrough brigade. He hears that the reconnaissance commander has been killed, and that command is to be transferred to his nephew, but doesn't know that Rafi Bar Lev lies dead.

Two more tanks of Rafi's company sustain direct hits. Agam collects the wounded, pulling them into a dug-out prepared by the Egyptians. The armored battalion commander orders his remaining tanks, and the reconnaissance company, to organize for all-round defense. Within the circle lie the wounded, among them Ami Freedman suffering from burns and his previous eye injury. Three APCs evacuate them. Ami is loaded on the last one and all set out southwards to the battalion casualty clearing station set up in a retaken stronghold.

Unfinished Journey

Ami's APC doesn't arrive at the clearing station. Again, he is unlucky. But this time he won't get away with a wound alone. For some reason, the driver of the third APC runs off the road into a nearby ditch. The two forward vehicles sense nothing. All their men remember is a salvo of bazooka rockets close to this spot. They continue down the track, link onto the rear of other vehicles carrying wounded, and don't notice the absence of the third APC.

In a few days, the APC to which Ami was transferred will be found with two bodies inside. The other passengers lie dead all around. Their documents are missing and their watches have been taken. They continued to travel along the ditch till they strayed into an Egyptian position. From the places where they lie, it appears that most of them, including the wounded, jumped from the vehicle to organize for all-round defense. They were killed in battle by bullet shots.

INTERLUDE: THE ARAB WARRIOR

Negative Image

Repeated IDF victories created a negative image of the Arab as a soldier, at least in the eyes of the Israeli public. The accepted opinion was that he possessed low motivation, wasn't resolute, had a low average intelligence and therefore found it difficult to handle sophisticated weapons, wasn't prepared to take over-many risks and tended to abandon wounded comrades. His officers mostly made lying reports, and their attitude to their men was poor. Professional military men also made this generalization, though not all IDF officers subscribed to it. The determining factor was public opinion, since this public furnished both officers and men of the reserve army. Till the Six Day War, this opinion may have been shared by few, but the great victory of 1967 turned it into common concensus. Senior military men said that the quality gap, which determines the soldier's level, is a matter for generations.

The Arab success in achieving surprise and some of their military objectives, therefore shocked the Israelis. The Arab soldier was expected to perform as in the past, and misuse his immense quantities of modern arms, because of his poor level. Events took a different course, or so it seems. But, did an improvement really take place in the Arab soldier? And, no less important, did the changes indicate a trend for the future?

Brainwash Pride

The most obvious improvement was in the Arab's motivation. By comparison with past wars, the Egyptian and Syrian armies of 1973 demonstrated a greater willingness to make sacrifices. An almost revolutionary change had taken place; but the Egyptian soldier's willingness to charge Israeli tanks, and his officer's to stand fast, didn't derive from social changes in their country. Quite the contrary.

In recent years Egypt suffered economically, with a detrimental effect on many aspects of life. True, since the Six Day War, the Egyptian Government took care to recruit educated men into the army; the literate were not as easily released from military service, and did find their way to officers' schools. Yet, the improvement was more a result of intensive indoctrination on the significance of

228

soldiering and Arab pride. War on the Suez Canal, or 35 miles from Damascus, instilled a sense of fighting for the homeland and not for the benefit of others, though they may be considered Arab brothers. Frustration possibly also served as an important stimulant for both the Arab officer and individual soldier. National survival was, and is an important motivation for the Israeli soldier; the feeling of national insult—following repeated defeats, and universal contempt — could just as easily impel the Arab soldier to display spiritual resources never before revealed.

Blame the Tools

This war indirectly affected another affair of pride—the honor of Russian weapons. After the Six Day War, the Arabs blamed their defeat on the inferior quality of Russian armaments, Soviet generals argued that the Arabs hadn't learned to use what they were given; many of the weapons were not even tried. Arab officers responded that Russian armaments were inferior to Western counterparts in IDF hands. The decisive Arab defeat of 1967 roused doubts elsewhere; soldiers in the Soviet satellite states feared that their weapons were not as good as Western arms.

When the Arabs started the 1973 war, it was clearly a renewed arms test. The Soviet Union did not want an Arab defeat, partly because the prestige of the Russian armaments industry was in their hands. **Tass Press Agency** hastened to comment: "It was with the help of Soviet weapons that the Egyptians broke through the Bar Lev Line; a line described by Israelis as impregnable. Syrian soldiers are also successfully repelling Israeli attacks with the help of Soviet arms."

The Soviet Union fed the Arab states with quantities of tanks, aircraft and artillery far beyond the reach of countries the size of Great Britain, France and West Germany. But did the improved Arab motivation and the vast arsenals turn the Arab into a better soldier?

But Check the Workman

The technical preparation of Arab armies for the 1973 war was undoubtedly better than in the past. The Arab soldiers are regulars who can be trained over long periods. Exercising in the operation of anti-tank missiles became the daily bread of Egyptian infantrymen. The relative simplicity of Russian weapons made it easier for poorly-educated Egyptian soldiers. Technology closed quality gaps and, to a certain extent, converted their war into one of "button-pushing".

The Egyptian Engineering Corps also performed satisfactorily in bridging operations that it had had exercised in a regular manoeuver repeated thousands of times.

If the technical preparation of the Egyptian and Syrian soldier was better, the same cannot be said of maintenance where almost no progress had been made. Equipment that fell into IDF hands gave ample proof of this, and the percentage of serviceable Arab aircraft was low compared with any European army. The Arab staff officers knew this, and tried to compensate by the availability of considerable quantities. In place of complicated repairs, and complex maintenance, they issued new weapons and equipment. Instead of repairing a broken-down truck, they replaced it. The vast quantity of "factory-new" weapons used in the Day of Judgement War was evidence of this approach. Many of the vehicles captured by the IDF hadn't travelled more than a few miles from warehouses to the front. This system could not, of course, always work. Quantity will not always compensate for faulty maintenance of sophisticated and complex weapons.

Modern Inconvenience

The operational level of sophisticated weapons was not uniform. Sophisticated weapons systems sometimes tended to hamper the Arab soldier more than they helped him. This was especially true when there were technical hitches and a need for rapid improvisation. First lessons from the

230

war teach that, in static weapons systems, the Arab armies overcame problems, and manned them properly—though not excellently. But, in mobile weapons systems—such as modern aircraft and missile ships—there was no tangible improvement and a substantial gap still remained.

There was a noteworthy improvement in planning. From the Six Day War and the War of Attrition, the Egyptians learnt to locate their weaknesses and find appropriate operational answers. This was possibly done with the assistance of thousands of Soviet advisers, yet it makes no difference; the fact is that they did learn from their mistakes. Strategic planning was thorough, as proven by the successful integration of their military plans and political efforts.

Their operational plans appeared to be better and more complete than before. From captured Egyptian documents, the crossing plan appeared to be of an acceptable Western standard. There were discrepancies between planning and implementation, yet they cannot detract from the improvement in the high command planning echelons.

However, the operational plans were schematic, and contained no specially brilliant strokes or unconventional concepts. The moves were based exclusively on optimal fire power, and almost inexhaustible manpower. The schematicism became apparent whenever there was a hitch, or when the IDF presented the Arab command with an unexpected problem; as, for example, when an Israeli force crossed Suez, in the second week of war. The Egyptian forward HQ and Supreme Command had difficulty in reading the battle picture, and their reactions were no less confused than in the past. Some 48 hours elapsed from the beginnings of the Israeli crossing until the Egyptian Supreme Command understood, perhaps thanks to Soviet spacecraft, the danger that faced them.

As in the past, the Arab armies began to disintegrate when the IDF penetrated their rear. In the Day of Judgement War, the Egyptian Third Army started to crumble— and 8000 of its men were taken prisoner— after the IDF crossed the Suez Canal and moved to encircle.

Management-Labor Relations

The "distance" between the Egyptian officer and soldier did narrow. It still existed but, in the Egyptian Army, it was not what it had been. In the Syrian Army, there was no noticeable change. Officers' privileges on the battlefield were frequently at the expense of their men and their lives. One Syrian Army order determined that wounded officers should receive medical aid before their men, irrespective of the type of wound. It went on to say that officers were to be transferred to a special hospital. Wounded soldiers would be evacuated by vehicle, but not before it was completely loaded.

Exceptions Don't Prove Rules

A student of Arab-Israeli wars would find it impossible to generalize about the Arab soldier. Because of their defeats, there is a tendency at the end of campaigns to forget that Arabs have often fought properly. This was true in the 1948 War of Independence, especially with reference to the Palestinians. In the Six Day War, there were frequent examples: the Syrians on Tel Fahar; Jordanians in the Old City of Jerusalem and the armored battles in Samaria; and the Egyptians when the IDF broke through the Jiradi, at Shekh Zewaid and on the Gaza Strip. The Egyptian soldier always excelled in defense—witness the Faluja Pocket in 1948 and Abu Ageila in 1956.

Even after the 1973 war, some senior Israeli officers still believed that no significant change had taken place. Three of these are Yitzhak Hofi, Raphael Eitan and Baruch Harel. The former were on the Syrian front, while Harel—who won a mention in dispatches in the Six Day War for his share in the Sinai breakthrough—fought on the Egyptian front. They started out from the fact that this was the first war in which the Arabs determined the shape and time of battle; they enjoyed both a preferential situation in weapons and fire power, and total surprise with the privilege of the first blow—and their combat standard should be examined in this context.

Maj.-General Hofi said: "All the preliminary data were in the Arabs' favor. They had a significant and important advantage in artillery, yet in armor clashes they displayed no special ability. They moved tanks at night, with the assistance of infra-red, but fought little. The Syrian commando succeeded only once—on the Hermon. When we attacked they made a ferocious and obstinate stand, but this had happened before. The Iraqi forces on the Syrian front displayed low level."

Maj.-General Eitan was more extreme: "There is no change in the Arab warrior. They were not outstanding, in armored warfare—neither in flanking movements, nor in the use of tank guns. It was mass that created force, and gave impetus to their assault. There are two yardsticks for standard. One—the number of abandoned tanks which were undamaged, or very slightly damaged—and the other, the number of tanks each side lost in armor-armor battles. For every two Syrian tanks burnt in battle—crews abandoned another one which was intact and serviceable. On the Syrian front alone, the IDF seized hundreds of intact tanks. As for damaged tanks, the ratio was 4:1 in favor of the IDF."

Mixed Opinions

Veteran armor commander Brigadier Uri Benari expresses a different opinion. He was released from the IDF after the 1956 war, and fought the Six Day War as a reservist on the Jordanian front. In this war, he served as Deputy Commander of the Egyptian front. Benari said: "One thing became clear. The Egyptian Army can be considered a good army, and there is no room for contempt. The improvement was considerable, both in the standard of the individual soldier, and of his officers. The Egyptians were always good at defensive battle. A change has clearly taken place in the Egyptian Army's attack capability, and it was especially noticeable in their infantry. In armored warfare, the Egyptian Army still lags behind considerably. There were places where. immedi-

233

ately after an abortive attack by an Egyptian infantry battalion—a heavy price being paid in blood—another one which witnessed the failure, came in to renew the attack. We have no memory of this from previous wars."

In certain aspects the Arabs did fight better, and the outstanding example was the Egyptian infantry. Senior Paratroop and Infantry Officer, Brigadier Emmanuel Shaked also contended that the Egyptian infantryman proved himself beyond any doubt in the 1973 war. The Egyptian soldiers were courageous; they manned missile batteries and anti-aircraft guns in the face of diving Israeli aircraft. Egyptian commandos also acted boldly, though this bordered on expendability of manpower; their achievements were minimal, and hundreds were lost en route to missions. The Syrian commandos showed greater tenacity and willingness to fight, but their achievements were limited to Mount Hermon.

Good Shooting

Certain improvements were also noticeable in Egyptian gunnery. The Egyptians made concentrated use of massed artillery, over small sectors, and layed faster fire on specific targets. partly thanks to the use of forward artillery spotting officers. The Egyptian artillery has made a slow and modest entry into the computer age—evidence of future trends. They have considerable gun-laying equipment, some of it Western in origin.

In armor, on the other hand, neither the Egyptians nor the Syrians showed any impressive improvement, possibly because the use of armor is primarily in mobile war where the IDF excels. In the air, the gap still remained. The Arab pilots were noticeably better trained than ever before. They were bolder, but still couldn't be compared with their Israel counterparts. More than 90% of the Israeli planes that were downed were hit by missiles and other ground fire. The Arab air forces didn't succeed in hitting targets within Israel, or in disrupting the movement of reserves towards the front. Their activities were solely on

234

the forward sectors, with almost no effort to operate aircraft at night.

In the war at sea, there was no noticeable Arab improvement. Though they had considerable modern equipment, the Arab navies did not threaten Israeli shores, and failed in every naval battle. Their sole success was recorded in the Bab el-Mandab Straits, beyond the reach of Israeli forces.

Clearly, the results of the Day of Judgement War will contribute to a "morale revolution" in the Arab armies, especially among the Egyptians. This is the first time in the history of the Arab-Israeli conflict that Arab armies have recorded any kind of military achievement. They will obviously be spurred on to additional investment and effort, primarily based on intelligent use of quantities of fire and manpower—to narrow the quality gap.

OCTOBER 16, 1973

The Compound

Towards morning, the self-propelled ferrycraft arrive at the compound. An excavator pounds away with its big shovel on the crumbling west ramp, and the way to the canal is open. Another excavator scoops out the earth embankment, and a lighter slips into the water as the first tank impatiently races forward. The lighter engine begins to beat, and it ploughs across to the west bank—to Africa. This is a great moment. The paratroops on the other side are no longer alone. Tanks provide them with a cloak of armor. More lighters arrive, with additional tanks. This isn't the rapid transit of a bridge, but the thin stream persists.

By the canal, the work goes on quietly. Apart from one short mortar bombardment, the Egyptians haven't bothered the paratroops on the west bank. But the two main roads — west to the bridgehead and north to the Chinese Farm — are a different matter. They are virtually

235

impassable. The track across the dunes from the south is the only route that remains open. Silent witnesses to the heavy battles of the night lay strewn along the roads and to the north; dozens of scorched vehicles and burnt and holed tanks. Egyptian and Israeli tanks yards apart, and sometimes even touching. The Egyptians have been harder hit, but they have closed both roads. The southern road is swept by machine gun and tank fire. The northern one — which is no more than an 18 ft. wide dirt track — is controlled by nearby Egyptian units. Towards morning, hundreds of Egyptian soldiers swarm out from the Chinese Farm to dig-in along the roadside, while tanks deploy behind and between them.

Revised Plans

Many tanks of the breakthrough brigade have been hit during the night, and now only 27 remain intact. The casualties are heavy and there is a disturbing lack of ammunition of all types. Nevertheless, Sharon receives orders to seize the junction of the road north along the Bitter Lake, and the other from the east. He is promised air support, but the planes do not arrive. While the orders for the seizure of the junction are still being debated on the radio waves, shells begin to fall around Sharon's command post, in one of the heaviest barrages since the crossing began. The explosions are so loud and frequent that it's impossible to hear the signallers. The orders are now amended; Sharon's forces won't attack the junction. The breakthrough brigade will pull back to the shores of the Bitter Lake to reorganize, fuel up and renew ammunition supplies. The section north of the bridge will be taken by a battalion of Adan's Centurions, that was to have been the first of his corps to cross the canal bridges.

Agam XI

Rafi Bar Lev's reconnaissance company also pulls back to reorganize; its remnants collect in the compound. They

all know that Rafi is dead. Many friends have died, or been
burnt before their eyes. The mood is grim and fatigue
takes its toll. The company's tank commanders are youngsters, immediately after conscript service, and this is their
first war. Men fall asleep in the vehicles, and no one
bothers to open iron rations. Yitzhak Agam, now the
senior officer, senses the heavy mood, and collects his
company together in a corner of the compound and says:
"I order you to eat. Each of you will take a C Ration, and
eat a proper meal. We haven't finished the war yet."
Danny, the doctor also obeys the order. The men slowly
recover, but cannot rest. Their present task is to protect
the compound against Egyptian attack.

Tenuous Affair

"In my view, this isn't a bridgehead," Maj-General Adan
reports to Southern Command HQ. And indeed, it is a very
tenuous affair. Alongside the Suez Canal, Sharon's units
are holding, and have even transferred 20 odd tanks to the
other bank but the Egyptians are between Adan's men,
who are supposed to cross, and the compound. On the
southern road, the tanks can shoot their way through in a
fire fight, but without the light vehicles and their precious
loads of ammunition and fuel. The bridging equipment is
held up to the rear, and cannot pass down roads covered
by heavy Egyptian fire. One part of the bridge is broken.
Armorers are working on it, while the tow tanks have been
ordered by Sharon's HQ not to wait; they are to race to
the canal, and cross to the other side. Command Engineer
Officer Johnny and Haim Rason, an armorer, are left with
the bridge which they promise to repair within an hour or
two.
   The feeling in Southern Command HQ is that the crossing operation is about to fizzle out. Eighteen hours have
passed since the offensive opened − and not one bridge has
been erected. By noon, Sharon has reinforced his paratroops on the west bank with only 27 tanks, and their
lifeline is easily cutable. The IDF has so far only poked a

thin needle into the enemy. And this is no ordinary crossing onto an enemy held bank, but one in which the opponent occupies both sides of the water barrier.

Rejected Suggestion

Moshe Dayan has been in Southern Command War Room since the early hours of morning. He has been scrutinising maps and listening anxiously to the reports. Now he says: "I suggest bringing the force back — the paratroops and the tanks." The room falls silent. This isn't an order — only a suggestion — and they sense the difference.

Gonen is the first to reply. He is against the suggestion; he believes that Sharon and Adan will clear the roads, and the bridges will be erected. Bar Lev also opposes the suggestion to recall the paratroops: "They won't be slaughtered, and even if it doesn't go — we'll bring them back by the same route. At most, we'll leave a few dozen burnt tanks behind."

"I accept," Dayan says. "But we must set a red line, a time at which they will be recalled if a bridge isn't built by then."

Arik IV

While this debate is in process, Sharon is on the other bank. This morning, he "thumbed" a ferry ride into Africa. His men tell him about the first battles on the west bank, and the Egyptians' shock at encountering them. Sharon is now formulating a change in plan; his corps, instead of holding and enlarging the bridgehead, will immediately move across. Transit will be hard and slow, since the bridges aren't ready, but it can be done with ferries. Meanwhile, Adan will smash through the blocked roads and consolidate the flanks to protect the bridgehead. In other words, in place of Adan's corps crossing first — as the bridges are built — Sharon will take over his role. Later, the third corps will move in. This was Sharon's original idea which was replaced by the Southern Command plan. Sharon believes that time is pressing: better risk the transfer of additional forces, even without the bridges, before the Egyptians recover from their shock.

Bar Lev's Party

Southern Command now faces two contrary proposals. Dayan's—to stop the crossing and bring the force back, or set a time at which—if the bridges haven't been built— the operation will cease. And Sharon's diametrically opposed plan to continue despite everything, and transfer additional armor without the bridges. Dayan's proposal is shelved, and Sharon is in the minority. Bar Lev sets the tone, and the decision is to continue as originally planned. The forces that jump the canal will continue to operate, though Adan will not cross yet. Instead, he will take responsibility for opening the roads to the bridgehead, and transferring the fording equipment. Adan's deputy is entrusted with the protection of the bridging equipment, and its transfer to the compound.

The breakthrough brigade commander is clearly dissatisfied. He doesn't want to settle for the role of trailblazer alone, but would like to cross over with his tank crews — immediately. He turns to Bar Lev and asks: "Sir, what's more important — a tank battalion here by the bridge, or next to Cairo?"

Bar Lev is annoyed. He answers in a thunderous voice: "A tank battalion near Cairo is a dead battalion if we don't have an open road and a bridge. I don't need any wisecracks. Carry out the task as written!"

Surprise Visitor

The Egyptian High Command doesn't know exactly what is going on north of the Bitter Lake, and west of Suez. From the Second Army comes a report that a small Israeli force has penetrated west of the canal; a tiny raiding force, which will quickly return to base. And if not — then

239

it will easily be destroyed. President Sadat is making a speech to a special session of the People's Council describing developments, but without mentioning the IDF crossing. It is the first time that the Egyptian President speaks of cease-fire, on condition that Israel withdraws to the 1967 borders. The reports from the front aren't bothersome, and Sadat has a distinguished and unexpected guest.

Soviet Prime Minister Kosygin has come unannounced to get direct impressions. The Kremlin realises that the Middle East war is at a turning point. The Arabs can make no more substantial military achievements; they are exhausted. From here on, they can only decline, while Israel may pull some surprises out of the bag. The Israelis are within artillery range of Damascus. The Russian airlift is pouring considerable military equipment in to Syria, but Israeli aircraft are interfering with its movements, and with roads throughout the country. Four large road bridges have already been hit. All that now remains is to preserve the Egyptian Army's achievements on the Suez Canal. The Soviet Union will soon have to act for a cease-fire. Nothing could be better than for a high-level Soviet leader to be on the spot. He can put his fingers on the pulse, and immediately know what is going on. The day he arrives, nobody bothers Kosygin with stories about the Israeli force on the west bank.

Egyptian War Minister Ismail Ali orders the O.C. Second Army not to allow the Israelis freedom to do whatever they please. There is no way of knowing their intentions, so it would be best to strike as early as possible, with armor and commandos. The Second Army Commander calms his War Minister. He promises an attack today, but by evening — there is still no action. The Israeli paratroops and their armor escort operate without interference, striking at vehicles and gun positions — and at two missile batteries. As evening falls, they are ordered back towards the canal, when the tanks are already more than 12 miles into Egypt.

Debut

The first intimation of events on the other side of Suez is supplied by the Israeli Prime Minister. In a Knesset speech, Golda Meir says in one short sentence: "At this time, an IDF force is also operating on the west bank of the canal." Opposition leader Menachem Beigin, who speaks after Golda, also refers to the IDF's activities beyond the canal. This morning, Beigin spoke to Arik Sharon by radio, and heard of the crossing for the first time. Golda Meir's announcement disperses some of the fog of batle and, though no special details or objectives are noted, Southern Command HQ is not exactly delighted; it would have been better to wait with the news, and confuse the Egyptians even more.

All eyes are on the two roads by which the bridging equipment must move. Hundreds of Egyptian infantrymen are deployed across one route, and infantry are assigned to sweep them off it. Memories of the first days — when the Egyptian infantry struck at Israeli armor with missiles and bazookas — are still fresh and painful. In the Gulf of Suez, a paratroop brigade sits waiting. It will now be thrown into the fray together with armor. Helicopters are sent to bring the paratroops to the central sector.

Red Beret Improvisation

When the paratroops arrive towards evening, Bar Lev communicates with their commander: "Opening the road is most essential. The entire operation depends on it, and without the crossing, I don't know how this war will finish!"

The paratroop commander repeats Bar Lev's remarks to his staff. A heavy burden rests on their shoulders. Time is pressing, and they're going in to battle without serious preparation and with little information. The paratroops are told, in general terms, that the Egyptians control the north road, but no reference is made to their positions, weapons, or strength.

A battalion takes the lead, followed by brigade head-quarters; there is no artillery, air or tank support.

The paratroops traverse a third of the way under heavy fire, and then bog down. From the north, more than 20 Goryanov machine guns cover the road. The paratroops seem to be inside an extensive Egyptian defense work, which stretches from the road to the Chinese Farm. The paratroops have no alternative but to assault the machine gun nests. They push the Egyptians back but, for every yard of road, they leave bullet-riddled bodies behind. The clashes are at ranges of a few yards. The Egyptians have the advantage in fire power, and need not move from their positions. Paratroop companies are dispersed over the terrain, and all are engaged in cruel and bitter combat.

By dawn, four company commanders are dead, and another seriously injured. Shells fall within the command group, killing some men. Now the problem is to find shelter. Close to the road is a wide ditch, which used to serve the nearby farm. There is an Egyptian force at the end of it, but the paratroops push them out and find cover. It gives protection against flat trajectory weapons, but the Egyptians — realising where the Israelis are — call down artillery and mortar fire, which grows more accurate by the minute. One man in the ditch took part in the Beirut operation against the Popular Democratic Front headquarters. Then he thought no fire could be denser, but now he knows that Beirut was a child's game compared with the Chinese Farm.

Dawn finds the paratroops pinned down in the long ditch. In place of opening the road, they are in a fire trap. Many have run out of ammunition. Some are left with only one or two bullets, and their cries for supplies are so far unanswered.

OCTOBER 17, 1973

Thin Armor

Daylight neither helps the paratroops, nor lessens the bombardment. The entire Egyptian effort is directed at the dirt track, and the road south of it. On the canal banks, where the first paratroop unit crossed into Africa, it's much quieter. Overnight, and at dawn, the ferries carried additional vehicles across and there are now 36 Israeli tanks on the west bank; a force capable of inflicting injuries, but hardly an armored fist for a major offensive.

The paratroops know nothing of the canal. They have full-time problems of their own and they want out. Their commander realises that his men have reached the limit of their endurance. The objective now is not to open the road, but to hold out and save the men. First, he contacts Maj.-General Adan, to whom he is attached, and asks permission to evacuate and regroup. Adan hesitates; he doesn't want to agree without approval from HQ. He reports the paratroop losses to General Gonen.

Command Misunderstanding

The paratroop officer repeats his request to Gonen. This time, the answer is clearer: "Only wounded to be evacuated!" Clearly, Southern Command HQ sees the battle picture differently. The paratroop commander is shocked at his men's ordeal. Bar Lev's comments on the importance of this battle are fresh in his memory and he wouldn't request permission to evacuate were it not for the situation of his men. He doesn't want to abandon the road, but only to be relieved by a fresh force; HQ don't realize this. They believe the paratroops are protecting the flank of the bridgehead and that removing them will allow the Egyptians to completely close the corridor.

It isn't that way at all. The paratroops no longer hold the flank. An Israeli armored force is fighting on a line parallel to them, preventing the Egyptians from isolating

243

the bridgehead. Finally, Haim Bar Lev comes to visit General Adan and realises the true situation. He gives approval for evacuation of the paratroops.

The paratroops cannot break off contact and move back while exposed on the ground. The only way is to take them out in armored personnel carriers, squad by squad. The last to remain are two groups fighting close to the Chinese Farm; one of eight men, and the other of ten. The paratroops are now replaced by tanks, but HQ – commanded as it is by men with an armor background – very well understands that without infantry, the IDF will have extreme difficulty in extending the bridgehead and repelling the Egyptian infantry. Paratroop companies are hastily pulled in from all over the place, and assembled in the rear, ready for continuation of the battle.

Water Intrusion

Another special IDF force – the naval commando – tonight carries out a daring action in Port Said at the northern entrance to the Suez Canal. Its anchorages are extensive, and the difficulty is to locate the pools where enemy naval craft are to be found. Two pairs of frogmen enter the harbor from the sea, swimming hard against the strong canal currents. The Egyptians are awake to the possibility of Israeli frogmen operating in this, the closest port to the front line. Patrol boats prowl between the anchorages and the canal, from time to time dropping depth charges. Guards on the piers throw explosives into the water close to the few ships at anchor. The muffled explosions create pressure waves that are fatal below surface.

One pair penetrates a pool where two large landing craft are moored. They decide to concentrate on one to guarantee a sinking. The explosions tear huge holes in the hull and the craft sinks rapidly. Its neighbor is also damaged.

The second pair, Amir and Kimchi, sneak in to another anchorage, where a missile ship and a torpedo boat are moored. Nothing more is known of their fate; the two ships are sunk by limpet mines, but Amir and Kimchi do not return. It seems they fell victims to one of the charges.

Their comrades wait at the port entrance, in vain. Night passes — the two do not return. The other team risks a search in daylight, under the eyes of Egyptian look-outs. Israeli boats come to the port entrance, but there is no sign. The Egyptians notice the movements and open artillery fire. A few days later, the Egyptian press will publish a photo of the body of an Israeli frogman found — according to their reports — in the waters of Port Said Harbor.

Late Launch

Bren Adan's tanks slowly push the Egyptians back from the roads north of the Bitter Lake. They are operating from south to north, fighting for every inch. First, the Egyptians relinquish the south road. Adan's deputy, now responsible for towing the pontoons, has been waiting for this moment. Close to 06:00 hours, the tanks pass through, towing the first pontoon and led by a bulldozer which shoves obstacles and burnt vehicles aside. At 06:25 hours, it is launched into the waters of the Suez Canal. The engineers responsible for bridging, and the tank crews who towed the pontoon, burst out in cries of sheer joy. More pontoons are moving down the road. At 07:55 hours, the compound reports the arrival of three more. Eight are needed to cover the width of the canal — 180 yards at this point — and assemble the first bridge.

Tropical Downpour

At 10:00 hours, the last of the eight arrives at the compound. They don't all belong to the same unit. Every pontoon that reaches the road, irrespective of origin, is rushed on its way. More are already being towed from Tasa, to form the second bridge.

At 10:05 hours, the Egyptian bombardment, which has been no more than a steady rain, suddenly becomes a tropical downpour of shells, mortar bombs and katyusha rockets. The Egyptians have pinpointed the bridgehead and have brought scores of artillery batteries to bear. A huge hole is torn in the center of a pontoon standing in the compound. Four engineers stationed around it are killed. Salvos of shells and rockets churn the canal waters. The officer of a ferrycraft is wounded and then a pontoon-battalion commander is also hit. In the short pauses between salvos, the ferries try to cross with additional tanks. One takes a direct hit from a large caliber shell, lists to one side and quietly sinks with two tanks on board. The engineers who man the ferry jump into the water. The tanks are swallowed up in the water with their crews.

The waters teem with hundreds of fish killed by shock waves. The men face a similar danger. Four soldiers fall off a ferry. Luckily, they are wearing life-vests. Ohion from Kiryat Shmoneh is among them. The shells exploding in the water beat at his stomach like immense fists. He tries to evade the shock waves by turning on his back, but the next shell falls so close that he loses consciousness. His commander jumps into the water to haul him out.

The dangerous work of erecting the pontoon bridge falls on fourteen men; three officers and eleven soldiers. They work on despite the heavy fire. When one falls, another comes out to replace him. Major Shmuel Bruchiel works on the east bank, pushing the pontoons into the water, one after the other, with a bulldozer. Another group, led by Captain Yehuda Hodeda, links them one to another. Yehuda will survive all the bombardments up to the last day. In the final salvo before cease-fire, he will be hit by a katyusha rocket. His comrade, Dotan Yeshai, is working in the water directing the pontoons to the places where they are to be linked. He runs risks not only from shells and shrapnel, but also from the under-water shock waves.

Question of Hours

At noon, there is a battlefield consultation in Adan's HQ. Sharon, Bar Lev, David Elazar and Dayan arrive. It is now clearly a question of hours until the first bridge is linked up, and ready for transfer of forces. But the bridge-head hasn't been extended as planned, and Bar Lev suggests that — when the bridge is in place — Sharon will cross the canal with part of his force. His deputy will remain at the bridgehead, while he opens a general advance on the other side. Russian tanks, the spoils of war, will be added to his units. Bar Lev's proposal is rejected. The Chief of Staff is convinced that the plan must be followed. Sharon must hold the bridgehead and be responsible for the east bank. Adan will pass through first, while Kalman Magen will be ordered to prepare for movement today.

While the conference is in session, the battle for the roads continues. The Air Force assists methodically and in great force. Its planes dive, one after the other, on the Egyptian positions around and to the north of the Chinese Farm. Thousands of bombs have already been dropped on this web, many directed against the Egyptian infantry.

News has just been received that the Egyptian 25th Armored Brigade is approaching from the south, along the lake, to support the Second Army in its attempt to cut the roads. Bren Adan is to take care of this brigade, and will postpone transfer of his forces. He receives an additional brigade that has been held in reserve. Another unit, commanded by Natke, joins the gigantic tank ambush. One force blocks from the north while the other waits on the east flank. The Egyptians move northwards in a long column and fall easy prey to the Israeli armor. Thirty eight tanks and armored personnel carriers are set ablaze. The remaining force tries to retreat, but the Israeli tanks surge forward to demolish many more.

Dawning Recognition

The Egyptian Supreme Command faces a serious problem. From aerial reconnaissance, they now know that this is clearly no ordinary raid, in which the force will return to base upon completion of its mission. The question is whether to recall forces from Sinai, or to thin out the units protecting Cairo.

One sole mechanized division, including the tank brigade known as the Republican Guard, and a paratroop brigade, remain near the capital. An additional force from the Armor School, with obselete tanks, stands in reserve. The paratroop brigade and an armored brigade are sent to erect a new line across the road to Cairo. In parallel, the Second Army is ordered to attack from the north, with a mechanized brigade and two paratroop battalions. The Third Army is to move against the bridgehead from the south, with armored forces from the 4th Division, which will return part of its units to the west bank. The Egyptian Air Force receives orders for intensive action against the Israeli bridgehead.

The air arm today makes its second attempt at deep penetration into Israeli territory. The mission is entrusted to French-made Mirage aircraft, transferred into Egyptian hands by Libya. Six Mirages take off from Tanta, fly at low altitude across the sea and try to penetrate near El Arish — but Israeli planes lie in wait for them. The Israeli pilots are more conversant with the Mirages, and quickly down two of the Egyptian craft. A third plane hits the waves without even being scratched, while the fourth — which is lightly damaged — is abandoned by its pilot. Only two Mirages return to base.

Air Raid

At 15:00 hours, Yehuda Hodeda supervises the link-up of the last bridge pontoon. He doesn't need to push his men; they are working as though possessed. Suddenly, Egyptian MiGs swoop down in the most concentrated attack on the bridgehead — so far. The bombs fall wide apart, but the last pontoon is holed by a rocket. It is no longer safe for tanks, but taking it apart will require considerable time. An engineer officer guides a bridge carrier tank into position to drop its section over the damaged pontoon. The first bridge is ready for traffic at 15:30 hours. The Engineering Corps has beaten the armor to it. Adan's forces are not yet ready to cross.

Sharon exploits the lull around the bridge to renew the proposal that his forces cross first. The time is 16:50 hours. The Chief of Staff is in Southern Command War Room to take Sharon's call.

Elazar: "Arik, your plan doesn't make sense to me. You must hold the bridgehead and let Bren (Adan) pass through!"

Sharon: "This is a historical mistake and a waste of time."

Elazar: "I'm not concerned with history. Pay attention to continuity, carry out and report!"

Sharon doesn't give way. Five minutes later, Sharon calls again to repeat his request. Elazar replies: "First make good on protection of the bridgehead, and afterwards we'll see!"

Lover's Lane

The delay around the bridgehead lasts a long while. Southern Command HQ presses Adan to complete his plans. At 19:45 General Gonen talks to Adan.

Adan: "I need another fifteen minutes!"

Gonen: "No good! You must pass through immediately, without delay!"

Adan: "We need to fuel the tanks before crossing".

Gonen: "First move to the other side. Fill up there."

Some of the tanks refuel in battle on the road close to the Chinese Farm, and at the position called "Missouri". The unit commanders want to cross with full loads of fuel and ammunition. Now, they receive an order to "speed it up".

The first tank races onto the bridge, but the driver is too enthusiastic about his historic task. Instead of five miles an hour, according to the standing orders for pontoon bridge crossings, he is moving at more than 20 mph. The tank suddenly swerves to the right and smashes the railing. More tanks cross, but the bridge weakens at the

249

point where the damage was done; another hold-up until the repair is finished. To prevent further delays, the ferries continue to float tanks across.

Close to 22:00 hours, after the repair, Adan moves across the bridge with his command group. A full moon shines on the water. But for the noise of exploding shells, it could be a romantic stroll. Somebody in the APC pulls out a whiskey bottle, says **"Lechaim"** and passes the bottle around. On the African shore, the short romantic interlude comes to an end. The corps staff are caught in their heaviest and densest bombardment since the beginning of the war. Shells fall around the bridges, killing some of the engineers in the compound.

Keener Eyes

The Soviet advisers attached to the Egyptian General Staff sense the danger of reversal on the front. This evening, they report to the Soviet Prime Minister in Cairo. Russian activity in the Mediterranean has increased. Five Russian landing craft passed through the Bosphorus today, on their way to the Mediterranean. No men were to be seen on deck, but American Intelligence is convinced that more than two battalions of marines are on board. The remaining space is taken up by tanks. The Red Fleet in the Mediterranean now numbers a record 95 ships. Weapons supply to Syria and Egypt has also reached its peak with the arrival of additional Russian ships in port. In Syrian ports – 15 freighters have already unloaded cargoes which include 400 new tanks to replace those lost in battle.

Holiday IV

Long columns from Bren Adan's corps, scheduled to cross the canal tonight and tomorrow, are piling up on the roads to the bridgehead. At the tail-end of one column, a medical aid unit is waiting to cross. Dr. Uri Freund has just finished a letter to his children, Rachel and Yaakov. A letter of joy and sadness, in the best traditions of the

Children of Israel: "You must certainly know that tomorrow is the Feast of the Rejoicing of the Law. Tomorrow, we pray for rain. Tomorrow is also a day of remembrance. Each of us remembers his parents, his ancestors, his family and the dead of our nation. Tomorrow, **Yizkor** is said in memory of soldiers who fell in war – and also in this war. This evening and tomorrow, the festive circling with the Scrolls of the Law will take place, and I hope you will be in synagogue. Next year, we will rejoice for this year too."

In an Air Force base, pilots give way to the beseeching of Habad **Hassidim** – and lay phylacteries before going off on sorties. Some of the bearded **Hassidim** carry palm hearts and citrons, to let the pilots make the traditional blessing associated with this festival. **The Hassidim** say that the palm heart, in the numerical mysticism of Judaism, is equal to the word "life". This blessing will therefore be a virtue for long life. Among units in the field, many comply with requests from their religious comrades to pray with them, lay phylacteries and recite a special injunction written by the Military Rabbinate for those going into battle. On the Golan Heights, where there is far more foliage, many soldiers lay tree branches across their half-tracks, in order to keep the ancient commandment: "Thou shalt build a tabernacle." Many commanders note that the religious among their men are more tranquil and relaxed. Their faith apparently helps them through the most difficult hours with a far greater peace of mind.

OCTOBER 18, 1973

Modified Media

Egyptian official bulletins are no longer the balanced reports of the first days. The official spokesmen mention bitter battles on the central sector, but give little space to the IDF crossing. One communique does say: "During the battle, seven Israeli tanks infiltrated Egyptian lines near the Bitter Lakes, west of the canal. Three tanks were destroyed, and the other four dispersed."

Soviet Prime Minister Alexei Kosygin, spending his third day in Cairo, knows that the Egyptian Army can expect no more victories — only failures. Kosygin's assessment confirms Soviet intelligence information gained from the espionage satellites that criss-cross the battlefield. Once every two days, a satellite lands with photographs of troop movements and the course of battle on the front lines. The Russians made their first attempt to use espionage satellites in deciphering tactical moves — during the India-Pakistan War. Now, they are improving the technique.

Minute to Midnight

The time has clearly come to press for a cease-fire. The Russians have so far refused to respond to American proposals. But, in a phone conversation, Leonid Brezhnev today tells the President of the United States that it would indeed be desirable to stop the Middle East war immediately. He adds that his ambassador in Washington will relay Moscow's cease-fire proposals and a solution for the Israel-Arab dispute to the State Department. An impending cease-fire is the main subject of conversation in State Department corridors, and among Washington newsmen.

Israeli Ambassador Simcha Dinitz, again invited for a talk with Henry Kissinger, hears of the Soviet approach. Israel's timetable is about to come to an end, but the fact isn't yet grasped by the country's political and military leadership. Foreign Minister Eban tells newsmen that he knows nothing of preparations for a cease-fire.

Missile Hunt

As dawn breaks on the west bank of Suez, Adan's forces are smashing through the front lines. The first tanks across were recalled to the Sweet Water Canal and, meanwhile, the Egyptians have poured armor and commando

252

units armed with anti-tank missiles in to the area, so the gaps have to be reopened.

The picture at the front is somewhat different from that described by spokesmen in Cairo. The Egyptians, at a desperate pace, dispatch an armor brigade from the Second Army in the north, to block Adan's speeding tanks. From the south comes a force of Palestinians attached to the Egyptian Army, but they can't stop Adan and Sharon. The air support is better than any as yet given IDF ground forces on the Egyptian front; planes come in waves, and operate near the vanguard.

The Egyptian missile batteries are placed in a mosaic to offer mutual defense; a close umbrella much denser than that erected around Hanoi by the North Vietnamese. As the tanks roar down the west bank, the mosaic is broken, and the planes can choose comfortable approach angles. But the area is still packed with missile positions, shaped like flower petals, and — as Adan's forces move westwards, and then turn south — his tanks are ordered to race from one missile "rose" to another.

Crowded Sky

The second clash with the North Koreans takes place today. There are 30 North Korean pilots stationed south of Cairo, but they make do with defensive missions, in planes bearing Egyptian markings. As on the previous occasion, the Koreans evade battle. There is an exchange of fire, and then they break off contact.

The Israel Air Force has achieved aerial supremacy in the arena. It has already flown 10,000 sorties. Benny Peled, asked by Dayan how long his air force can continue to fight at this rate, replies: "There's no problem. We've got plenty of breathing space!" The Air Force has more planes and pilots than in the Six Day War, and — despite both the prolongation of the war and the losses — the pilots need not fly the same number of daily sorties as they did in 1967. However, the tasks are many times more difficult. The Egyptians and Syrians have already used

253

many thousands of missiles, and some pilots have had scores fired at them.

The Egyptian Air Force is making a special effort today — mainly directed against the Israeli bridge north of the Bitter Lake. Fifteen MiGs attack, immediately followed by four helicopters that try to drop napalm on the bridge. The fate of the helicopters is cruel. Anti-aircraft gunners at the bridge open fire with all weapons, and Israeli aircraft join the chase. All the helicopters are brought down between eucalyptus trees west of the canal. Eight MiGs are also downed. An hour and a quarter later, the Egyptians attack again, only to lose more helicopters and seven MiGs. A third wave comes in the late afternoon. The damage is greater this time, but they still do not succeed in destroying the bridge.

Fallen Friend

The bridgehead area is under incessant bombardment, mostly from the east bank — north and south of the bridges. As a shell falls in the center of the bridge, an armored personnel carrier races across to the west side. The soldiers' eyes pop out as they see Moshe Dayan straighten up inside the APC, and look out over the canal and the men. He's not even wearing a steel helmet. Dayan is going to visit Arik Sharon at his new command post on the west bank. It's an especially difficult day for Arik. An old friend and brother in arms, who reported to Sharon's corps without being mobilized, was struck down near him by the bombardment.

Agam XII

This is Yitzhak Agam's last day of war. Yesterday, his reconnaissance unit again moved north to extend the bridgehead. It is now taking part in the effort to repel the Egyptians from the Chinese Farm. This morning, they are on the same plateau where Rafi Bar Lev's burnt tank is

254

standing. Egyptian shells hunt them out, and there is no hill or dip where they can hide.

Yitzhak Agam will have a clear remembrance of the hour when he is hit. An Israel radio announcer begins reading the 11:00 hours news bulletin, and the broadcast is picked up on a transistor in the APC. The announcer is reporting IDF successes on the canal — as the APC suddenly shudders under a terrific blow. The shock rings like a thousand bells and a fire-ball, crossing through the walls of the APC, blinds the eyes. Agam makes an effort to rise and jump from the burning vehicle. He runs forward and then falls — with spinal injuries. Another five jump out with him. Two more remain in the APC — dead.

Chain Gang

Tank units have begun to tow the bridge parts along the north road where the paratroops fought, following a decision to step up the erection of additional bridges. An offensive by an armored corps cannot be based on one bridge, which has already sustained direct hits. The engineers race to fill each new hole with sand. The second bridge that they intend to erect is the one that was held up on the first day of the crossing, 11 miles from the Canal.

The towing isn't easy. No less than 12 tanks are involved. Cables break from time to time, and they must stop to repair them. Three tractors, noticeable for their bright yellow color, travel before them along the dirt track. These are civilian tractors assigned to removal of any obstacles, and levelling the roadside earthen embankments which interfere with transit of the bridge. The column is led by a jeep in which sits Johnny, the Command Engineer Officer responsible for getting the bridge to the canal. Alongside him sits Chief Engineering Officer Yitzhak Ben Dov.

The road is ostensibly open, but IDF tanks are fighting alongside the neighboring Chinese Farm. A company of tanks has been assigned to protection of the bridge and the towing party. The crews aren't happy. They must

255

travel at the pace of the bridge, converting themselves into almost static targets for Egyptian missiles. Last night, the Egyptians strewed mines along the track, scattered at random, without holes being dug for them. Sappers, travelling in three half-tracks, deal with them. While they are at work, Egyptian shells drop on the road. Defusing mines under shellfire isn't easy. There is no way back as long as the bridge blocks passage. The only option is to remove the mines quickly. Instead of removing the detonators and checking for booby-traps, the sappers must risk lifting and laying them, armed as they are, by the roadside.

Valley of Death

The bridge moves on again. The towing party is passing the area where the paratroops fought yesterday. Scores of Israeli and Egyptian bodies are scattered around. The Israelis are recognizable by their red paratroop boots, while the Egyptians wear black.

"There's another of ours, and another!" Johnny points at bodies of Israeli paratroops.

"Keep moving! Don't look around!" Ben Dov orders. He fears that shock will distract them from the vital task of transferring the second bridge to the canal.

Where the dirt track crosses the road along the Bitter Lake, they pause for a moment. Ben Dov climbs on a big water conduit. The tractors and the bridge are lagging behind. The jeep and three half-tracks stand nearby. Fifteen Egyptian MiGs choose this moment to cross low over them with guns firing and spewing rockets that hit an empty half-track. As they return to drop bombs, two Israeli Mirages appear. The damaged half-track is burning, and some of the Egyptians are already on their bombing run. Ben Dov hears Johnny call "After me", and sees him run towards the entrance of the conduit. Some of the men are behind him. Ben Dov pulls his head down between his shoulders, and waits for the explosions. There is a heavy thunder, and somebody shouts: "Johnny's wounded! Johnny's wounded!"

256

Combat Engineers

Johnny is lying at the entrance to the water conduit. Ben Dov at first believes him injured by the bomb. Then, he notices a huge Egyptian commando lying near Johnny. Both are badly injured and breathing heavily. Blood pours from Johnny's temple. It seems that he encountered Egyptian commandos in the conduit. They must have opened fire simultaneously. Johnny hit the first of them, but was wounded by a bullet in the temple. His men are now cleaning out the conduit with hand grenades.

Johnny dies a short while later. One hour after him, another engineering officer, Yehuda Deleon from Sharon's corps, is killed while directing traffic by the bridge. At 23:00 hours, the bridge slips slowly into the water and across towards the other bank like a giant dinosaur. Now two bridges cross the Suez Canal, 200 yards apart. Men of the naval commando, as a precaution against Egyptian frogmen, throw hand grenades into the water from time to time, and dive under the bridges.

Second Thoughts

While the bridge is still being lowered into the water, a number of helicopters fly the corps commanders to Southern Command HQ. A meeting is set for midnight to discuss coming moves. All now agree that it is worth risking a large part of the third corps. Other forces will remain in Sinai to pin the Egyptians down at their bridgeheads. Bar Lev's plan is for Kalman Magen to replace Sharon at the bridgehead. Bar Lev knows that Sharon has handled the most difficult battle so far — and wants to relieve him. One of Arik's brigades is still fighting by the **Missouri** entrenchment that includes the Chinese Farm and the area north of it.

Adan's corps is to move on the Egyptian army camps alongside the Bitter Lake, while Sharon breaks through towards the town of Suez and the gulf port of Adabiyeh. Sharon's spearhead brigade is already west of the canal, with the paratroops who crossed first. The meeting ends, and the corps commanders part, each to his own command. Bar Lev walks into the small dining room next door. A few moments later, Sharon comes back for a talk with Bar Lev which now leads to a change in missions. Bar Lev calls Magen back to the command post to tell him that his forces will move on Suez and Adabiyeh. Sharon, who already knows the terrain, has requested to enlarge the bridgehead and push north to Ismailia, at the center of the Suez Canal.

INTERLUDE: THE AIR FORCE

Flying Steamroller

On the eve of the Six Day War, there wasn't a single officer in the IDF General Staff or land forces who imagined that the Israel Air Force could achieve such a decisive victory over the Arab air forces. Some senior officers believed that victory was achievable on land, even if the Air Force only scored a draw in the skies. Maj.-General Ezer Weizman told the Command and Staff School that the IAF would destroy Arab air forces in six hours — but he was considered mad.

The result may even have surprised the Air Force. Within 80 minutes, the Egyptian Air Force was eliminated, in practice deciding the outcome in Sinai. One result was greater expectations of the Air Force. Since 1967, it was assumed that the Air Force could, in the event of war, achieve aerial supremacy quickly, serve as the IDF's strategic arm and supply full support to ground forces. Defense plans were based on the Air Force as the major factor. So great was their self-confidence that no other possibility was conceivable. Their success in the War of Attrition, in which the Israel Air Force was the major offensive factor, only served to strengthen the feeling. The missile problem

258

at the end of the War of Attrition was considered a mere episode.

Short War

Since the War of Attrition, I have heard many Air Force officers assess "the next war", and if I sum up what was said — it was a mixture of correct foresight and error. They all assumed that the next war wouldn't be a repeat of the Six Days, or the War of Attrition, but a more massive clash, at a faster combat rate — with higher casualties. However, it would be a short war. The IAF, like the rest of the IDF, didn't believe it could be otherwise. They were right about the nature of the war, but off the mark as far as its duration was concerned. Mordechai Hod, the past O.C. Air Force, said that victory wouldn't be achieved quickly, but the outcome would be obvious much earlier than it was in 1967. Hod's successor, Maj.-General Benny Peled, correctly assumed shortly before the war that the Air Force would have to face more elaborate and massive defense systems. The Air Force clearly felt that the Arab anti-aircraft system wasn't similar to that encountered in the War of Attrition, yet they believed that it could be overcome far more easily than was indeed the case.

The War of Attrition ended when the clash between aircraft and Egyptian and Russian operated missile batteries resulted in stalemate. While the IAF only had to fight SA-2s operated by Egyptians, the planes still enjoyed supremacy. Russian crews, with SA-3 missiles, modern radar equipment and SU-23 radar-guided guns, changed the balance of power.

Washington helped Israel with modern anti-missile electronic equipment, but the War of Attrition ended without a comprehensive answer to the new missile system. The Americans were interested in an immediate end to the conflict — because they also lacked a good enough answer to the Russian missiles. American Deputy Defense Secretary Packard told Israeli Ambassador Yitzhak Rabin that cessation of combat for a year would permit the United States to complete development of counter-missile weaponry.

When the cease-fire took effect, the Air Force started intensive training and development of attack exercises against missile systems. From the U.S., Israel received Shrike missiles — intended to home on missile battery radar. A half a year later, on February 22, 1971, an Air Force officer told military correspondents: "We are convinced we have a full answer to missiles. In July 1970, we didn't have it. Now there will be no serious problems. There will be losses, but smaller than those we sustained on the eve of cease-fire. This should be proven within the first two or three hours of war. We will overcome the whole system within two or three days."

One Thing at a Time

The estimate was over-optimistic. The Air Force could not deal properly with the missile batteries in the beginning because of the burden of interception and ground-support, deep strategic bombing and airfield strike missions. Nobody thought the tasks would be so complex. As a result, attacks on the missile systems were carried out piecemeal. On the day of the canal crossing, there were still dozens of operative missile batteries on the Egyptian front. Six Day War Chief of Staff Rabin said: "The experts painted a different picture of the missiles!' Past O.C. Air Force Ezer Weizman commented: "The Air Force didn't find a full solution to the missile problem, maybe because they didn't learn the subject, and maybe because they were surprised."

Friendly Competition

Yet the Air Force did know a lot about the missile batteries. Their surprise was apparently at the quantities of modern SA-6 missiles, and the appearance of the SA-7 — the shoulder-fired Strella missile — now mounted on trucks like a Katyusha, and fired in salvos of four or eight. The

SA-6 was credited both in the international and Israeli press, with the best results, but analysis of Israeli losses — of 102 planes — teaches that his hasty conclusion is somewhat exaggerated. The SA-6 — defined by experts as a camouflaged weapon, difficult to locate and destroy — downed less aircraft than did the other types of missiles, and the anti-aircraft guns in no way lagged behind. Yet this does not prove that the Russian missiles are poor. Anti-aircraft defense includes both missiles and guns as one system. Each factor in the system complements its partner by covering different ranges and altitudes. The planes damaged by anti-aircraft guns were of course flying at low altitude, but were compelled to do so by the very existence of the missiles.

On the Ball

The IAF started the war with more planes and pilots than ever before; the latter both in absolute terms and in ratio to each plane. Since the Six Day War, the Air Force's carrying power had increased by hundreds of percent. Each sortie involved four times more armaments and yet there was no lack of basic munitions like bombs. The only shortages were in special types of armament, used in immense quantities.   At noon on **Yom Kippur**, the Air Force was at full alert, due to prior warning of a pre-emptive strike. If there was a certain delay in scrambling planes against the Egyptian crossing, it derived from the aborted pre-emptive strike; the planes were armed for an operation of a different type. The Air Force later destroyed most of the Egyptian bridges, and inflicted heavy losses on commando carrying helicopters. But it didn't save the canal. On the Syrian Heights, air power did contribute at this stage. It was the IAF that blocked the Syrian armor on Southern Golan — until reserve ground units arrived.

The IAF's great achievement was undoubtedly the relatively rapid attainment of aerial supremacy over and beyond the front line. The lines weren't hermetically sealed against Arab aircraft and, from time to time, they did penetrate — but they always paid a heavy price. The home front was totally closed; mobilization of reserves, and movement of units to the front progressed without interference, though the Arab air forces possessed 1000 planes. In aerial clashes, the Israeli Air Force held unchallenged supremacy, though it went into battle outnumbered three to one. Israeli pilots achieved by aerial combat what they had done in the Six Day War by surprise attack on airfields. Some 450 Arab aircraft were downed by planes, and another 50 by anti-aircraft fire — missiles and guns. By comparison, the IAF only lost a small percentage of its total casualties in aerial combat. Towards the end, when the Egyptians cast most of their aircraft into the fray, there were days when they lost the equivalent of squadrons. While in the Six Day War, most enemy aircraft were damaged while empty, many Arab pilots were killed in this war — almost half of those whose planes were hit.

Communications Gap

The IAF's success wasn't so indisputable as far as ground support was concerned. The aerial presence was felt in the critical stages on the Golan Heights, but less so on the Southern front. There was an impression that current operational communications between the air and ground forces were sometimes incomplete. Ezer Weizman comments that, in some situations, the Air Force seemed to be reading the battle picture incorrectly.

On the Egyptian front, the Air Force was hampered by the dense missile system though it didn't affect the approach to targets deep in enemy territory. From the moment of political approval for deep strategic bombing, the Air Force reached every assigned target. The approval was only given for Syria — the minor Arab partner. In the case of Egypt, the IAF limited its action to the front lines alone, though Egypt waged war elsewhere, as for example, the blockade of Bab-el-Mandab Straits. The political echelon hesitated to approve missions deep in Egypt.

Cheap at the Price

The war ended with Air Force losses of 102 aircraft; a large number when compared with the total available, and with those lost in previous wars. Nevertheless, Air Force officers claim that, by comparison with the duration and intensity of this war — the losses were not great. The yardstick must be the ratio of aircraft lost to the number of sorties flown. During six days of combat in 1967, the Air Force lost 45 of its planes. In this war, Israel lost more than a quarter of her initial aircraft — in 18 days of most intensive combat. The Air Force operated for three times as long, and flew 12,000 sorties. By comparison with the number of sorties, the Six Day War percentage of losses per sorties reached 1.9, against a smaller number of missile batteries. In attacks on airfields alone, the losses per sorties reached 4%, despite the complete surprise enjoyed by IAF planes. In October 1973, the ratio was 0.9%. The number of crewmen lost was higher, but some of the planes now flew with two-man crews — a pilot and navigator.

OCTOBER 19, 1973

Higher Echelons

The IDF's front-line successes have transferred the point of gravity to Washington and Moscow. The Kremlin wants a cease-fire on the Egyptian front, before it is too late. There are only a few score Egyptian tanks facing the IDF forces on the west bank, and the Russians have no way of knowing that Israel isn't interested in Cairo. No relationship exists between Israel and the Soviet Union, but there are unofficial contacts between Washington and Egypt. If the Kremlin could be sure that Israel doesn't intend to take Cairo, her reactions might be less sharp.

Alexei Kosygin hastens back to Moscow, while the Russian Ambassador to Washington is informing Dr.

Kissinger that the Soviet Union is interested in a cease-fire
— today: "It's a matter of hours, and not days!" Ambassador Dobrynin already has a draft resolution to place
before the U.N. Security Council. Dr. Kissinger points out
that the resolution necessitates preliminary discussion. The
Russian now resorts to a menacing tone: "The Soviet
Union will not allow Cairo to fall. The problem must be
solved today." Washington already knows that the
Russians transferred MiG 25 squadrons to Egypt yesterday.

Lay it on the Line

Dr. Kissinger already met Israel Ambassador Simcha
Dinitz an hour ago, to discuss the time needed for Israel to
complete her missions on the Egyptian front. Kissinger's
latest information is that the Israeli Chief of Staff believes
he needs another four or five days. Dinitz stressed that
each additional day would be another blow against the
Egyptian forces; the objective is not to seize territories,
but to break the Egyptian army. Now it looks as though
Israel will not have the required time.

Dr. Kissinger now phones Dinitz to tell him of the
Dobrynin meeting, and the Kremlin's demand. The United
States has reason to believe that — without an immediate
cease-fire — the Russians are likely to intervene, and
Kissinger explains that he doesn't want them to appear as
the Arabs' saviour: "The Russians demanded immediate
debate, here in Washington, implying a cease-fire to take
effect tomorrow. To gain an extra day for Israel, I
informed them that the debate will be in Moscow. Please
inform your Prime Minister that I am going to Moscow."

Friend in Need VII

Washington also isn't particularly interested in Arab
degradation. The United States neither wants an Israeli
failure, nor a decisive victory that will make later negotiation difficult. A hint is to be found in President Nixon's

speech to Congress, as he requests $2.2 billion defense assistance for Israel: "The United States is making every effort to end the dispute quickly and honorably, in days and not in weeks." Before coming to Congress, he sent a letter to Golda Meir, clarifying that cease-fire is also necessary for the United States. The U.S. arms airlift has already caught up with some IDF needs. Israel is back to her original number of Phantom aircraft, priority having been given to these planes — which were flown across the Atlantic and the Mediterranean, with stops on American aircraft carriers to refuel. Some Skyhawk aircraft have also been flown in from Europe; the rest will come by ship together with helicopters, guns and other equipment.

The only aspect in which the Americans have been tight-fisted is in the number of tanks supplied to Israel. Together with electronic equipment supplied to neutralize Russian missiles, Israel is also receiving American electronics experts; electronic warfare is now a focal point of interest for experts from various armies.

Three Lane Highway

Israel is now dictating the moves on the battlefield. The Egyptians continue to bombard the bridgehead, but mainly from areas under Egyptian control in Sinai, and they cannot prevent the army engineers beginning a third bridge across the canal, on pontoons, like the first.

The Egyptian Army has failed to block IDF forces on the west bank, so the Supreme Command is now throwing most of its air reserve into the breach. Planes so far kept south of the battle zone are now brought up to forward airfields. As in previous days, the Egyptian aircraft are attacking in large waves: Sukhois with MiG 21s protecting them from above. But the Egyptian Air Force is clearly suffering a lack of pilots; many have been killed in battle, and veterans from among command and staff echelons are being recruited to fill the gaps.

Today's top IAF score is held by a reserve pilot who is a trainee in an attorney's office. Yesterday, he downed 4

MiG 21s in two sorties. Today, his luck is still in. In one sortie, he hits and downs 4 MiG 21s, three by gunfire, and one by a missile. He now holds the Israeli record for 14 enemy planes to his credit.

West of Suez, the offensive is gaining impetus. Magen's corps is already 16 miles into Egypt. Adan's forces have turned southwards, and are attacking rear echelons of the Egyptian Third Army. In one place, Adan's tanks have penetrated a division command post which is still occupied. In Sinai, the Egyptian forces show no signs of withdrawal, but on the west bank — they are in flight.

Within two days, 1000 prisoners have been taken in Egypt. Following the Syrian example, the Egyptians are now blaming their failure on the United States. The Egyptian Army spokesman in Cairo claims a captured Israeli pilot told his interrogators that 35 Phanton aircraft with American pilots have reached Israel.

Arik V

While Adan and Magen's forces probe southwards to encircle the Egyptian Third Army, Arik Sharon is turning north towards the Second Army. The terrain through which he must operate is thick with foliage, villages and water canals. He has to advance on both sides of the canal, but understands that to cut off the Second Army, and approach Ismailia from the rear — he must place the emphasis on the west bank. To the east — his mission is to push the Egyptians from the **Missouri** entrenchment to enlarge the bridgehead.

The Chief of Staff today meets Sharon for the first time since establishment of the IDF's bridgehead over Suez. The rendezvous takes place in Africa, north of the bridgehead. Sharon tells Elazar: "Dado, it's a terrible war. A terrible war, I tell you. We never had anything like it. The Six Day War was only one battle."

The two draw aside for a private conversation. Four months ago, Sharon decided to leave the IDF, after Dado made it clear that Gonen would be appointed OC Southern

Command in his place. Sharon wasn't offered another job, and the Defense Minister didn't find it necessary to intervene on his behalf. Up to his retirement from the IDF, Sharon had maintained correct relations with Elazar, and on General Staff operative planning – their viewpoints were for the most part identical. The quiet conversation in no way reveals the tension that now exists between the two.

The Chief of Staff's helicopter is making its way back, over the canal and the bridges. The pilot inadvertently strays into the area of the Egyptian Third Army in Sinai. Suddenly, Egyptian soldiers and vehicles appear below. The helicopter is fired on, with damage to the hydraulic system, but the pilot succeeds in evading. Not long ago, on the same route but in the opposite direction, another helicopter was hit. This one carried a medical team. Its pilot reported being under fire, and then – silence.

OCTOBER 20, 1973

Talkfest

Cease fire discussions between Leonid Breznhev and Dr. Kissinger open in the Kremlin today. Israeli representatives in Washington are making an effort to persuade the Americans not to mention Resolution 242 – which speaks of withdrawal from territories conquered in the Six Day War – in any proposed Security Council resolution. The Americans say they will try but will not insist if it endangers chances of a cease-fire. President Nixon is prepared to guarantee rejection of any proposal for discussions under the auspices of France and Britain.

The Israeli Ambassador in Washington is periodically informed about the Moscow discussions – until he is told by the State Department that there is a technical hitch in communications with Russia. The partial details are enough for Israel to conclude that, within a day or two at most, a cease-fire decision will be taken in the Security Council, with the agreement of both the US and USSR. Nevertheless, Dayan in a television interview repeats Abba Eban's comments that he knows of nothing special about any US initiative for cease-fire; in Dayan's evaluation, the Arabs aren't yet prepared for peace or cease-fire.

The Truth will Out

Soviet radio for the first time reports an Israeli victory on the Egyptian front: "Israeli groups are breaking through near the Bitter Lakes!" There is no more chance to deny or ignore the IDF presence west of Suez, or relate to it as a small commando raid. Clearly, a large-scale encircling battle is in progress, and the problem isn't the IDF's proximity to Cairo, but who will hold the main roads. The more northerly Cairo-Suez road is already under heavy IDF artillery fire.

Closing Noose

The force of two army corps that is on its way to encircling the Third Army is the most successful; it is operating with ease in convenient terrain. Sharon's progress is slower. South of Ismailia, the Egyptians have breeched the Sweet Water Canal, converting a vast area into heavy mud and quicksand. Israeli and Egyptian tanks have floundered up to their turrets. Infantry have to be used to mop up in the foliage, and advance along the single track, where they present easy targets for Egyptian fire.

This morning, the IDF's third bridge is complete. All three are within 500 yards of each other. Transit is now convenient and quick, and the IDF has already transferred some 50% of its available tanks on the Egyptian front. The Egyptians are also withdrawing armor from Sinai, apparently in the hope of blocking the IDF offensive.

The Air Force now has freedom of the skies over the front lines. The armor has accounted for 10 missile batteries, though in a number of other places, the tanks only found dummies. The Air Force has taken care of most of the other batteries — around Port Said, Qantara District and in the south — around Suez town.

The Supreme Command believes that, by cease-fire, the IDF will control the west bank from Ismailia to Suez, forcing the Egyptians to evacuate Sinai; if they don't — they will fall in the bag like ripe fruit. Then Israel will control most of both banks, while the Egyptians will only hold the sector north of Ismailia.

Cat and Mouse

On the Mediterranean, the Egyptian Navy isn't operating east of the Nile but, with the front line crumbling, they have apparently decided to try their luck against Israeli shipping at sea. This is no simple matter because, with active maritime traffic on the Mediterranean, the Egyptian submarines must be sure that the ships in their sights are Israeli.

They choose to hunt the sea passages close to Crete. Till now, 115 freighters have reached Israeli ports since **Yom Kippur** — including many bringing arms and war equipment. All passed safely, without sighting Egyptian submarines, but today — two submarines are tracking a ship. It succeeds in evading them.

OCTOBER 21, 1973

Relentless Clock

On this, the sixteenth morning, the Israeli commanders feel that their time is running out. Early today, Elazar phones Gonen, to tell him that Israel will accept the cease-fire proposal. Kissinger is reported as having already agreed with the Russians, and the UN Security Council will resolve on cease-fire tomorrow evening. At Southern Command HQ, the subject is raised to Deputy Prime Minister

Yigal Allon, who is visiting today. Allon estimates that they have another three days. He later tells Sharon that there is enough time to complete his missions.

Southern Command staff are aware that they must hurry. The corps commanders are under constant pressure to complete their tasks. Magen's forces are moving up onto the main Cairo-Suez road. His tanks are now in the westernmost sector, deep in Egyptian territory. Adan's corps is fighting by the Bitter Lakes, in an area of Egyptian army camps and airfields built by the British in the two world wars. South of the lakes, Adan is trying to get to Suez town and the canal, to complete the first encirclement. Magen is to make a wider and deeper move, aimed at trapping the entire Third Army. Sharon's men are still fighting every yard of the way to Ismailia. Arik has moved five miles up the west bank of Suez, but — in Sinai to the east, the bridgehead is still narrow; it extends a mere two and a half miles from the compound.

In Southern Command War Room, the coming moves are being debated. The Defense Minister, Lt.-General Elazar, Bar Lev and Gonen are surrounded by officers and staff members. Bar Lev is chairing the meeting. Elazar wants most of the effort devoted to the south; encirclement of Ismailia and the Second Army doesn't seem realistic to him. The chances in the south look better, though he isn't interested in over-extending himself even in this direction. He would prefer smaller yet more certain achievements. Encirclement of the Third Army looks like work for another three days, so Elazar thinks it best to advance close to the Bitter Lakes, then southwards along the canal itself.

Gonen is more optimistic, and more demanding. He suggests encircling the Third Army in a wide sweep, well to the west of the lakes. Then, he wants his forces to race south along the Gulf of Suez. He is against surrounding Ismailia and the Second Army for both technical and tactical reasons.

Moshe Dayan is the only one in favor of a parallel movement north towards Ismailia. As far as the south is concerned, he doesn't like the idea of an advance along the Gulf of Suez coast. He also doesn't think a wide westward sweep, as Gonen suggests, will be worthwhile. He prefers to stick close to the lakes, according to Elazar's suggestion, and perhaps the erection of another bridge over the canal south of the Small Bitter Lake.

Storm Brewing

Most attention is being paid to the west bank — the Egyptian hinterland — but something is happening in Sinai which is going to cause endless headaches to the Supreme Command. The Egyptian entrenchment code-named "Missouri" on IDF maps is north of the bridgehead, on the flank of the Egyptian Second Army. It extends over five miles, and is two and a half miles deep. Its northern sector is a line parallel with the Timsach Lake, while the southern is the Chinese Farm.

Missouri has been spoken of since the moment that the canal crossing was planned north of the Bitter Lake. Its conquest was proposed, and nobody disagreed — for it was essential. An Egyptian infantry brigade is positioned in Missouri, and threatens to foray southwards, onto the roads to the bridgehead. Even without straddling the roads, the Egyptians in Missouri can cut them by anti-tank missile fire. Sharon's forces were intended, on the first night of the crossing, to gain control over part of Missouri, and push the Egyptians back north of the bridgehead.

If I had a Hammer

Missouri hasn't yet been taken. So far, all the effort has gone into the bridgehead and the two roads south of the entrenchment. The paratroops blunted their teeth on the Chinese Farm, and the armor hasn't penetrated much deeper. Elazar has been repeatedly asking Bar Lev and Gonen: "What's happening at Missouri? Why hasn't Missouri been taken?"

271

Yesterday Egyptian soldiers were still holding Missouri, though the Air Force allowed them no respite. Since October 17, planes have incessantly dropped bombs — more than on any other position. The ground is now pitted with craters, but the Egyptians are staying put. Yesterday, Sharon thought they were finally leaving and reported to Bar Lev that the reatreat had already begun. He was informed, by his forward units, that Egyptian trucks were collecting soldiers in Missouri.

Sharon's eyes are on Ismailia. When he asked permission for his corps to operate northwards, he hoped to achieve in Ismailia what Bren Adan and Magen are now doing to the Egyptian Third Army. His emphasis was placed on the west bank, on the assumption that the Missouri entrenchment would fall by itself in the second stage. This morning, he is specifically ordered to stop his advance on the west bank — and to deal with Missouri. At 09:48 hours, Gonen tells Sharon: "Transfer the main effort to Missouri. Move the vanguard brigade from the west, and even part of another unit. Missouri must be taken. It needn't be done in minutes. Let the Air Force work for an hour or two, and then move in ..."

The Air Force continues bombing. Meanwhile, one of the ships trapped in the Great Bitter Lake is engaging Sharon's attention. Katyusha fire has been opened on IDF units from this ship. The Egyptians seem to have taken it over, and permission is now given to return the fire.

Arik VI

At noon, the attack on Missouri hasn't yet started. At 12:17 hours, Arik Sharon is again pressed to begin. Now he insists that he sees no military logic in the order. Arik: "In place of investing Missouri, we should move directly to cut their supply lines. I prefer to go northwards instead of east."

Gonen: "Listen, we want Missouri. It takes priority. It's already been more attacked from the air than any other place in this war."

Arik: "That may be, but I think that attacking Missouri is a mistake. It's possible to go north and cut off Ismailia and the roads to it, and not go eastwards."

Gonen: "Then the order is to go for Missouri, and not north."

Arik: "See here, we are carrying out orders. The order is really not logical, but we'll carry it out."

Gonen: "If you want to appeal, Haim (Bar Lev) will be with you in half an hour ..."

The Defense Minister is in the War Room while this debate is going on, but departs without comment. The argument with Sharon now moves to his own HQ. This time, he tries to convince Bar Lev; assaulting Missouri is banging our heads against a wall, while Ismailia is an important objective, and its encirclement will be a psychological shock to the Egyptians. Bar Lev agrees in principle, but says: "We're approaching cease-fire, and a bridgehead like this one isn't good for us."

At 15:00 hours, Sharon attacks Missouri, with a brigade that has remained on the east bank. At first, the attack goes as planned, but then the tanks run into mines, and three roll to a stop. Others are hit by missiles and RPG rockets. Four tanks reach the heart of the entrenchment, while the assault force seizes about a mile of the Egyptian trenches, but the attack slowly wanes; the force isn't sufficient. Fourteen damaged tanks are trapped on the field, with no possibility of rescuing all their crews.

The news of the failure is traumatic. Southern Command HQ is convinced that the attacking force should have been augmented, and given more serious support. Sharon will later say: "I still curse myself for carrying out the order. It leaves me no peace. I objected and objected, and finally carried it out. It ended in heavy losses."

Do Not Disturb

Gonen's staff demand of Sharon that he returns to the attack. Gonen himself tells Arik that the Egyptian force is low on ammunition. Sharon is again ordered to transfer units from the west bank, as support for a renewed assault. As time goes by and nothing happens, Gonen calls again, but is told that Sharon is too busy to answer; he is describing the situation for newspapermen who have reached his HQ. Later, the OC Southern Command is told that the corps commander is asleep, and can't be disturbed. Southern Command learns, from members of Sharon's staff, that the corps doesn't intend to renew the assault on Missouri. Close to midnight, Gonen finally talks to Sharon. The hour is 23:59:

Gonen: "Good evening! "

Sharon: "Good evening! "

Gonen: "Do you intend to reinforce T (the unit already at Missouri, which was to renew the attack) for the assault? "

Sharon: "No! I have nothing with which to reinforce it! "

Gonen: "With A (the vanguard unit)."

Sharon: "Under no condition whatsoever! "

Gonen: "Then I tell you to reinforce it! "

Sharon: "Definitely not! "

Gonen: "Then know that this is insubordination! "

Sharon: "What? "

Gonen: "Insubordination! "

Sharon: "Really, leave me alone. Don't bother me with things like that! "

Gonen: "Alright then, I am ordering you to reinforce! "

Sharon: "I don't have with what."

Gonen: "With A."

Sharon: "I don't have with what."

Gonen: "O.K., goodnight! "

Sharon: "Goodnight, goodnight! "

Gonen (to those present in the War Room): "It won't end like that ..."

Gonen turns to Bar Lev. He is noticeably angry at such a blatant disregard for his authority. "Listen here, I am the front commander. You are an ex-chief of staff, and a representative of the present Chief of Staff. It's not pleasant to have to tell you that the order isn't being carried out. I'm asking you to tell him. This isn't a matter of prestige. They'll attack again and won't take it. This will be an unsupported assault."

Bar Lev talks with Sharon, who announces that he will reinforce the forces. Five tanks do cross the canal eastwards but still the attack doesn't take place. While the tanks are moving up to join the assault force, Sharon contacts the Defense Minister. It is 04:00 hours, and Dayan is in the Supreme Command post in Tel Aviv. Sharon explains what has been demanded of him, clarifies his position and asks for the order to be rescinded.

In the early hours of morning, Maj.-General Tal contacts Gonen and says that the Defense Minister told him an assault on Missouri would be suicide. "The Minister asked me — what do we want with Missouri?" Now, Tal orders Gonen not to assault Missouri, based on the Defense Minister's recommendation. Tal has also received the Chief of Staff's approval to hold up the attack. Elazar is convinced that the assault is being carried out with insufficient force, and it would be better to let it drop.

After the war, Gonen will press charges of insubordination against Sharon. In a letter to Elazar, Gonen will say that Sharon refused to carry out a battlefield order, and bypassed the chain of command. (He has twice approached the Chief of Staff with a demand to dismiss Sharon; on October 9, and after the battle for the bridgehead and the crossing.) Arik Sharon will answer Gonen's charges with an admission of insubordination, justified by his concern for his men.

Relief of Hermon II

The war with Syria began and is to end with a battle for Mount Hermon. The fall of the mountain fortress — since the Six Day War, Israel's most reported holding — was a shock so great that, up to October 15, the censorship allowed no publication. Now the Israeli public learns of it indirectly; the Syrians cannot be pushed back, unless they are there in the first place.

Despite Golani's earlier failure, the Supreme Command and Northern Front HQ know that the IDF must try time and again to repel the Syrians. They now decide that the Israeli Hermon will not be enough; the campaign must include the higher peaks of Syrian Hermon. For this purpose, two crack brigades — Golani and the paratroops — are assembled. Golani is to make another attempt at taking the Israeli position, while the paratroops seize the three higher points that overlook it.

Each force is allowed to choose its own method of attack. Golani decides to operate independently head on to the fortress; the same direction from which they assaulted it on the third day of war. As proud infantrymen, they elect to advance on foot. One battalion will climb the mountain by two paths, and another force will move up the asphalt road, led by tanks and half-tracks; exactly the routes they used the first time. The OC Northern Command and his deputy approve all the details of the Golani plan.

First Class Passengers

After considerable thought, the paratroops opt to travel by helicopter. They have to reach the rear of the Hermon — its western rib. On foot, they must cross "Fatahland" on the Lebanese-Syrian border, wasting many hours, and fighting terrorists en route. One way or another, they will arrive exhausted. In any case, in the event of failure, they will have to be evacuated by helicopters. This way, the force will reach its jump-off point fresh, but —

will have to traverse ravines and wadis that teem with terrorist groups, who are likely to lash out at the overloaded craft.

Two different attack methods, and each brigade believes the other has chosen the more dangerous way. In Northern Command HQ, the anxiety is for the paratroops, because the helicopters are more vulnerable on the way to the target. Before the paratroops embark, Maj.-General Hofi asks two battalion commanders: "Now, my veteran foxes, will you do it?" Haka Hofi is a paratrooper himself and easily finds a common language with the two, both of whom are reservists. Elisha from **Kibbutz** Ramat Yochanan is a veteran of the paratroops' retaliation actions in the 1950s. Hezi, an economist and senior executive of Nesher Cement Company, participated in the airborne attack on Um Katef in the Six Day War. They answer: "We'll do it, and perhaps without losses!" Hofi, troubled by the long flight along the flank of Hermon, senses more than a hint of braggadocio. "I don't ask you to say that," he retorts. "If you cross through enemy territory, over Fatahland, and reach a landing — you'll have done the main job ..."

Shuttle Service

The use of helicopters obliges the paratroops to start their operation in daylight. While the men of Golani are assembling near the Druse village of Majdal Shams and waiting for nightfall, the paratroops embark on their aircraft. The pilots say they cannot negotiate the deep canyons after dark, and the transfer and disembarkation of the two paratroop battalions must be completed by 17:30 hours. They have their work cut out; a 9000 ft. climb by a twisting route exposed to terrorist positions, quick location of the landing site, and a return for another trip.

While the paratroops crowd into their helicopters, Israeli artillery begins to soften-up the Syrian positions. A relatively large number of guns and mortars have been assembled, and Air Force planes are lending a hand.

The first helicopter lands at 14:20 hours. It isn't really

a landing; because of the slope of the terrain, the helicopter rests on two wheels. The paratroops burst forth and race forwards as far as possible from the landing zone, which will certainly soon be a target for Syrian artillery. A helicopter brings a few dozen paratroops every 15 minutes. The air support is very close and successful. The planes fire rockets and cannons at the Syrian positions, and drop smoke bombs. Syrian commandos are a few hundred yards from the landing zone, prancing around on the ridges, and apparently surprised by the Israeli entry through the back door. Syrian help arrives very quickly. Artillery shells begin to probe around the landing zone. As Hezi's helicopter rises out of the canyon, he can see two enemy MiGs flying overhead.

View from the Gallery

A large-scale aerial battle has been going on above the paratroops' heads for 10 minutes. Three MiGs fall and the paratroops cheer. Another four crash deeper in the Syrian valley. The paratroops aren't worried by the aircraft. Their anxiety is over the artillery shells, against which they are defenceless. Hezi orders them to lie close to the spine of the ridge on the west side, where it's like a long knife blade; short-ranged shells must fall on the eastern slope, while the others will drop on the west slope far below the men. This assumption proves correct. The heavy bombardment only claims one casualty, an officer who is walking along the ridge.

At 15:30 hours, the Syrians try another tactic; five heavy helicopters, loaded with Syrian commandos, attempt to land in the area — but are easy prey for the Israeli aircraft. Two are downed by missiles, and a third crashes while beating a hasty retreat. The other two get away. The aircraft also pound a number of Syrian tanks on the winding road up from the valley near Arna village. Meanwhile, an Israeli helicopter is climbing from the landing zone, at an altitude of 7200 ft., to the highest peak of Hermon, at 8500 ft. In the helicopter are a small group of

278

soldiers and a gunnery officer. They will spot Syrian movements from above, and direct Israeli artillery fire.

Dress for the Occasion

As evening closes in the mountain air is colder, and prolonged prostration on the ridge doesn't help the body heat. Despite the heavy fire, a soldier in Hezi's command group suggests changing into the long woollen underwear from their packs. The first to pull off his pants and don the long johns is Paul Meiberg. Rafi Sivoni, a Moroccan immigrant and Tel Aviv women's hairdresser in civilian life, jokes at the sight of Paul in underpants while shells are falling all around, but shortly afterwards follows his example.

At 17:00 hours, Hezi's battalion begins to move. This battalion is to take the "Serpentine" and "Crevice" positions. Elisha's battalion, which will follow in reserve, will later move through to take the Syrian Hermon position. Before setting out, Hezi repeats: "Work slowly. I don't want heroic charges. We'll use fire power and cover each other. You've got plenty of time." He has cover from batteries of 160 millimeter mortars and 155 millimeter guns. A rolling barrage will precede him.

Downhill Stroll

Uzi Zur, a member of **Kibbutz** Shamir at the foot of Hermon, commands the vanguard company of veteran paratroops, most aged 30 or over. They have considerable combat experience, and are no longer at the age for wild charges. The thin mountain air also discourages fast movement or running. To get to the Serpentine position, at a height of 5400 ft., they must descend a steep slope. The position is alongside the road that snakes up from Arna. Movement is slow, and enemy fire heavy. The only man lost from Hezi's battalion is killed here. Menachem Fineblat from Pardes Hanna leads the point section. He is hit in the forehead by a shot at close range.

279

Two and a half hours after the start of the action, the Serpentine Position is in the paratroops' hands. The Syrian commandos have bolted, leaving seven bodies behind. Uzi's company places a road block on a nearby curve – at just the right moment. Within minutes, a convoy of 6 Syrian trucks draws to a halt by the block. This is a heavy mortar unit sent, too late, to aid the Syrian commando. One truck escapes the ambush, and the men of the convoy all bolt.

The paratroops must still climb to the Crevice Position, 1800 ft. higher than the Serpentine. Shai Lyn's company is now in the lead. Shai is a member of a **kibbutz** – Afikim – like many others in the battalion. The tall Shai with his ready smile is an electronics engineer. He also ensures a slow advance, allowing the artillery screen to move in front and do its own work.

The struggle for this position lasts four hours. Every crevice is deluged in lead as the paratroops advance. Shai's men find the bodies of 15 Syrian commandos in the crannies and emplacements. The rest have run down the eastern slope. The Syrian commander and two men are lying in the command post, killed outright by a mortar bomb. Some of the dead Syrians are wearing items of IDF uniform, apparently taken from the Hermon position and Israeli prisoners of war. Some have Israeli identification papers and disks in their pockets.

Esprit de Corps

Shai is obviously advancing steadily, so Hezi decides to proceed with the next stage. Close to 02:00 hours, Elisha's men pass through on their way to the Syrian Hermon. This position overhangs in a threatening fashion causing considerable anxiety. However, it soon becomes clear that the Syrian commandos abandoned the position, when they realized that the Israelis were moving from the inside outwards. The Syrian Hermon falls without a shot.

Now, Elisha's paratroops would like to move on to the Israeli Hermon as rear support for Golani. The fire there is denser and heavier, but Golani opts to finish the job alone, without assistance from paratroops. At first light, commandos begin to appear — retreating from the Israeli Hermon. This isn't disorderly flight; they even exchange fire with the paratroops, killing one of Elisha's men. A Syrian wants to surrender, but his comrades shoot him in the chest. With a curse, he drops his gun and marches towards the paratroops as blood pours down his body. When the Syrians realize their road is blocked, they surrender.

The Hermon is again demanding blood from Golani Brigade. Its men are conscripts aged 18-20, in first-rate physical condition. They successfully stand up to the effort of an eight-hour climb up the Hermon slopes. But, the Syrians are waiting for them and, as in the previous attack, have chosen a correct tactic. They don't fight from within the position itself, but sit on the ridges in front of it, and the road that curves round the mountain.

A number of tanks lead the column along the asphalt track. The first goes up on a mine, while others are hit by bazooka shells. Close to the upper station of the skiers' cable railway, the road is sown with land mines. The battle is bitter and the column draws to a halt.

The climbers engage the enemy at dawn. At first light, the column is passing by the hill under the fortress, where the Syrians have stationed a unit of 28 volunteers, commanded by a company officer. They're well hidden on the slope, and pick off the advancing men at close range. Other Syrians are sniping from the many crevices and rocks. Artillery support is no longer effective as the soldiers are strung out over an extensive area, close to the Syrian commandos. There is no alternative but to stop the gun fire.

Golani Grit

Daylight finds the men of Golani pinned to the ground. Hand grenades are being thrown from side to side over distances of a few yards. The rising sun blinds the attacking force. The toll of wounded is mounting by the minute, and dozens of dead are strewn across the slope, some lying upon each other — where men hastening to save their comrades are also hit. The number of combat-fit men declines hour by hour. Wounded must be evacuated quickly, and each stretcher needs four bearers.

The men of Golani sense that the brigade's pride depends on this battle. Before moving out, their commander explained the importance of the Hermon, and described Golani's blood bond with it. Many of the soldiers nickname the Hermon position "The Eyes of Israel", and fight for it as though it was the Wailing Wall. The brigade commander, one of the first into battle, is now among the wounded. The men charge again and again. Squads try to outflank the Syrian snipers. At 09:00 hours approximately, on the morning of October 22, the Syrian commandos begin to give themselves up. Among them is the company commander whose men sniped at and hit scores of Golani soldiers. The mountain is covered in a pall of smoke. The men of Golani enter the Israeli position, where so many of their comrades have given their lives. At 10:53 exactly, a soldier named Ali climbs the flag-mast, to unfurl two flags — of Israel and of the brigade. The Hermon is again in IDF hands, but the price is heavy. This time, Golani has paid with 61 dead. While the helicopters still evacuate the many wounded, men are combing the tracks around the fortress — looking for bodies of their comrades from the previous battles.

OCTOBER 22, 1973

Suicidal Scandal

The Missouri affair still persists. Moshe Dayan, after acquiescing to last night's intervention on Sharon's behalf, comes early this morning to visit Arik's army corps. He chats a while with Sharon, and then proceeds to Southern Command HQ. He races down the bunker steps, his bodyguard – armed with a Kalachnikov made in China – chasing behind him. He is plainly angry. Inside the War Room, he convenes a number of the senior officers. His remarks are obviously directed primarily at Maj.-General Gonen. Lt.-General (Res.) Bar Lev isn't present. He has gone to a meeting with the General Staff, and the Prime Minister.

Dayan opens his broadside: "You told him to take Missouri. It's a scandal. An attack on Missouri is suicide." The Defense Minister isn't satisfied with a mere military assessment. He goes on to level a serious accusation: "There is in this command a political reaction to all Sharon's proposals." Gonen retorts: "Arik is waging a private war."

New Teacher

Dayan appears to have adopted Sharon's operative approach for himself: "I prefer Ismailia to encirclement of the Third Army. It's important to isolate the Second Army. Ismailia is important politically." Dayan looks at the map and, with his finger traces downwards, southwards, inside Sinai – to stop on the Egyptian positions facing the Small Bitter Lake: "Capture that entrenchment! What is G. doing? His force hasn't operated through the whole war. Tell him to take that position."

A professional discussion ensues. Gonen only explains military considerations, but the accusation of political bias has obviously offended him deeply. He explains that to take Ismailia, and isolate the Second Army is a new war, while the encirclement of the Third Army is almost complete. A move north necessitates fording two sweet water canals. The Second Army flanks, in an area of swamps and dunes, are packed solid with missile batteries and artillery. Total encirclement is impossible, since the Second Army will be able to receive supplies from Port Said to the north. Gonen goes on to say that the conquest of the Egyptian positions, inside Sinai, facing the Small Bitter Lake, is impossible. The Israeli force facing it has insufficient tanks, and those that it does have are obsolete Shermans. Such an assault would necessitate a force of corps strength. The cease-fire will take effect this evening, and there isn't enough time.

Dayan sticks to his opinion, unconvinced by Gonen's reasoning. Gonen tries to stall by passing the buck: "Give an order to the Chief of Staff. If Dado instructs me to carry the plan out, I'll try to convince him that it isn't worth it."

Dayan is furious. He stalks out of the War Room, leaving a heavy pall behind him. This is his last visit to Southern Command HQ. He will not return until Gonen is replaced by the Deputy Chief of Staff, Maj.-General Yisrael Tal.

Command Confirmed

As Dayan leaves, Gonen calls the Chief of Staff. A short conversation, and Elazar orders him to continue the missions previously allotted. The objective now is to gain as much as possible before the cease-fire.

Encirclement of the Egyptian Third Army isn't yet complete, but IDF forces are in full attack. Magen's deputy, who has replaced a brigade commander injured in battle, has reached Kilometer 101 on the Suez-Cairo road. His Centurions are fueled, armed and ready for a move west towards Cairo. He asks permission to continue, but is ordered to stay put at Kilometer 101.

Adan's forces are fully engaged with the enemy in the verdant area close to the canal. His brigades are fighting among army camps, west of the Bitter Lakes, where pockets of Egyptian, Palestinian and Kuwaiti units still remain. Air support makes it easier, and the area has been cleansed of most of its missiles. Of 61 anti-aircraft missile batteries at the beginning of the war, only eight remain. Most of the job has been done by the Air Force, but land forces have hit and taken more than ten batteries, some intact — including an almost complete SA-6 missile.

The planes supply substantial support in armored

battles, but not when the tanks encounter Egyptian infantry. Despite the panic-stricken flight of many west bank Egyptian units, multitudes are still prepared to fight Israeli tanks at close quarters. The dense foliage along the canal makes it easy for them. As darkness falls — and the cease-fire approaches — the Egyptians become even bolder. They inflict heavy damage on nine tanks and two APCs in one of Adan's armored battalions. The rest of the unit is only with difficulty extricated from the trap of foliage, water canals and mines.

Arik VII

Sharon's forces have the main Ismailia-Cairo road covered, but Arik isn't satisfied. His reconnaissance units and paratroops are advancing slowly in the suburbs of Ismailia, followed by a column of vehicles and armor. Their way is blocked by the town's sewage plant, at the southern entrance. Two Egyptian commando battalions, with a sizeable quantity of anti-tank missiles, hold the road. The fire is heavy, and the casualties mount. Darkness falls. The hour of cease-fire approaches. Magen and Adan's forces are ordered to stop firing at exactly 18:52 hours — the time set by the UN Security Council — but the order doesn't extend to Sharon. The struggle for Ismailia is at its height, and cannot be stopped while wounded still lie on the battlefield; yet another case where disengagement has become more complex than the start of battle.

Sharon demands air support for his rescue teams. The answer is negative. Bar Lev explains that the night is dark; the planes will have difficulty in giving close support, and will themselves be vulnerable. Sharon doesn't accept the explanation. He doesn't know that Bar Lev has a very personal interest in the battle raging in Ismailia. His son is fighting at the head of the column. Maj.-General Hod also tells Sharon of the difficulties involved in operating aircraft under such circumstances. The paratroops and scouts must extricate themselves, with the help of heavy artillery.

No More Initiative

At 19:33 hours, Southern Command HQ informs Sharon that the other corps have ceased fire. His orders are not to initiate any more action, but to limit himself solely to removal of wounded, preferably without firing. Rescue operations continue for another four hours, until all the dead and wounded are removed. Here, dawn will reveal Israeli paratroops and Egyptian commandos — 20 yards apart.

Close to midnight, the front near Ismailia is calming down but, on the southern sector, Egyptian commando and infantry teams are penetrating Israeli armor laagers, to strike at tanks and vehicles with their RPGs. They apparently intend to prepare a way through to the Egyptian Third Army. Israeli soldiers, believing the cease-fire in effect, are being killed in these attacks. Southern Command HQ comes to the conclusion that cease-fire is meaningless. Towards dawn, and, with the Prime Minister's approval, Adan and Magen are ordered to continue the offensive.

OCTOBER 23, 1973

Borrowed Time

The Egyptian violations of the cease-fire are permitting the IDF to complete encirclement of the Third Army. More than 20,000 Egyptian soldiers, with 300 tanks, are trapped in a pocket in Sinai and a part of Suez town. Another 8000 have already been taken prisoner.

The entire Egyptian effort is now aimed at preventing encirclement. Third Army engineer units are laying bridges across the canal — this time in the opposite direction — to permit transit westwards out of the closing ring. Adan's forces disrupt seven Egyptian attempts at bridge-building. This afternoon, Bren Adan opens his last great attack. Two armored units from his corps assault in a wide arc, undermining the Egyptian disposition across the Suez road. Scores of Egyptian tanks are damaged. Vehicles and artillery are abandoned. In its impetus, this battle is reminiscent of the Six Day War. Upon completion of this manoever, Adan's forces are standing on the approaches to Suez. Tanks surround the town's industrial area, the fertilizer plant and great refineries that were mostly destroyed in the War of Attrition.

The penetration into Suez opens the road southwards to the Gulf. Magen's forces pour on, faced by Egyptians and a Moroccan unit recently arrived in Egypt. The Israeli column is led by an armored brigade that was stationed in Sinai on the Day of Atonement. Many of its men have fallen, and their places have been filled by reservists. This brigade is destined to reach the southernmost point of the encirclement: the port of Adabiye on the Gulf of Suez. At 23:40 hours, Magen reports to HQ: "Adabiye is in my hands!" The encirclement of the Third Army is complete.

Sports Meet

Shortly after Magen's arrival, naval patrol boats enter the Egyptian port. Two merchant ships, one Saudian and the other Yemeni, are tied up alongside the wharves. Apart from them, there are three small Egyptian warships. One of them is smoking, and a dead sailor lies on deck. The commandant of the naval base, Colonel Nadar Diab, salutes an Israeli naval officer and offers surrender. The young Israeli officer tells Diab in English, in a tone of apology: "I'm sorry to meet you under such circumstances." The Egyptian answers: "That's the way war is!"

Later, on the deck of the Israeli patrol boat, as it returns across the Suez Gulf, Colonel Diab mentions that he is national champion in Dragon class sailing boats. An officer remembers that Israeli champion Yair Michaeli is in his unit. He orders Michaeli summoned to the quayside to greet the Egyptian prisoner.

No Stalingrad

Completion of the encirclement isn't the end of the war. The orders are to maintain cease-fire and not initiate new action, but to continue mopping up the area in IDF hands. Small Egyptian pockets are dotted across the desert expanses and in the town of Suez. Here and there, Egyptian soldiers try to break out, assisted by fire from within.

In Suez, Adan's forces are steadily penetrating inwards, street by street. At 01:30 hours, Brigadier Uri Benari, Gonen's deputy, contacts Maj.-General Adan: "We want you to take Suez, but on condition that it's not Stalingrad! If it is Stalingrad — then don't do us any favors. If it's easy, then O.K...." Adan accepts the guideline, but prefers to start the action in daylight, before noon.

Stolen Victory

The feeling throughout the army is that war has ended too soon; complete victory has been stolen at the last moment. The Chief of Staff's Order of the Day — the last of the **Yom Kippur** War, carries a hint of this: "We now control the roads that lead to the enemies' capitals. We have come out of the battle victorious, but have not yet completed the victory. As long as the Arabs were attacking, as long as they and their supporters believed they could defeat us — the Security Council didn't even see a need to meet and discuss their aggression. But when they realized that defeat was imminent, our enemies and their friends were immediately alerted to demand a cessation of battle."

At dawn, the IDF Spokesman publishes a communique on the encirclement of the Egyptian Third Army, and the IDF occupation of Adabiye. This communique will later serve the Soviets as proof that the encirclement was completed after the first cease-fire deadline set by the UN Security Council.

Ominous Preparations

Soviet military intervention in the Middle East today takes on a more tangible and threatening aspect. For the first time, the heads of the Soviet military mission to Egypt are sending panic news to the Kremlin. The cease-fire, resolved on by the Security Council following Soviet pressure on Washington, isn't being kept. The last day has resulted in a serious change on the front. In 24 hours, the Israeli Army has achieved what it couldn't during the whole war. The Third Army is encircled, and its rear echelon has been smashed and dispersed. There are only a few tanks between the Israeli columns and Cairo. The IDF has a number of possible alternatives, one of which is towards the Egyptian capital. There is nothing to stop them since the Second Army is in the north, far from the main roads to Cairo.

American intelligence services are noticing Soviet preparations for military involvement in the Middle East. It sometimes seems that the Russians are making little attempt to conceal their activities. American listening posts record movements of Russian forces in East Germany and Poland. Seven divisions of paratroops and infantry have received orders for hasty flight to the Middle East, and a prolonged stay. Some divisions begin to move to airfields, from which they are to be flown to their objectives. In parallel, fighter squadrons are alerted for transfer to the Middle East.

The Russian airlift, which up to now has been moving equipment, arms and ammunition to Egypt and Syria, this morning stopped completely. The intention seems to be to direct the transport planes to transfer the seven Russian divisions. American espionage satellites add details from the Middle East. Two Russian brigades, equipped with ground-to-ground Scud missiles, have deployed east of Cairo. When the missile brigades passed through the Bosphorus, sensitive recorders noted nuclear weapons aboard their ships. Now the Russians seem to want to display the atomic weaponry they have brought to Egypt. Nuclear warheads can clearly be seen on the satellite photographs.

War of Words

This disquieting information is accompanied by suspicious declarations. Sadat now suggests a joint Russian-American force to maintain the cease-fire. The Kremlin rushes to endorse the Egyptian President's proposal. In a conversation with Dr. Kissinger, Soviet Ambassador Dobrynin completes the evidence of Soviet preparations. He states openly that his country intends to dispatch forces — together with the United States — to police the cease-fire broken by Israel. Kissinger reacts firmly: "If the Soviet Union joins the war, in the air, on sea or land, she will find the United States facing her."

After his conversation with Dobrynin, Dr. Kissinger convenes the National Security Council. One assessment is that the Russians do not intend to send an army to the Middle East; it's a bluff aimed at returning the IDF to the lines held on October 22, and preventing an additional offensive. However, the National Security Council isn't prepared to take unnecessary risks. President Nixon declares an emergency in the U.S. Army. The Strategic Air Command is alerted and additional American ships make flank speed into the Mediterranean. In the States, the 82nd Airborne Division is put on stand-by for transfer to the Middle East.

Softly Spoken

The Russians hold back. If they intended to transfer an army — they aren't doing it. They have indirectly achieved their objectives. The encirclement of the Third Army will not be absolute. "What the United States and Israel need is tranquillity — cease-fire. Withholding food from the Third Army will result in the dispatch of Russian ships to the port of Suez," Kissinger explains to Israeli leaders during his visit to Jerusalem. Kissinger doesn't present an ultimatum, but an Israeli refusal, followed by Russian intervention, will obviously result in Washington holding Jerusalem responsible for the declining situation. "It will be your problem," Kissinger explains. Israel thereby loses an important card. Kissinger agrees that the IDF shouldn't retreat to the October 22 lines but the Third Army must be saved. A few hours before Kissinger's arrival in Israel, the Defense Minister emphasizes in a Government session that the encirclement of the Third Army is the IDF's most important achievement: "We must be obstinate about it. It should at least lay down its arms and evacuate the territory." Yigal Allon joins the Defense Minister in stressing that anxiety over the Third Army is the factor that will bring the Egyptians to the table for immediate talks.

This vigorous stand can't be maintained more than one day. Soviet intervention has created increased Israeli dependence on the United States. Israel's only hope is that — this time — direct talks with Egypt might bring something more meaningful, and not just another weak arrangement.

Gaping Jaws

Meanwhile, the Egyptians are fighting hard to break the ring. Close to the main Cairo road, near Kilometer 101, an Egyptian force is attacking Magen's westernmost unit. The bitterest battle of all is taking place inside Suez town; the only one of this war in a built-up area, and the IDF is drawn into it unwillingly. Scouts this morning probed around the Egyptian positions, reaching the conclusion that either Suez is a ghost town — or the force within is small and disorganized. They didn't see any anti-tank gun positions, and reported no response to Israeli tank fire.

There are in fact a few thousand Egyptian soldiers in Suez, some from units that were deployed on the west bank, but including at least one properly organized

291

brigade. The Israeli commanders on the spot are convinced that the few residents and soldiers in Suez want to surrender. The telephones in the town are still working. From the suburbs, they phone the Civilian Governor who is prepared to capitulate, but — according to him — there is no point without approval from the Military Governor. He promises to report together with his military counterpart, but no more is heard from him. Another phone call is made to an Egyptian officer near the port, who says that his men will lay down their weapons when Israeli forces reach them. Everything seems simple and guaranteed.

At 10:30 hours, the advance begins from two directions; one column from the north and the other from the west. They are to meet alongside the beach. Confidence is so great that there is no preliminary artillery softening-up. The lead unit is a battalion of tanks, and not the infantry who customarily probe and check against ambushes. The tanks are followed by half-tracks and armored personnel carriers, manned by paratroops and the men of a reconnaissance unit. The route is down narrow streets, banked on both sides by high buildings. There is no interference. The Egyptians allow the Israelis to move into the trap.

Closed Door

Suddenly, a hail of heavy fire from all sides. From windows and gardens, the Egyptians throw thousands of hand grenades into the open half-tracks. From behind fences, and balconies — they fire anti-tank missiles, hitting many of the tanks and half-tracks. There is no way out — but to retreat. The tanks turn back and escape. The more exposed paratroops jump from the damaged vehicles and occupy nearby houses.

As in the Chinese Farm, and alongside Ismailia — the problem is now how to disengage; to pull out paratroops bogged down in a battle for which they were insufficiently briefed. All efforts are again devoted to rescuing men and their wounded. The brigade intelligence half-track rushes in and is hit. Its men are last seen leaping onto one of the nearby fences. Tank companies are sent in, time and again, to link up with the paratroops who are retreating group by group. Tanks are damaged and the number of wounded mounts. Helicopters land alongside the town, within firing range, to facilitate rapid evacuation of the wounded.

From Fayid, a big helicopter takes off for Suez with a senior doctor who organized three corpsmen and decided to evacuate the wounded personally. The helicopter doesn't arrive. On its way in to land at Suez, it is hit by a Strella shoulder-fired missile, and crashes with all eight occupants.

More and more groups are extricated from the fire-swept town. The dead already number 30 paratroops and tank crewmen. As darkness falls, and the men of the UN Emergency Force plant a flag at Kilometer 101 on the Cairo road — to mark the westernmost point of IDF advance, three groups are still trapped in Suez; the men from the intelligence halftrack with whom there is no contact, a group of paratroops led by H., and a larger group in one of the houses. The battalion commander, who is badly wounded, is with this group. A company commander directs the defense. Communications with the two groups of paratroops are functioning. As darkness falls, H.'s group decides to walk out, carrying their wounded with them. They are led by a relatively strong force, against a chance encounter with Egyptians, and another such force brings up the rear. After two hours of slow progress, the group comes out of the town.

The second and larger group is a more serious problem. The Egyptians have concentrated considerable forces and they seem to be completely isolated. In one attempt at rescue, the paratroop deputy brigade commander is wounded and dies. All rescue operations using tanks fail. Five tanks and two APCs do reach within 100 yards of the group, but the Egyptians have erected a large barrier and sown mines across the road. The column has to turn back under a hail of anti-tank missiles.

Midnight Chat

Close to midnight, a consultation takes place on whether to suggest to the encircled force to come out on foot with their wounded — or wait for daylight and Air Force and artillery cover. Gonen asks to talk with the commander.

Gonen: "How are you?"

Force commander: "Meanwhile everything's O.K. We are in a well-defended house. Our situation inside the house is alright. The problem is that coming out will take us into an area of army camps. There are forces dug-in all around. I therefore request to stay here until tomorrow morning. Over."

Gonen: "Have you got supplies and ammunition?"

Commander: "Almost no supplies. We'll try to take from our burnt vehicles, if there's anything left. The ammunition position is critical. In my opinion, the solution is tomorrow morning. To come in with a serious shock force of tanks, followed by small vehicles to get us. Perhaps air support is also possible?"

Gonen: "I've got another question. Is there another way out at night?"

Commander: "In my opinion, it's not worth it. We're surrounded."

Gonen: "What's your name?"

Commander: "David, Dudu."

Gonen: "Dudu, perhaps we'll accept your suggestion. How do the men feel?"

Dudu: "Very tired. But relatively speaking the situation is O.K."

Gonen: "Badly wounded?"

Dudu: "Two."

Gonen: "Are they being looked after?"

Dudu: "Yes. I have a doctor who's doing marvellous work. I've got a good team here. There are no problems as far as the wounded are concerned, apart from two whom it will be important to evacuate."

Gonen: "Is the roof of your house flat?"

Dudu: "Yes. I'm in Suez Police Station. The building can be identified from an aerial photograph."

Gonen: "I'll be in touch with you. Stay by the radio."

In the War Room, aerial photographs are pulled out and a search begins for the building where Dudu and his men are trapped. The objective is to identify an exit route, and try and guide Dudu out.

Dudu: "Forgive the interruption. We are at a road fork. The map I have isn't accurate. It will be worth using aerial photographs."

Gonen: "Have you got a photo?"

Dudu: "I only have one map, and that's not in a very good state."

Gonen: "Is the house at a crossroads — square with a hole in the roof?"

Dudu: "Yes."

Gonen: "I've found it, hold on."

In the War Room, Gonen asks how much artillery can be brought to bear on the area around the house.

Gonen: "I want to bring down artillery around you. Are you following me? Can you see the enemy around you?"

Dudu: "I see the enemy. I have observation posts. I've also caught a prisoner."

Gonen: "Are you being fired on now?"

Dudu: "Everything's quiet all around. I have good guards."

Gonen: "Are you prepared to attempt bringing out a small force? Perhaps they're not awake."

Dudu: "I weighed that idea. It seems to me that the men are in no state to come out at this stage. I've collected some of our men who were in a house to the east, and there's been exchange of fire all day. I'm now going up to the second floor, and I'll try and identify what's happening all around."

Walking Tour

Meanwhile, Gonen is in conversation with the Command Intelligence Officer, Adan and the airmen. They again conclude that the best way is to bring them out by night. Dudu and his men have about a mile to go, and night has its advantages. It's decided to encourage him to come out quickly. Again they make contact.

Dudu: "I didn't see any movement. There were a few shots."

Adan (intervening in the conversation): "I ask you to come out immediately. Organize your force! Decide from which direction! If you don't move now, you're likely to get into an abnormal mix-up. You must come out immediately."

Gonen: "Make a note — you go 200 yards south to the end of the third block from the crossroads."

Dudu: "Clear. Over."

Gonen: "After that, 250 yards west along the alley. Before the end of the street, there's another alleyway. Turn into it and continue another 200 yards north. You'll reach a railroad, a water canal and a bridge. From there, it's straight to the crossroads that we're holding. Now you must decide if you want support or not."

This conversation continues until after 02:00 hours. Finally, Dudu decides to try without artillery support; to surprise the Egyptians by a quiet exit. The decision proves correct. The slow progress takes two hours. Yard by yard, with the wounded on their backs. At 04:00 hours, the force approaches the crossroads held by the IDF where ambulances are waiting to evacuate the wounded. The last major battle of the Yom Kippur War is at an end.

OCTOBER 25, 1973

No Surrender

The war is over. Another war. But men continue to die. Egyptian commandos this morning attack a brigade HQ. The commanders are in a meeting when RPG rockets begin to explode around them. A number of men are killed.

Desperate and panic-stricken Egyptian soldiers are trying to make a way through their own lines. Many are killed, but in the exchanges of fire they also hit Israelis. In the Third Army, some Egyptians are prepared to surrender, but their comrades shoot them as they try to give themselves up. Within the two besieged Third Army divisions, courts martial are judging any soldier who tries to surrender, and the penalty is fifteen years imprisonment with hard labor.

The Fathers and the Sons

Israel's fifth war has ended. The War of Independence, 1948; the Sinai Campaign, 1956; the Six Day War, 1967; the War of Attrition, 1969-70; and now — the Yom Kippur War. This time, Israel has paid a very heavy price — 2600 dead. Only the War of Independence cost more. Many remain lying on the battlefields from which the IDF retreated.

This is the second generation that fights for Israel's existence; a war of fathers and sons. The fathers who as youngsters fought the War of Independence, are now commanders sending their sons onto the battlefield — into the inferno. Many senior officers fight on the same front with their sons. In the War of Independence, the parents were at home.

Now, the fathers have time to ask after their sons. They — civilians and military men — comb the battlefields. Many IDF officers have lost their sons; others — have boys among the badly wounded or on the list of missing. Close to the Hermon position, Colonel Avraham Ayalon, a veteran of Givati Brigade in the War of Independence, discovers his eldest. Alongside the trenches of the Egyptian Third Army, in the deep of night, Maj.-General Amos Horev drags out the body of his son-in-law — a tank commander. On the Golan Heights, they search for the body of Yonathan Peikes — eighteen and a half years old. His father isn't among the searchers. He fell commanding a battalion of reservists in the battle for Jerusalem, in the

Six Day War. The wars of the fathers and sons — generation after generation.

POSTSCRIPT: THE ISRAEL THAT WAS – WILL NOT BE

Let the Victor Beware

In March 1960, the well-known British military commentator, Liddell Hart, told Israeli senior officers that the greatest danger facing the IDF was the fact that it was a victorious army. Successful armies usually swell with exaggerated self-confidence, and prepare for future wars in the pattern of their past victories. The IDF had then fought two wars and won two victories; since then, two more have been added. The impressive Six Day War, and the frustration of Arab plans for the War of Attrition and the terrorist organizations. Israel's cup of self-confidence overflowed, especially after the Six Day War. Victory made Israel arrogant. The Yom Kippur War proved that Liddell Hart's warning had come true.

Silent Service

Significantly, the IDF's only arm that won a complete and undisputed victory, the Navy, was the same unit for which the Six Day War was considered a failure. The Israeli Navy's victories had not gone to its head; there were two failures to prevent this happening. In 1967, the Navy went to war unprepared, and its achievements were infinitesimal. Late that same year, the destroyer Eilat was sunk by missiles off Port Said. The Dakar submarine tragedy — it vanished in the Mediterranean — also added nothing to the Navy's complacency.

Failures impelled the Navy to rely on itself. It tried hard to overtake other units of the IDF, and stand shoulder to shoulder with them. It wasn't over-confident, and did draw conclusions from its mishaps. The O.C. Navy, Maj.-General

Benyamin Telem, said: "We, perhaps more than any other element in the IDF, were busy examining ourselves."

The Israeli Navy won the world's first missile battles at sea. It succeeded in operating modern weapon systems — missile ships with sophisticated electronics — at night. And it was the only unit to make full use of operational darkness.

Earthquake

The Day of Judgment War shook Israel from its foundations to the very summit. A deep lack of confidence suddenly replaced the exaggerated arrogance, and was most noticeable among leaders and senior officers. Questions that had been perpetually pushed off at a tangent, resurfaced. Will we always live by our swords? Can we withstand more wars, when the quantity gap is ever widening to the Arab benefit?

Israel returned overnight to stage one — the State's existence was again threatened. Old fears reawoke and, within the shock, smaller crises.

One moral crisis was in the IDF. After years of fostering the sacred tradition of not leaving wounded on the battlefield, the IDF now found itself having to abandon both wounded and fit in enemy territory.

Unfulfilled Mandate

The war exposed the full hopelessness of Israeli leadership. In the most difficult hours, there was no one to talk to the nation. Israel had no leader with the 1948 stature of Ben-Gurion. The Moshe Dayan of 1967 was also lacking. The main burden of directing the war fell on the shoulders of a 75-year-old grandmother.

The Defense Minister was towed along behind the war, trying to dispell stories of his personal breakdown. For this purpose, he released for publication the minutes of an October 9 meeting with the Israel Newspaper Editors' Committee. Moshe Dayan didn't break down in this

299

meeting, but his mandate from the nation wasn't to direct the Editors' Committee. The mandate was for proper preparation of the IDF, master-minding of the defense plan, a correct view of reality — and the direction of the IDF in war. Moshe Dayan wasn't up to it. By contrast with the Six Day War, Moshe Dayan in 1973 was a part of the leadership that suffered from a credibility gap.

Some people linked the credibility crisis to the IDF communiques during the war. But this wasn't where it began; it was much more complex than that. It began in promises that social gaps would be closed, that the status quo between Israel and the Arab states would continue to Israel's benefit, that war wouldn't come for many years, and if it did — the Egyptians would be unable to push the IDF back from the Suez Canal. The crisis was revealed in war, but its seeds germinated long before.

Island Fastness

The passing years had given birth to a myth: "The IDF is a different matter. What happens among the general public doesn't happen in the army." The Army is an isolated island fastness, unswept by the high waves of murky water. There is a concensus of Israeli national opinion about security and defense, unlike other spheres, but the IDF is no exception among the nation's institutions. It is the nation's army, and as such it has acquired the vices and virtues of the nation that created it. The moral sclerosis that afflicted Israel since the Six Day War could not, therefore, by-pass the IDF. If Israeli administration and society were noteworthy for depressing bureaucracy, the IDF could be no different.

The army was no less able to avoid the civilian chase after luxury and affluence; it is enough to compare the post-Six Day War offices of senior commanders with those built by their predecessors. And this — painfully — while the IDF obviously lacked new tools of war because of "a shortage of budgets". Such phenomena could be manifest, not only because of the comprehensive process in Israeli

300

society, but because the IDF and the defense establishment weren't subject to criticism. The army enjoys a preferential status as far as public censure is concerned, and the little criticism that was levelled was usually received in acrimony, and an atmosphere of revenge.

Sloppy Discipline

The low level of national discipline and public responsibility simply had to permeate the ranks of the IDF. In recent years, there was a noticeable decline in discipline, and there was no clearer proof of this than what happened to the alert declared on the eve of Yom Kippur. Orders to reinforce front line positions, like the Hermon, weren't carried out. Soldiers went into battle without identity disks, and improperly dressed.

Weakening of thought processes, and undermining of moral values — most noticeable in the civilian population — didn't escape the IDF. It would be unjust to contend that senior officers didn't perform their functions, but many took things much more easily than in the past. Phenomena that had previously nauseated the IDF, like army chauffeurs becoming officers' family servants, now happened while nobody sensed that they were in contradiction to the spirit of the nation's army.

Mr. Minister (Res.)

A process of politicization took place in the senior command echelon. The political parties encouraged it cynically and the military leaders exploited it to their own ends. The process reached its peak under Dayan, for he was known for his political approach to Defense Ministry problems. In public life, there was a new love of military men.

Personal struggles in the high echelons of government accelerated the phenomenon. Ministers sought their own generals and military advisers, thereby stimulating the military love-in. Generals were hauled direct out of military service into political life — and right to the government table. Negotiations between senior officers and parties took place while the former still wore IDF uniform. This politicization was revealed in its full significance during the war. The political debates between senior officers, who on the eve of the war had been engaged in electioneering, exposed the full extent of the damage.

Nothing Succeeds Like...

Politicization, weakening control, bureaucracy and moral erosion — were the symptoms of arterial sclerosis, which had to manifest itself **inter alia** in the preparation of the IDF for war. Much was known about the Arab armies, but the information was neither fully utilized nor always translated into the language of practice. Everything was known about the Soviet doctrine of warfare, as adopted by the Arab armies, and about their missiles, yet the proper preparations to deal with them weren't made.

The responsibility must fall on the shoulders of the Supreme Command. Whoever contends that he saw things clearly but remained silent — his guilt is double. Wisdom after the fact is akin to advice given by pathologists; it can only prevent future diseases. Few dared to criticize or disagree with what was happening, and their job was all the harder because they had to argue against the men who had won the Six Day War; their success was used as a convincing argument in every debate. I clearly remember one incident when a senior Armored Corps officer got to his feet at the end of a corps exercise and spoke out in terms of withering criticism. His remarks, in January 1973, were an angry prophesy: "I believe there must be a change in the consciousness of IDF senior officers. I think we are neglecting our jobs. We have a consciousness of the Six Day War, and in my opinion — we will eat very bitter pills on the battlefield if we do not prepare. l pledge my word here that this is what we can expect. I say in front of witnesses, that if we do not ..."

302

At this point, the senior commander was cut short by a famous general, who said: "There will be a meeting of senior staff officers about these subjects. This is an exceptional opportunity while the Chief of Staff, the Defense Minister and all the defense-military leadership are present. You can get up and say anything you want, but what is the connection between this exercise and your remarks?" The senior officer would not give way. He added that the IDF was, in his opinion, below the red danger line in establishing additional units, emergency stores, and so on, while on the other side — a new army was growing.

Culpable Media

After the war, public criticism of the IDF became a kind of national sport. The Israeli press began to dredge up all yesterday's sins. Yet the press had no right to chastise the IDF for not seeing the shape of things to come, when the newspapers themselves performed no better.

Did the press forecast the oil crisis, or the collapse of Israel's diplomatic front? These two subjects weren't subject to the tender mercies of military censorship, and yet the press didn't foresee coming events. Most Israeli papers participated in the arrogant mockery of Sadat whenever he spoke of war. As far as defense was concerned, the press no less than political leadership was party to the transgression. The Editors' Committee was a partner in concealing information from the public, by agreeing to a "vow of silence" in return for knowledge of secrets.

Empty Committee Rooms

Despite the threat to her physical existence, Israel on occasions relates contemptuously or apathetically to her security. There is no better proof of this than the fact that many cabinet ministers were still unaware of Egyptian and Syrian concentrations along the borders on the eve of the

Day of Atonement. Months after the war, Golda Meir's government hadn't yet found time to discuss such burning subjects as the lessons to be learnt from the war, and the possible shape of the next one. Because of party and prestige problems and matters of jealousy, the Government didn't establish a ministerial committee for defense affairs. Instead, the full Cabinet was considered to be such a committee. Clearly, this complexity could only hamper decision-making.

In place of suitable staff work, appropriate to a modern age, the Government dealt in improvisations and combinations. After the shock of Yom Kippur, Israel's leaders were finally prepared to agree that the country, after five wars, needed a national security council. Golda Meir was no exception. Her predecessors had also been reticent to accept such a council, because they feared intervention in sensitive subjects.

The Knesset Foreign Affairs and Security Committee became a rubber stamp, for automatic approval of measures requested by the defense establishment. The civil authority's supervision of the IDF was limited to the hearing of secrets, and its practical jurisdiction barely stretched to budgetary change of insignificant items. It was no wonder that this committee became a laughing stock among IDF officers.

Short Hindsight

Among the IDF's apparently most serious mistakes was the Intelligence Branch evaluation that the Arab concentrations of force were not intended for war. Intelligence Branch didn't see a distance of 200 yards across the Suez Canal. It ignored simple and clear indications, like the bringing-up of fording equipment in immense quantities, and the holding of briefing sessions close to the water-line.

Israel's situation would have been even more critical, but for the one piece of news, before dawn on the Day of Atonement, which upset the apple-cart. One single announcement that could just as easily have not arrived. Had it not done so, the tragedy would have been many times worse. The fact that correct intelligence appraisals were dependent on one piece of information must provoke bitter questions.

In hindsight, it is clear how the mistake developed. The warnings, the indications and the data were artificially classified into two separate stories. The Syrian concentration of forces was seen by Intelligence Branch as the result of the downing of 13 planes, and Syria's desire to exact revenge. The massing of forces in Egypt was viewed as a large-scale exercise. The two stories weren't put together, because of the assumption that the Arabs wouldn't dare start total war, since Israel has absolute air supremacy. At most, they planned for one day of battle on the Syrian border.

The fact that Israel had acquired territorial depth and augmented her aerial warning system, blurred for many the importance of early warning. Before 1967, it was enough for an army to cross the Suez into Sinai. But after the Six Day War, the entire Egyptian Army was regularly stationed along the front line. Changeover to war didn't require considerable movement, as it had in the past. Intelligence warnings therefore had to be shorter in duration, though the strategic differences were in Israel's favor.

Know Your Enemy

Nevertheless, the Intelligence error between the Jewish New Year and the Day of Atonement was nothing but an accident, no matter how serious. There was a more fundamental and deeper seated mistake than that; a faulty evaluation of the balance of power. The unawareness that the Arabs were not only prepared to go to war, but were also capable of pushing the IDF back from the Suez Canal and off the Golan Heights, and of hampering the strategic air arm. Israel neither sensed nor understood what was happening "on the other side of the hill". The Arabs themselves were astonished at the extent of Israel's surprise. In a research paper published by the Institute of

305

Palestinian Studies in Lebanon, Riad el Ashkar wrote: "The surprise was that Israel did not correctly evaluate Arab intentions and power."

Fertile Ground

This grave misconception was far more than an Intelligence error; it was shared by all the senior command echelons. It developed naturally on the fertile ground of the War of Attrition, and analyses of border incidents, operations and raids in recent years, including aerial battles. The IDF's professional level was consistently higher than that of the Arabs. The Israeli Supreme Command was noteworthy for boldness and initiative. But it seems that all this wasn't enough. Sporadic and limited clashes couldn't possibly give a complete picture, either of Arab armies operating in large masses, or of a situation in which they would strike the opening blow, and force the IDF to fight defensive battles, after being surprised.

During the tension of May – June 1973, I heard a senior officer say that a few days would be enough to rout the Egyptian Army, and reach the approaches to Cairo. On the eve of war, a senior armor officer contended that the number of tanks sent to the Golan Heights was an exaggeration; 100 would be enough to cope with a Syrian general offensive. The debate on the morning of Yom Kippur, over the number of reservists to be mobilized, showed that the misconception of Arab power had reached the very top, including the Defense Minister. The contention that the non-execution of the Sinai defense plan was lucky, because the losses would have been heavier, is in itself an additional proof of Israel's critical mistake.

Misty Glass Ball

Perhaps the IDF's most serious failure was that it did not read the future battle, as it should have done, after the War of Attrition. This failure cannot be attributed solely to Intelligence Branch. The share of the operational echelons was no smaller. Everything was planned for fast victory, and nobody foresaw blocking battles involving all the IDF's available divisions. The army relied too much on the Arabs remaining true to tradition, and making mistakes that would allow the IDF to utilize its talent for improvisation – and on the post-Six Day War territories to absorb the first blow and block the Arab advance.

The mistakes weren't failures of techniques or doctrines, but of the Supreme Command, in that it didn't anticipate and prepare for the future battle. But the same command that failed in preparation of the army and in its strategic conception, did display military talent and ability after the blocking stage. The IDF's recovery evidences its high operational standard, and command abilities – especially the junior command – in adapting to a new situation. And the rank and file fought boldly and bravely. The IDF broke the Arab blitzkrieg and developed successful offensives on both fronts, though it attacked – as ever – at a numerical disadvantage.

Decisive Decisions

In the blocking stage, the Supreme Command was taken by surprise – and it took iron nerves to withstand the pressures of pessimistic suggestion; this was where David Elazar's contribution made itself felt. The direction of the war – after October 8 – was good. Mistakes were made, and not all objectives were achieved, but the important decisions were correct. Up to the end of the blocking stage, the Supreme Command and regional headquarters made three critical decisions: to send the tactical reserve to the northern front; not to evacuate the Suez Canal strongpoints; and to stage a gradual offensive with Adan and Sharon's army corps, on October 8.

Only the first decision now seems entirely correct. But for the reserve that moved north, the outcome on Golan might have been very different. The same cannot be said for the other two decisions. Had an order been given on the night of October 6 to evacuate the strongpoints, since

307

they no longer fulfilled any important function, IDF losses would have been smaller — and there would have been no need for hazardous rescue attempts in the three following days.

Elazar's unwillingness to commit the two army corps simultaneously on October 8 is understandable in the light of the initial shock on the first days, and the anxiety over the future — but this important offensive clearly suffered from diffusion of forces. Sharon's criticism was justified beyond any doubt. Inability to concentrate forces — whether because of the lack of reserve and the need to wage desperate war simultaneously on two distant fronts, or whether because of command errors in the field — was to haunt the IDF throughout the war.

There were more critical decisions in the next stage: To transfer Air Force effort and give top priority to the northern front; to bomb strategic targets throughout Syria; to cross the 1967 cease-fire line on Golan; the timing of the Suez Canal crossing — after transfer of the mass of enemy armor into Sinai, and the Egyptian offensive of October 14; and finally — the direction of the IDF offensive on the west bank. All were correct decisions considering operational circumstances and diplomatic conditions.

Important Lessons

Can it be concluded that the gap between the IDF and the Arab armies is now closing? There are factors by which the gap can be gauged precisely, but for data such as command level, motivation and talent to improvise, there is no yardstick. So it is possible to indicate trends, but not to determine precisely the extent of the gap and the rate at which it is closing.

Following the Six Day War, Israel clearly erred in not attaching sufficient importance to the Arab quantity reinforced as it was by modern and sophisticated weapons systems. An important lesson of this war is that even relatively poor quantity becomes quality when equipped with modern and suitable weapons systems. Arab quality, as revealed in war, wasn't expressed in ability to overcome, but primarily in a capability of causing heavy losses. In this, the Arabs — with Soviet assistance — succeeded in closing the gap between them and Israel.

Electronic War

The Day of Judgment War was a push-button conflict to a far greater extent than Israel had expected: An electronic war, which found expression — in anti-aircraft missile systems, and the weapons used against them; in naval warfare; in the numerous anti-tank missiles used by the Arabs; in the multiplicity of night vision equipment; in missiles that home on radar stations; and even in electronic interference and monitoring of communication networks.

The Arab armies embarked on a new era. Electronics had played a minimal role in the Arab armies during the 1967 war. Israel, during the War of Attrition, spoke of "electronic destruction", and the Arabs — led by Egypt — decided to prepare for electronic warfare. They acquired novel easily-operable weapons systems. They invested staggering sums in equipment and training, both at home and abroad. Captured documents included training manuals with a foreword by the War Minister, who quoted President Sadat's promise that the coming war would be electronic.

When the war came, Israel realized that this was a battle against Arab masses assisted by modern Russian electronics. To Egypt's credit, they learnt many lessons from the Six Day War and the War of Attrition. The Arab success in operating modern electronics systems does indicate a closing of the gap, and Israel's tendency to see her opponents as unchangeable must now be amended.

Arab maintenance of the new systems is poor by comparison with European armies or the IDF, but they are apparently not over-worried by it. In the event of breakdown, they waste no time on repairs, but simply replace the entire system with a new one.

309

Population Implosion

The war again stressed that Israel is a small nation, and its army is like the wage-earner who balances his budget, yet always finds himself short at the end of the month. The IDF will always lack a division or two with which to end the war in a better position. Egypt can permit herself combat techniques in which many men must be sacrificed, while the IDF must always act with much smaller forces.

One conclusion to be drawn is that, as long as the IDF will be committed to frontal moves, quantity will talk against it, and Arab mass will be of considerable influence. Israel's only chance to maintain the quality gap is by the indirect approach of "by stratagem make war".

The Arabs improved by virtue of technical sophistication. Modern equipment — like their immense quantities of night vision instrumentation and missiles — helped them close gaps. The overcoming of infantry, previously considered easy, became very difficult. The quality gap did remain as long as weapons systems clashed with their own counterparts; in aerial combat, in armor-armor battles and in sea confrontations between missile ships. Where the commanders' ability to manoeuver and improvise played a decisive role, the IDF held a clear advantage.

Ever-Elusive Victory

Unluckily for Israel, the results of war are not determined solely on the battlefield, nor even by the situation in the arena. What happens in the field is very important, but not decisive where a small country is concerned — and especially not when it faces a "Great Power", and depends on another.

On the Syrian front, Israel undoubtedly won a major military victory. The IDF drove the Syrians back from the Golan Heights, and penetrated deep into their own territory. The Syrian Army wasn't destroyed, but damaged and decimated. Damascus came within range of IDF guns. These were serious achievements. but Syria was the second

310

front in order of importance. And Israel can never expect to vanquish her enemies − or even one of them. At best, she can rout and decimate them.

On the Egyptian front, the results were different. Thanks to the IDF's rapid recovery, a kind of territorial draw was achieved. Two Egyptian armies continued to hold bridgeheads in Sinai, while the IDF gained control of a large tract of land west of the Suez Canal, cutting off two divisions of the Third Army. Had the war continued, the IDF would undoubtedly have seriously mauled the Egyptian Army, and perhaps advanced towards Cairo. The draw was clearly balanced in the IDF's favor, but it wasn't maintained for long. Under pressure and following various agreements, the siege of the Third Army was lifted, and the IDF withdrew from the west bank. But the Egyptian bridgeheads in Sinai remained − and were even expanded, and Egypt was handed the entire Suez Canal. This was her strategic victory, her success at undermining the **status quo** in the Middle East, not by military victory, but by the very fact of her going to war.

Israel's post-war trauma primarily derives from the feeling that the country had returned overnight to square one − where it all started. Despite all her past victories, Israel suddenly found herself again pondering dangers and realizing that defeat in large-scale local battles can endanger her existence.

Noticeable Disymmetry

Despite her victories and growing military power, Israel cannot deter her enemies from attacking, and so the second part of the Israeli formula must be capability for victory if initial deterrent doesn't work. From Israel's viewpoint, this − as we have already seen − could not be decisive victory but rout, as proven by the great victory of 1967. This noticeable dissymmetry has always existed between the parties to the dispute. While the Arabs talked and planned "destruction", Israel had to concentrate on "time-saving attrition".

Prior to the 1956 Sinai Campaign, Israel had no deterrent power. Nasser blocked the Tiran Straits and sent fedayeen into Israel, because he didn't fear a clash with Israel. Ben Gurion himself then doubted Israel's capability to achieve decision. He feared that the Israeli Air Force couldn't supply meaningful defense to Israel's cities and civilian targets. Hence, the source of his willingness to conspire with the French and British, for a joint Sinai-Suez operation in which Israel received pilots from France to defend her skies.

Following 1956, Israel took care to develop her Air Force, which she justifiably saw as her deterrent-strategic arm. But it didn't work on the eve of the 1967 Six Day War. Nasser believed that weakness of Israel's political leadership would result in no reaction to closing of the Tiran Straits, and placid acceptance of no free navigation – or navigation under United States patronage. His calculations were proven wrong.

In the War of Attrition, Israel did enjoy deterrent capability, as evidenced by Nasser's fear of total war; he was only prepared to risk restricted, static war along the Suez Canal. As Israel's losses mounted, she threw the Air Force into battle on the front lines, and then – deep in Egypt. Egyptian vulnerability to the IAF marked the end of the War of Attrition. Then it was the Egyptians who invited foreign – Russian – pilots to defend their homeland.

The Israeli intelligence error on the eve of the 1973 war very possibly derives from an assumption that the Egyptians were exactly where Israel left them at the end of the War of Attrition. In other words; they were not prepared for total war, from fear of the Israeli Air Force. But Egypt and Syria had concluded that limited war wouldn't achieve their objectives, and so it would be better to challenge the IAF.

Territorial Illusion

The contention that the Day of Judgment War was limited because it was waged in small arenas close to the

Suez Canal and on Golan is the result of an optical illusion. The closing of Bab el-Mandab Straits — a step the Egyptians didn't dare take in the War of Attrition — disproves the contention. Up to the Day of Judgment, Israel's deterrent was based on Egypt not daring to strike at navigation far from her borders, for fear that it would provoke reaction elsewhere — maybe in Alexandria. The Arab assumption was right; Israel couldn't react "elsewhere".

The strategic change was effected when the Arabs, again under Egyptian leadership, were equipped with Soviet-made ground-to-ground, long-range missiles — and the Israeli leadership was unwilling to face this challenge. The Arabs were unsuccessful against the Israeli Air Force, so they acquired Scud missiles that could cover any target in Israel. Though they are only of medium range, their impact on the Middle East is greater than it might be elsewhere.

The Egyptians and Syrians also recruited pilots from other Arab countries and — with Soviet help — from North Korea and North Vietnam. Israel's deterrent capability primarily achieved by her superior air power, was now balanced by a counter Arab deterrent. Yet, it was the Scuds that neutralized Israeli reaction "elsewhere" — rather than imported pilots or ground-to-air missiles. Whether the Israeli Air Force would have been capable of operating deep in Egypt is irrelevant; the ability did exist, but the political exchelon decided not to use it this time — and not because of any moral compunction; after all Israel did use this technique against the junior partner — Syria.

Israel thereby returned to her situation of the 1950s, despite all the changes in relative force and geographic conditions. A symptom of this was Israel's willingness, after the 1973 war, to change her attitude to UN forces. After the Sinai Campaign, it was Nasser who wanted to hide behind the UN, and who allocated Egyptian territory for the purpose. Now Israel is the country that gains satisfaction from a buffer zone of UN troops, thereby confirming that she senses her loss of deterrent power.

New Tone of Voice

The Arabs broke the fear barrier. They weren't victorious but, for the first time, they didn't fail. Since October 1973, the Arabs have been saying that whoever succeeded this time can try again; Israel can be eliminated by stages. President Sadat speaks of peace under his conditions, including the return of the Palestinians' legitimate rights. In Israel, no one yet knows what is Sadat's concept of "rights". Does he mean a Palestinian state in Judea and Samaria, and the Gaza Strip? Or perhaps to push Israel back to the UN partition boundaries of 1947; in other words — Jaffa, Lydda, Ramle and perhaps even Western Galilee excluded from Israel? Leaders of the Palestinian Liberation Organization define their legitimate rights as "the total liberation" of Palestine — in other words, elimination of Israel. Therefore — as long as there is no true peace between the parties, Israel must be prepared for the next war.

After the earthquake of October 1973, Israel must be much more cautious. It will be on her conscience if the next war is planned on the pattern of its predecessor — the Day of Judgment. The IDF is devoting considerable thought and resources to the building of a new defense line in Sinai, but the next war may not take place there at all. It might well be primarily a war of missiles and rockets, in which the ground movements take place on different tracts of land, such as on the Jordanian border.

Third Front

Exact prediction of the nature of a future war is impossible, but the general trends may be deduced. It will obviously be more difficult than its predecessor, more vicious and bloodier. The civilian rear will be hit, and Israel must assume that she will have immediately to fight on three fronts. In October 1973, Jordan's Hussein was not over the shock of the Six Day War, in which he was the greatest loser. He eventually met his moral commitment by

314

sending two armored brigades to Syria, but he may now see this as a mistake. Maj.-General (Res.) Ezer Weizmann defined it as a double mistake. Firstly, because Hussein did involve himself in the Six Day War. And secondly, he didn't participate in the 1973 war. If Hussein dared send armored brigades to Syria in 1973, what is to prevent him allowing the Syrians to station missiles in Jordan?

Israel fought on both flanks, on one of which was her most powerful enemy, while on the other stood the most extreme. Neglect of the central Jordanian front — the most important geo-strategically — could be a critical mistake. In facing the future, the IDF must allocate more forces to the central front, and ensure greater reserves than those available to the General Staff during the Day of Judgment War.

Opponent's Bid

If no compromise will be achieved, Israel must assume that the military initiative will again be in Arab hands. The Arabs will seek to surprise Israel by the opening move, and attain their major achievements in the first stage. Israel will probably not be free, as she was in the past, to utilize pre-emptive war.

The concept of preventive action has changed fundamentally since Yom Kippur. At best it is possible to speak of a pre-emptive strike, or of maintaining a strategic force to guarantee a bold and painful second strike if the Arabs start a war. Israel will not be as free as she was in the past. Her political leadership will have to consider new data; the Arabs' new found ability to strike at the civilian home front, which was previously at least partially immune thanks to the supremacy of the Israeli Air Force. Aerial supremacy will persist into the future, but the Arabs now have ground-to-ground missiles, which are difficult or impossible to intercept — and the warning of approach is extremely short.

315

Home Guard

In preparing for a coming war, the IDF must remember the importance of defense. This doesn't mean that the army needs to divert all its efforts to fortifications. In defense, the purpose is not necessarily to defeat an enemy, but to inflict heavy losses during his offensive and follow through to his destruction by appropriate manoeuverability on the terrain. The IDF will of necessity have to accept that it cannot solve every problem by bold blitzkrieg. Moreover, the importance of spatial defense will increase. Israel will have to return not to **kibbutzim** defending themselves — as they did in the War of Independence — with rifles and machine guns, but to a spatial defense adjusted to the new conditions.

Instead of hasty evacuation of settlements, as was the case in the Day of Judgment War, the men of these settlements may be used to operate anti-tank defenses, equipped with the best of modern weaponry. Evacuation at the onset of war was a by-product of the concept that the new territories would solve all problems. Israel has taken a giant step forward since the War of Independence — when small settlements were prepared to stand, alone and surrounded, against regular armies — but regional defense in a new context will again be important in the effective use of Israel's available manpower.

Balance of Local Terror

Israel must assume that, with their immense funds and petroleum reserves, the Arabs can buy almost any new weaponry from either East or West. It follows that electronic warfare will be further developed and the use of missiles will become a matter of routine, giving a new dimension to Middle East wars.

Optimists may hope that ground-to-ground missiles on both sides will create a balance of terror that prevents war. But it is doubtful whether this will be the case. Firstly, if Israel indeed has missiles that can cover the essential Arab

316

targets, she must declare the fact. Unless the Arabs are aware of the fact, Israel cannot create the balance of terror. A more troublesome question is whether these missiles will create such a balance of terror. The Arab rulers may have reconciled themselves to civilian losses for the sake of military gains, but any Israeli government must be many times more sensitive. The Arabs entered the Day of Judgment War with insufficient Scud missiles. But what is to deter them when they have enough weapons to cover the whole of Israel?

A conventional balance of terror, in Middle Eastern conditions, is unlike the one that exists between the Great Powers. Not only do the Great Powers deal in terms of total terror, based on atomic weaponry, but the Arab world is fertile ground for a "mad ruler" capable of anything. Only recently, Arab leaders declared their preparedness to sacrifice millions of their countrymen.

Missiles with conventional warheads cannot resolve a war, but can wield great influence not only in terms of the ultimate price of war. The chances of advance intelligence warning against sudden missile attack are very slight. Yom Kippur taught that the best of intelligence services can be mistaken and, now, chances for prior forecast are even smaller.

Shortened Lines

The new circumstances will compel reorganization. Israel must adapt her reserve mobilization system to the possibility of interruption by missile attack. In past wars, Israel could mobilize without interference – and this was even the case on October 6, 1973, when she was surprised. The situation may be different in a missile war. So the IDF must organize on a territorial basis, cutting to a minimum the movements of reserve cohorts to emergency warehouses and the front line. The army must allow for a possible hold-up in the flow of reserves and a blocking stage that will engage the standing army for a longer period of time and be much more complex.

Consequently, the importance of terrain in a war of this kind will increase rather than decline. as many believe. The Arab capability of striking from a great distance at Israel's essential centers doesn't reduce the vital importance of defensible borders. Quite the contrary. If the Arab armies have weapons of immense destructive capacity, Israel must ensure that she isn't defeated on the ground. Territories and frontiers may not prevent missile attacks on the home front, but when the destruction is augmented by ability for quick thrusts into the heart of Israel, the Arabs' chances grow. Their potential for disrupting reserve mobilization obliges Israel to take much greater care over her ability to block land attack.

Doubtful Supremacy

Israel's military supremacy has been placed in doubt by the Day of Judgment War, and she cannot foresee the future to the degree that was possible in and after the Six Day War. Israel will always be limited in her military capability compared with the Arabs, whether for reasons of quantity or as a result of political factors. Even if she doubles or trebles her stock piles, she cannot match the logistic support that the Soviet Union gives the Arabs.

In the new conditions, the importance of political settlement obviously increases. Time isn't on Israel's side, and she must make greater efforts to achieve a true peace. Yet not everything depends on her. Those Arabs who are prepared to settle with Israel are either incapable of granting true peace, or their conditions contain the seeds of great danger.

Conventional Weapons

Meanwhile, Israel must prepare for a war that the Arabs may again force on her. Her military supremacy may have been placed in doubt, but this doesn't mean that her defensive capability has been impaired. The IDF can control the battlefield, blocking numerically superior Arab

318

armies and routing them while inflicting heavy losses. To increase its future power, the IDF must be based more on quality; weapons that will guarantee battlefield advantages, even if temporary or local, and despite the gap in quantity. It is a mistake to believe that the Day of Judgment War marks the end of the aircraft or tank. The value of air power will perhaps decline, but it will still provide the striking force, and the emphasis will be on its armaments. The tank may be more vulnerable, but it remains the major factor on the battlefield.

New Page

Yet, Israel's steadfastness does not depend solely on weaponry, no matter how high the quality. Quite apart from weapons, superior organization and intelligence, Israel needs social quality and moral fiber to face the Arabs. And she has no chance without fundamental change in these. If the Day of Judgment will only result in improvements in things done yesterday, then it will be no change. Israel needs to open a new page, not only in the IDF, but in the entire fabric of her life; education, immigrant absorption, economics, the political system, the electoral system and in leadership. Without fundamental revision — there is no value to change within the IDF. The State of Israel and the IDF are interwoven.

The earthquake of October might yet be the cure for Israel's ailments.

Tel Aviv, Summer 1974.

CPSIA information can be obtained
at www.ICGtesting.com
Printed in the USA
FSHW021956150219
55722FS